The Search for Roots:

C. G. Jung and the Tradition of Gnosis

The Search for Roots

C. G. Jung and the Tradition of Gnosis

Alfred Ribi

Foreword by Lance S. Owens

GNOSIS ARCHIVE BOOKS
LOS ANGELES & SALT LAKE CITY

© Alfred Ribi, 2013

Foreword © Lance S. Owens, 2013

First English Edition
Published by Gnosis Arhcive Books – Visit us at *gnosis.org/gab*

ISBN-13: 978-0615850627
ISBN-10: 0615850626

Original edition in German published as:

Die Suche nach den eigenen Wurzeln: Die Bedeutung von Gnosis,
Hermetik und Alchemie für C. G. Jung und Marie-Louise von
Franz und deren Einfluss auf das moderne Verständnis dieser
Disziplin. (Bern, Berlin, Frankfurt/M., New York, Paris,
Wien: Peter Lang Publishing, Inc., 1999).
ISBN 978-3906761602

Biographical note: Alfred Ribi was born in 1931. He studied medicine in Zurich, followed by specialization in Psychiatry and
Psychotherapy FMH. In 1963, he began analysis with Marie-Louise
von Franz—a close associate of C. G. Jung—and subsequently
worked for many years with Dr. von Franz as a colleague. He is a
diplomat of the C. G. Jung Institute, Zurich, where he has served as
Director of Studies, and as a teaching and control analyst, lecturer
and examiner of the Institute. He is a past President of the Foundation for Jungian Psychology, and of the Psychological Club Zurich.
Since 1968, Dr. Ribi has been in private practice in Meilen, and now
in Erlenbach.

Cover Illustration: Frontispiece from Wilhelm Schultz, *Dokumente
der Gnosis* (Jenna, 1910). This book was one of Jung's earliest sources
on Gnostic tradition.

If you don't understand this speech, don't trouble your heart over it. For as long as a person does not become this truth, he will not understand this speech. For this is a naked truth, which has come directly out of the heart of God.

Meister Eckhart

Contents

Preface to the English Edition

The distinguished Gnostic scholar Gilles Quispel once prefaced a lecture by saying, "It is difficult to speak about Gnosis." I would add to that statement, "And it is even more difficult to *understand* Gnosis." So be warned, this book is heavy reading, and it is probably not the book to take to bed for casual company before sleep. It needs your full attention and all your wits. But if you give it that, it will open to you both a new spiritual world and a new dimension of your psyche.

The original German edition of this study was titled *Die Suche nach den eigenen Wurzeln,* and published in 1999 by Peter Lang. With the generous financial support of Judith Harris and Tony Woolfson, Don Reveau thereafter prepared an English translation. However, a publisher interested in that English edition was not then found; those who dealt in books related to Jungian studies judged this book "too scientific" (to quote one publisher's words) for their audience. So it sat, waiting for this time.

Of course, this is a complex and "scientific" book. But then, the subject of Gnosis and C. G. Jung requires a careful treatment. This work was instigated at the insistence of my late friend Gilles Quispel, a renowned scholar who—with the personal support of Jung and financial assistance obtained through the C. G. Jung Institute—both acquired and facilitated a first publication of the Gnostic texts discovered at Nag Hammadi. Quispel introduced me to the scholars working in Gnostic studies, particularly those working with the Gnostic texts recovered at Nag Hammadi. So, perhaps Quispel is responsible for the scientific tenor of my book. I am especially indebted to Quispel for introducing me to Jean-Pierre Mahé of the Université Laval in Québec and the École superieure des Hautes Études in Paris; Prof. Mahé was the co-editor of the French edition of the Nag Hammadi Codices. Addressing scholars such as Quispel, Mahé and their circle, I was required to engage the Gnostic texts in a measure that met their standards; otherwise I would not have been taken seriously.

I honestly admit that I had some resistance when Dr. Lance Owens asked me to again review the English translation of my book in preparation for this edition. But as I started reading, I became more and more excited. Rereading this English edition, I engaged a deeper understanding of my original work. I am easily tired by thoughts I already know. When I can actually be excited reading a book of my own from past years, it confirms to me that the text is both well written and of ongoing value. As I read the book, often I caught myself wondering whether I had really written this. A new level of understanding of Gnosis developed, enhanced by my own personal development in the years since this work was completed.

Like my other books, this study was not written with my ego, but was dictated to me from a higher or deeper fact; it seems I was only the scribe. I am not proud of what I have written, because I have not written it: "It" has written it. Thus I feel a certain distance—a certain foreignness—when confronting the text anew. It is much more wise and clever than I ever could be; and it needs to be read and reread. So I am finally reconciled with Lance for forcing me to go over this work again. I have learned more about the Gnosis, and become more conscious of aspects and depths still awaiting understanding.

The ancient Gnostics were not heretics, though the Fathers of the Church called them that. The first two centuries of the Christian age where full of fights over the proper definition of Christianity and the epithet "heresy" was common. It appears now that the Gnostics were simply Christians who had an introverted attitude towards the "good tidings," the new evangelium of Christ. They did not take this evangelium concretely—as the developing orthodox church eventually demanded—but in a spiritual and symbolic sense. In this role, the Gnosis played an important function in the development and differentiation of orthodoxy.

A Gnostic attitude or interpretive approach remains relevant for us today, especially in understanding dreams and creative imagination. Dreams and images express their message in symbolic language. Every day we take in these images and events, and understand them concretely, at face value. But this is only the surface of reality, the outer glance. To find meaning, we have to see behind the façade; we have to dig deeper. Only through that effort will we find the "pearl of great price," and only then does life discover its depth and meaning.

That is what the Gnostics were striving for, and this is what makes understanding them such a crucial task for our current age. Many people are no longer satisfied with the old stories in the gospels. They ask, "What do we have to do with such fictions nowadays?" But when we understand the myths on a spiritual and symbolic plane, they burst out of the historical dimension, and into a timeless fact. They speak to us in their archaic and eternal voice. People who have lost faith and yet are able to discover this experience are hit by a sound that sings through the centuries. It is the eternal truth that lies behind the outward concrete reality. This experience is what has to be excavated in our modern age; this fact is what must hit home with those critical of religious heritage. The loss of Christianity is a disaster for our Western civilization. We cannot replace it by any substitute, be it a political system, a system of social welfare, or a philosophy. None of these reach the depths of human soul.

By returning us to the depths of the soul, the Gnosis can bring new meaning to our time. Gnosis is not a ready-made system, but an approach to the age-old myth of Christianity. It is the undeveloped potential of Christian myth, the myth that for centuries has awaited further development. Developing this myth is a task for people of our own time. It is an introverted task, a personal task.

I think most Christian believers have their own private convictions, although they confess believing in God. But tell me, what is the definition of "God?" Is He not the most unknown power directing our lives? For the Gnostics, the highest God—the Father of All—is indeed unknowable. This is a deep truth: God is the mover that we do not recognize, and yet, the origin from which we come. We can only speak about this primordial fact in mythological terms.

Of course, we cannot prove a myth; myth is beyond right or wrong. It is either a living truth in me—my truth, and meaningful for me—or it is just a belief that I have accepted from a traditional confession. In our age, it seems fewer and fewer people are satisfied accepting any religious belief or confession. Belief is not enough. But to move beyond belief, we must go on our own inner journey to find our truth, our myth, and our root. The Gnostics were doing this in their own private way, reposing on the mythic texts of Christianity.

A myth is not only a story; it is a statement made in symbols. The language of the unconscious is symbolic. A symbol speaks directly and immediately to the soul, and it is understood by the soul—even when consciousness does not understand. When a symbol touches the soul, it produces a change. Whether the psyche is disturbed or centered by this effect depends on the nature of the symbol. Symbols that center us are healing. Religions can be healing systems with a balancing effect on the soul. The religious myths and symbols of the ancient Gnosis still have this ability to powerfully affect and balance the soul. In this respect, they have a healing effect on a soul lost in the world. People need this balancing and centering root in order to live their lives fully.

It is not my purpose in this book to simply describe what the Gnostics had to say. That has already been done adequately by many other scholars specialized in the Nag Hammadi texts. My intention here is to clarify how C. G. Jung's depth psychology can assist students of Gnosticism in both understanding Gnostic texts and conveying that potentially beneficial understanding to our age. Modern people may actually find in the Gnostic legacy a religious orientation naturally akin to their own.

We witness a great lack of religious orientation in the current age, as evidenced by the intrusion of exotic or esoteric forms of religious belief into the culture. But instead of simply replacing autochthonous beliefs with foreign ones, would it not be better to question the nature of all belief, and turn instead to one's own foundational experience? What I experience, I do not need to believe; experience is the self-evident fact. With my experience, I stay on firm ground.

But can one experience something beyond the reach of extraverted consciousness? Consider this possibility. Every myth takes its origin in human inspiration. Inspiration—from the Latin *inspirare*—means a message from the spirit, the breath of life. The spirit is more than human; it speaks from the macrocosmos, the greater world, and not the limited world of our personhood. It can formulate truths of which we are not conscious. It can give us answers to the unanswered. So doing, it extends our personality into the immeasurable, into the infinity beyond time and space. By lifting us out of the restricted dimensions of our physical existence, the experience of such inspiration has a redeeming quality. Meeting this spirit, this inspiration, life fulfills a destiny beyond the dimensions of our sensible world. The Gnostics, if we understand their striving, can show us a way to this goal.

– Alfred Ribi

Foreword

by Lance S. Owens

I. Alfred Ribi and the Search for Roots

In November of 1960, seven months before his death, C. G. Jung suffered what he called "the lowest ebb of feeling I ever experienced." He explained the sentiment in a letter to Eugene Rolfe:

> I had to understand that I was unable to make the people see what I am after. I am practically alone. There are a few who understand this and that, but almost nobody sees the whole... I have failed in my foremost task: to open people's eyes to the fact that man has a soul and there is a buried treasure in the field and that our religion and philosophy are in a lamentable state.[1]

Looking back now over the last half-century, it appears Jung had reason to lament. He has not been wholly understood. But the cause lay not just in the sprawling scope and complex tenor of his writings. In retrospect, it is evident Jung had not revealed the whole. During his life, Jung cautiously and consciously elected not to publicly share the experiential key to his vast opus. He knew it, too, would not—at least, not then—be understood.

The missing key was, we now see, his long-sequestered Red Book, the work Jung formally titled *Liber Novus*, the "New Book." Begun when he was thirty-eight years old and based on experiences carefully recorded in his journals between 1913 and 1916, *Liber Novus* contained Jung's account of a life-altering journey into the depths of vision. At the commencement, he called his venture "my most difficult experiment."[2] For over sixteen years Jung labored at calligraphically transcribing and illuminating a compilation from his journal record into the exquisite folio volume known as the Red Book. This was his buried treasure; it is the foundation of Jung's oeuvre, and the Rosetta stone to decode his subsequent hermeneutics of creative imagination.

Nearly a century after its composition, the publication in 2009 of *Liber Novus* has instigated a broad reassessment of Jung's place in cultural history. Among many revelations, the visionary events recorded there expose the experiential foundation of Jung's complex association with the Western tradition of Gnosis,[3] a perennial praxis he identified as the historical antecedent of his psychology.

To understand the whole of Dr. Jung, it is imperative that we finally delve into the depths of his Gnostic vision and the ways in which that ancient rhizome nurtured his life task. This new edition of Dr. Alfred Ribi's multidimensional examination of Jung's relationship with Gnosis and its ancient textual witness thus comes at an important time. Initially authored in the decade prior to publication of *Liber Novus*, current release of this English edition offers a necessary bridge between the past and forthcoming understanding of Jung's Gnostic roots.

Ribi and Jung

Alfred Ribi is a formidable scholar, known to all those who have studied at the C. G. Jung Institute in Zurich over the last fifty years. His many books have however appeared heretofore only in German language editions, and he has not received due recognition from English readers. Since the historical importance of this volume is uniquely interwoven with the author's personal background, let me here introduce Dr. Alfred Ribi and tell a bit about how this book came to be written.

Jung traced the historical lineage of his psychology back to the Gnostic communities that had existed two thousand years ago at the beginning of the Christian age. That ancestry was important to Jung; he asserted, "the uninterrupted intellectual chain back to Gnosticism, gave substance to my psychology."[4] Alfred Ribi took Jung's assertion seriously; he stands apart in the analytical community for the erudition and intellectual rigor he has applied to investigation of Jung's association with the Gnosis. Allowing that Jung was correct, Ribi recognized that there was a natural and fraternal dialogue awaiting exploration between the burgeoning field of Gnostic studies and Jungian psychology.

Dr. Ribi is thus not here principally addressing colleagues in the Jungian fold, nor the casual reader seeking an easily digestible dollop of "Jung-lite." His purpose is much more focused. Ribi is trying to open a constructive dialogue between Jungian and Gnostic studies. If engaged, that interchange will eventually expose a hermeneutics attuned to the experiential nature of Gnosis, both ancient and modern. Such a dialogue will broaden the foundation, cultural location, and imaginative scope of modern depth psychology. This is a transformative undertaking. It is an undertaking true to Jung's vision of his work.

Dr. Ribi entered the C. G. Jung Institute in 1964 after having completed his medical training and a few years of scientific research in physiology. Marie-Louise von Franz, for many years Jung's closest associate, became Ribi's analyst. Jung had died three years before Ribi arrived at the Institute, but his memory was still a vital presence. Like many others of his generation in Zurich, Ribi was introduced to Jung not only through his writings, but also by the insights, private perspectives and very personal recollections of people who had known Jung well. For decades thereafter Ribi enjoyed collegial relationships with Dr. von Franz and others still active in Zurich who had worked closely with Jung.

During his association with the C. G. Jung Institute over the past fifty years, Dr. Ribi has worked continuously as an analyst, teacher and examiner of the Institute; he also served as the Institute's Director of Studies. He is an eminent past president of both the Foundation for Jungian Psychology and the Psychological Club of Zurich. After a half-century of engagement, it is safe to say that Ribi knows Jung and the Jungian tradition from the ground up. But even more noteworthy, he recognized Jung's deeper roots, and he carefully searched them out.

A natural scholar with a keen talent for research, Ribi committed himself not only to his work as an analyst and a teacher, but also to the study of the historical foundations of Jung's psychology. Jung's indispensible assistant during the twenty years he labored with the alchemical tradition, Dr. Marie-Louise von Franz, assisted Ribi in his early investigation of alchemical texts. In addition to studying all that Jung wrote about alchemy, he went further: he acquired and reviewed the original sixteenth and seventeenth century documents Jung had studied, ultimately accumulating a library of original alchemical works nearly equal to Jung's own.

Dr. von Franz eventually provided Dr. Ribi with the rare opportunity to closely study Jung's private alchemical notebooks, composed between 1935 and 1953.[5] Methodically working page by page through these notes and indexes, he observed the method underlying the development of Jung's hermeneutics of alchemy. He also discovered that throughout these notes, Jung continued to admix excerpts from Gnostic literature he was still reading—a revealing fact not previously known.

Ribi was searching for the roots of Jung's psychology, and they apparently ran back two thousand years to the Gnostics, Jung's purported "first psychologists." It was time, Ribi saw, to extend the historical understanding of analytical psychology into the textual tradition of the Gnosis. To do this, he elected to employ the same method Jung had used in his study of alchemy—the method he discovered while scrutinizing Jung's notebooks.

This was a natural continuation of Jung's prior effort. But Ribi now had available what Jung did not: an extensive collection of Gnostic texts recently discovered at Nag Hammadi. Although Jung had studied Gnostic materials for many decades, prior to the Nag Hammadi discovery there was a limited number of classical Gnostic writings available, and much existed only in recensions composed by ancient opponents of the tradition. Jung had stated as much, and therefore correctly judged that he lacked the adequate primary material to solidly link his own observations and experiences with the Gnostics in the first centuries. With the addition of the Nag Hammadi materials, the situation had changed, and Ribi saw the effort was now both possible and necessary.

Toward a New Hermeneutics of Gnosis

When I asked Dr. Ribi at what point during the course of his work he first perceived the importance of the Gnostic tradition to Jung, he responded without hesitation: "At the beginning." I then questioned if others around him in the Jungian community over the years had shared his interests or perceptions. His reply was, "No. Only Quispel understood; he was the only one I could talk with."

Gilles Quispel (1916-2006) was a Dutch scholar who in 1952—with financial assistance facilitated by Jung—acquired the first "codex" (as these ancient book are termed) from the cache of Coptic Gnostic texts that had very recently been uncovered at Nag Hammadi, Egypt. This manuscript is now known as the Jung Codex, or Codex I. It was formally presented to Dr. Jung and the C. G. Jung Institute in 1953 and remained with the Institute until being repatriated to Egypt in 1975. This was the first portion of the large collection of Nag Hammadi manuscripts to reach academic hands, and Gilles Quispel was one of the first scholars to fully recognize the immense importance of the discovery for Gnostic studies. Quispel would spend the rest of his long career working on the Nag Hammadi materials.

With the friendship and assistance of Gilles Quispel—by then a renowned scholar of Gnosticism—Ribi met other specialists studying and translating the ancient library of Gnostic writings recovered at Nag Hammadi. Before final publication of the entire Nag Hammadi collection in 1977, Ribi read every translation and commentary published in German, French and English academic editions and monographs.[6]

Over the years, Ribi worked methodically through each of the some fifty Gnostic texts recovered at Nag Hammadi, analyzing the translations in various languages, noting key words, concepts and recurring themes: essential, following techniques Jung used in his study of alchemy. Ribi indexed the terminological interrelationships and the visionary formations appearing in the texts. In the process he compiled thousands of pages of intricate notes, all transcribed in a beautiful calligraphic hand. These notes are now bound in several volumes as a witness to his work.

Ribi's study extended beyond the Nag Hammadi texts to Gnostic material that Jung had read, and to a careful examination of the usages Jung made of this material. Eventually, Ribi established that Jung had understood the core of Gnostic tradition very well, despite his lacking the supplementary material from Nag Hammadi. While the Nag Hammadi scriptures vastly broaden the textual evidence concerning the classical Gnostic experience, the writings Jung had available to him offered an adequate foundation for his conclusions. For the most part, the newly available texts garnered support for Jung's reading.

Throughout this labor, Dr. Ribi engaged dialogue with specialists working in the then still developing field of Gnostic studies. His interest was not only in their work, but also in sharing with them psychological perspectives on the nature of the experience underlying Gnosis. The wider field of Gnostic studies needed awareness of the psychological nature of the tradition, and in Ribi's judgment, Jung's hermeneutics served that need.

The efforts of Alfred Ribi, Gilles Quispel and others with like interests—notably including the independent scholar Stephan Hoeller,[7] and of course the globally influential efforts of Jung himself—were not without effect. In 2005, Dr. Marvin Meyer, the general editor and primary translator of the definitive 2007 international edition of *Nag Hammadi Scriptures,*[8] proclaimed that in Gnostic writings, "The story ...is as much a story about psychology as it is about mythology and metaphysics."[9]

Gnostic writings are a story about psychology. Coming from Marvin Meyer, the leading academic author in this field, and stated in an introduction addressed to the general reader, this is a transformational affirmation about the root of Gnostic tradition. If these ancient manuscripts reveal a story about psychology, then where in the modern world do we find a hermeneutics for, or an analog of their ancient psychology? Dr. Ribi offers an answer.

The Problematic Heresy

Over preceding decades, Jung's connection with Gnostic tradition naturally received comment, and occasionally it generated controversy. Plentiful evidence regarding his sympathetic interest in Gnosticism appeared throughout his published writings. More evidence came in comments he made in his private seminars.[10] And then, there was a little book he had printed, titled the *Septem Sermones ad Mortuos* (*Seven Sermons to the Dead*), which at a very early date robustly signaled the Gnostic foundation of Jung's vision.

Jung privately printed the *Septem Sermones ad Mortuos* in 1916, not long after their transcription in his journal.[11] In 1917 Jung added the Sermons—along with an amplifying Gnostic commentary spoken by Philemon—to the final manuscript section of *Liber Novus,* where they stand as a summary revelation of his experience. Jung gave copies of his 1916 printing of the Sermons to trusted students over many subsequent years. H. G. Baynes—at the time, Jung's principal assistant—prepared an English translation of *Septem Sermones* in the early 1920s. With Jung's approval, the English edition was printed in 1925 and it also was privately distributed for use by disciples who did not read German.[12] Numerous individuals working with Jung in those early years eventually read his Gnostic revelation.

In the mid-1930s Jung began his intense study of the alchemical tradition; over the next twenty years alchemy's symbolic language was a central theme in his many publications.[13] In alchemy Jung believed that he had found crucial evidence for an enduring Western cultural transmission of Gnostic vision spanning two millennia, reaching from the beginnings of the Christian age forward to his own experiences of psychic reality. Readers of Jung often overlooked the fact that this study of alchemy was wed historically with his Gnostic studies—at least in Jung's appraisal. Thus, in his writings on alchemy, one finds abundant references to Gnostic texts presented with parallel commentaries.

Near the end of his life Jung affirmed to Aniela Jaffe, "The main interest of my work is not concerned with the treatment of neurosis, but rather with the approach to the numinous."[14] For Jung, this was the primal experience of Gnosis. After a visit around 1955, his old associate Karl Kerényi remarked (perhaps partly in jest) that Jung then considered himself a kind of "Pope...of the Gnostics."[15] No joking was involved in 1952, however, when the philosopher and theologian Martin Buber published a vehement attack upon Jung's Gnosticism. Exposing pernicious heresy was serious business for Buber.[16]

Buber's assault and the publication of an evasive response from Jung undoubtedly dampened public discussion of Gnosis within the Jungian community over subsequent years.[17] But there were other issues at work motivating an amnesis of Gnosis. Following Jung's death in 1961, the analytical community, along with a growing number of C. G. Jung Institutes dedicated to clinical training, progressively became the primary custodians and propagators of Jung's work. Post mortem, Jung was institutionalized.

For the institution, the persistent and troubling issue was whether Jung's psychology would be viewed as a spiritual discipline or as a clinically validated therapy. There was obviously no professional profit in nominating Jung as a Gnostic prophet. Of course, many Jungian therapists continue to affirm the essentially spiritual aspects of their work, and they quote Jung in support. But culturally and professionally, it remains problematic to associate a school of clinical psychology with a widely anathematized heresy intimately entangled in the origins of Christianity.

The publication in 1982 of Stephan A. Hoeller's landmark study, *The Gnostic Jung and the Seven Sermones to the Dead,* aroused a wider general awareness and discussion of Jung's allegiance with classical Gnosticism.[18] Hoeller was, however, an independent scholar and a bishop of a modern Gnostic church, who stood outside the established Jungian analytical community. For many Jungian analysts, empathetic links between Jung and Gnostic tradition remain inimical to the scientific respectability of their profession. As Barbara Stephens stated in her 2001 reassessment of the Jung-Buber controversy, the issue of therapy as a spiritual praxis is the paradigmatic ground for "Holy Wars" within a fragmenting Jungian analytical tradition.[19]

A Modern Gnostic, a New Book

John Dourley, a Catholic priest and Jungian analyst who has written extensively about the controversy between Jung and Buber, concluded that Jung's only proper rejoinder to Buber—strangely not made at the time but evident in Jung's wider work—might well have been and should have been, "So, what's the matter with being a gnostic...?"[20]

Dr. Ribi is in essential agreement: within Jung's own conceptualization of the term, he was a Gnostic—but a *modern* Gnostic, creatively nurturing an ancient and perennial Gnosis into a new time. And there is *nothing the matter with that*—indeed, it deserves a much deeper acknowledgement and understanding than it has received in past years.

In his exploration of Jung's Gnosis, Ribi artfully traverses the two places where past ventures into this terrain have frequently mired down. First—and this discussion takes up approximately the first half of his book—Ribi dissects the multiple dimensions of the Buber-Jung controversy. His bold opening psychological analysis of Martin Buber, starting with his mother's abandonment of him, is likely to raise a few analytical eyebrows and objections. But Ribi declares his biases and intentions: he is a physician, psychiatrist and Jungian analyst, with decades of clinical experience, exploring a fundamental human conflict. And he is digging deeply into the psyche for understanding. To explain Jung's approach to the experience of Gnosis as a psychological fact, he examines Buber's own encounter with and interpretation of psychological facts—at least to the extent Buber publicly disclosed them. Buber diagnosed Jung as a Gnostic, and Ribi accedes. But what then in contradistinction was Buber? And why did Buber see such danger in the attitude he identified as Gnostic? The real subject of interest, Ribi explains, is the light this conflict casts on a vastly larger historical story: the two millennia long confrontation between *Belief* and *Gnosis*.

In the second part of his work, Ribi offers a probing study of the *Septem Sermones ad Mortuos*. By working together themes from the *Septem Sermones*, ancient Gnostic texts, and Jung's collected writings, he weaves a witness to Jung's intimate relationship with the historical tradition of Gnosis. Jung did not have available to him the Gnostic texts from Nag Hammadi quoted by Ribi in this section; nevertheless, Ribi demonstrates how the Nag Hammadi materials independently support Jung's Gnostic identification of his psychology.

But just as Jung did not have the Nag Hammadi texts, Ribi did not have *Liber Novus*. Ribi intuited the power of Jung's experience during the period he was composing *Liber Novus* and accurately regards the *Septem Sermones* as a signal of these experiences. He even identifies the volumes containing Gnostic texts that Jung had in his library and probably read during the period prior to writing the *Septem Sermones*. Nonetheless, Ribi was forced by the absence of primary documentation—material at that time still sequestered—to make a provisional reconstruction of events leading up to composition of the *Septem Sermones*. The depths Jung had probed and the power of his visions during this period simply could not be estimated. Only his private record could finally tell that tale.

Publication of *Liber Novus* now discloses the visionary foundation underlying Jung's life-long association with the Gnosis. This material supports and significantly supplements Ribi's study. In preparing this

English edition, it therefore was clear that the recently available material from *Liber Novus* should be discussed. That discussion could not, however, be integrated into the original text without radically altering the established work.

Therefore, in an extension of this foreword, I will add a discussion of *Liber Novus* and the story of Jung's initial encounter with the Gnosis. Putting the new pieces together with Ribi's probing exposition of previously apparent facts, we see Alfred Ribi did indeed construct a bridge to the future. His historic study opens the way toward a transformational understanding of C. G. Jung and the tradition of Gnosis.

II. The Perennial Rhizome

Writing in 1950, Jung explained his situation forty years earlier, at the threshold of the experience that produced *Liber Novus*:

> The psyche is not of today; its ancestry goes back many millions of years. Individual consciousness is only the flower and the fruit of a season, sprung from the perennial rhizome beneath the earth; and it would find itself in better accord with the truth if it took the existence of the rhizome into its calculations. For the root matter is the mother of all things.[21]

He recounts that his intense study of mythologies around 1911 forced him to conclude that without a myth, a human "is like one uprooted, having no true link either with the past, or with the ancestral life which continues within him, or yet with contemporary human society." Jung continues,

> So I suspected that myth had a meaning which I was sure to miss if I lived outside it in the haze of my own speculations. I was driven to ask myself in all seriousness: "What is the myth you are living?" I found no answer to this question, and had to admit that I was not living with a myth, or even in a myth, but rather in an uncertain cloud of theoretical possibilities which I was beginning to regard with increasing distrust... So, in the most natural way, I took it upon myself to get to know "my" myth, and I regarded this as the task

of tasks... I simply had to know what unconscious or preconscious myth was forming me, from what rhizome I sprang.[22]

So, beginning on the night of 12 November 1913, and continuing over the next several years, he confronted the portentous "task of tasks." C. G. Jung stepped to the rim of the world where, as he declared, "the mirror-image begins;"[23] he called it "a voyage of discovery to the other pole of the world."[24] And he found his myth, the rhizome from which he sprang. He explained, as reported in *Memories, Dreams, Reflections*:

> The knowledge I was concerned with, or was seeking, still could not be found in the science of those days. I myself had to undergo the original experience, and, moreover, try to plant the results of my experience in the soil of reality; otherwise they would have remained subjective assumptions without validity."[25]

In 1948, he described the event to Victor White: "I wanted the proof of a living Spirit and I got it. Don't ask me at what price."[26] The "original experience" and "living Spirit" of the Depths had led him to what he avowed in 1916 to be a "new spring of life."[27] But from the very beginning of his odyssey in 1913, Jung struggled with a rare hermeneutic task: translating his imaginative encounters—his visions—concretely into word and image. He had to plant what he had undergone in the soil of reality. The translators of *Liber Novus* comment:

> At the outset of *Liber Novus*, Jung experiences a crisis of language. The spirit of the depths, who immediately challenges Jung's use of language along with the spirit of the time, informs Jung that on the terrain of his soul his achieved language will no longer serve.[28]

The theoretical, didactic and discursive forms of his previous scientific jargon would not carry the fact of this experience. Jung confronts the challenge before him in his introduction to *Liber Novus,* and he makes this petition to the reader for understanding:

> My speech is imperfect. Not because I want to shine with words, but out of the impossibility of finding those words, I speak in im-

ages. With nothing else can I express the words from the depths.[29]

Near the end of life, Jung spoke of his visions as "the fiery magma out of which the stone that had to be worked was crystallized."[30] Jung's first task—his *primary hermeneutic task,* the first interpretive challenge—was a crystallization of the stone. That stone, the fact he would work for the rest of his life, originated in a protean visionary experience playing out over several years. It was a descent into mythopoetic imagination.

He was compelled to give this experience expressive form. Early in the experience, Elijah had said to him in a vision, "Seek untiringly, and above all write exactly what you see."[31] But how would he put in words the fictive facts of vision? In response, Jung entered an intensely focused and deeply considered formational process. The voice of the depths spoke in symbol and image. And so, in translating his experience, did Jung. Even the graphic form of words on the pages of the Red Book needed to speak with the voice of image.

Jung further intuited that his experience of the Depths was not unprecedented, but somehow linked with previous history, with a fact that had existed as lived event earlier in time. Where and how it had existed must have been ambiguous at the beginning of his journey in 1913 and 1914. Nonetheless, with parchment and paint, and archaic calligraphic pen, he had to bridge with word and image a chasm in time, thus linking past and present. And future.

The process unfolded in a dynamic progression. As the transcription of the manuscript of *Liber Novus* proceeded, parchment sheets changed to paper pages in the Red Book; the artistic images he imaginatively brought to form became more abstractly expressive, and the calligraphic hand became less cramped. Finally, around 1917 and 1918, a unifying symbol began to constellate in the form of cross and circle. And at the end of 1919, he crystallized in *Liber Novus* an image titled "the Philosopher's Stone."[32] In its sum, *Liber Novus* reveals these strata. But it is all stone from one same source. This was Jung's primary "hermeneutics of vision," a many-layered working of vision formed to image.

The Epochal Event

By late 1914, as the first draft of *Liber Novus* took form, Jung recognized that what he had experienced was of more than personal import. It was epochal. It was a new hermeneutics of human creativity, one made possible only by and through, and then in sensuous formation of an extraordinary human venture of vision.

In a letter to Kurt Plachte[33] dated 10 Jan 1929, Jung defined the symbol—and here he undoubtedly speaks of the living symbol formed from this own venture—as, "the sensuously perceptible expression of an inner experience." Jung continues and asserts that symbolic expression is the highest form of thought possible: "The highest form of intellectual process would be symbolic experience and its symbolic expression."[34] He explains this further by resorting to an ancient Gnostic vocabulary:

> The symbol belongs to a different sphere from the sphere of instinct. The latter sphere [of instinct] is the mother, the former [the sphere of symbol] the son (or God). For my private use I call the sphere of paradoxical existence, i.e., the instinctive unconscious, the Pleroma, a term borrowed from Gnosticism. The reflection and formation of the Pleroma in individual consciousness produce an image of it (of like nature in a certain sense), and that is the symbol. In it all paradoxes are abolished. In the Pleroma, Above and Below lie together in a strange way and produce nothing; but when it is disturbed by the mistakes and needs of the individual a waterfall arises between Above and Below, a dynamic something that is the symbol. Like the Pleroma, the symbol is greater than man. It overpowers him, shapes him, as though he had opened a sluice that pours a mighty stream over him and sweeps him away.[35]

A year later, in 1930, he wrote further about what happens when this mighty stream is let loose. Speaking about signal imaginative creations across the ages, he asserts that great imaginative art,

> draws its strength from the life of mankind and we completely miss its meaning if we try to derive it from personal factors... Whenever the collective unconscious becomes a living experience and is brought to bear upon the conscious outlook of an age, this event is

a creative act which is of importance for a whole epoch. A work of art is produced that may truthfully be called a message to generations of men... This is effected by the collective unconscious when a poet or seer lends expression to the unspoken desire of the times and shows the way, by word or deed, to its fulfillment...."[36]

Jung was speaking in kind of his own hidden book, *Liber Novus:* the primary translation to word of vision; a multifaceted layering of symbols; word in image and image in word, reaching back and forward in time, "a creative act which is of importance for a whole epoch...a message to generations of men."

Finding Gnostic Parallels

In 1912, C. G. Jung felt an urgent need to understand the "unconscious or preconscious myth" that was "forming him." Between November of 1913 and late spring of 1914, he began his extraordinary odyssey into the depths of the inner world. Though imaginative, mythic, apparently fictive, and ultimately subjective, what Jung met in his wanderings spoke with the voice of an objective fact. It was independent, ineffably ancient, and yet intimately and synchronously involved with human history. He perceived it as real, and the story it told had the tenor of a revelation.

The experience placed a weighty vocation upon him. He needed to link what had happened to him—both the experience and the new book it produced—to its root, to its history. He explains his situation:

First I had to find evidence for the historical prefiguration of my inner experiences. That is to say, I had to ask myself, "Where have my particular premises already occurred in history?" If I had not succeeded in finding such evidence, I would never have been able to substantiate my ideas.[37]

Analytical psychology is fundamentally a natural science, but it is subject far more than any other science to the personal bias of the observer. The psychologist must depend therefore in the highest degree upon historical and literary parallels if he wishes to exclude at least the crudest errors in judgment. Between 1918 and 1926 I had seriously studied the Gnostic writers, for they too had been confronted with the primal world of the unconscious and had dealt with its contents...[38]

By recognizing historical roots, Dr. Jung gave substance and sustenance to his psychology. The first place he searched and found those roots was in the Gnostic writers. *Memories, Dreams, Reflections* records he undertook his study of Gnostic writings between 1918 and 1926.[39] However, that initial date was incorrectly stated. His serious study actually began three years earlier, in 1915.

As Jung undertook the calligraphic transcription of the first pages of his draft manuscript into the Red Book in 1915, he was already searching the records of humanity for evidence that he was not alone in his extraordinary experience. He hunted it in history. At that point, Jung turned anew to reading the accounts of the ancient Gnosis. Sonu Shamdasani has noted that Jung began his close study of the Gnostic works while on military service in January and October 1915.[40] And now he approached the texts with a unique interpretive tool: his own experience of the prior two years.

This period in Jung's life has been his greatest enigma. He described it as the "numinous beginning which contained everything,"[41] but until very recently, we knew next to nothing about it. Disclosure of the primary records[42] now allows examination of the transformations that occurred in late 1915 and early 1916—the months after Jung had completed his drafts of the initial two sections of *Liber Novus,* and during which he started the calligraphic transcription of those drafts into the big folio volume that became known as the Red Book.[43] But to understand Jung's enormously important awakening during this period, the events must be carefully placed in temporal context. Without comprehending what happened to Jung during these years, I do not believe it is possible to fully grasp the motivation and focus of his later works. Indeed, it seems much has not yet been understood.

Barbara Hannah recorded: "He [Jung] told me more than once that the *first* parallels he found to his own experience were in the Gnostic texts, that is, those reported in the *Elenchos* of Hippolytus."[44] It is now evident that Jung studied the Gnostic materials preserved by Hippolytus in 1915 and saw then the parallels with his own experience. This connection with the Gnosis instigated intense interest and further reading of the then extant Gnostic literature. Gnostic myth thereafter supplied a vocabulary for expression of the experiences recorded in *Liber Novus*.

Of course, he had already crossed paths with some of this material during his feverish and wide-ranging study of mythologies four years earlier, around 1911, while working on *Wandlungen und Symbole der Libido*. But then, as he much later commented, he had not understood it.[45] The situation was different by the end of 1915. The events of the prior two years had granted Jung the interpretive key to Gnostic vision. He recognized the vision behind these ancient texts, because he too had experienced it.

Again, consider what had happened to him; order the events and their formidable effects. His contemporaneous ledgers of his visionary venture—as recorded in the journals known as the "Black Books"— began on 12 November 1913 with Jung's petition to his soul: "My Soul, where are you?"[46]   That supplication led in the next few months to a flood of imaginative material. The vision he called the *Mysterium*—the encounter with Elijah and Salome—came in late December 1913. Thereafter new encounters constellated almost nightly—the Red One, Ammonius, Izdubar, the Eye of Evil, the horde of dead Anabaptists on their way to Jerusalem, and Jung's first meeting with Philemon: all of this erupted over the weeks from December to February. By March the visions ebbed, and finally abated in June 1914.

In August 1914 came the outbreak of the First World War. During the following months of late 1914 and early 1915, Jung composed the drafts of what would become Liber Primus and Liber Secundus— the first two of the three completed sections of *Liber Novus*. Thereafter, he confronted a second onslaught of imaginative experiences; these commenced in the late summer of 1915. This second wave of visions was compiled in 1917 for inclusion as the last section of *Liber Novus*, called Scrutinies.[47] That last section included his summary revelation, independently titled *Septem Sermones ad Mortuos*, as mentioned earlier.

In the months following completion of the first two sections of *Liber Novus* and before the second onslaught of vision in later 1915— the middle or transitional period in the formulation of *Liber Novus*—a distinctly Gnostic voice and Gnostic myth powerfully entered into

Jung's vocabulary. This was apparently a period when Jung intensely identified the Gnostic root of his epochal revelation.

Reading Hippolytus

Jung stated repeatedly to his associate Barbara Hannah, that the *first* historical parallels he found for his experience were in the Gnostic texts recorded by the ancient heresiologist Hippolytus (170—235 CE), in his work *Elenchos*. Note that Jung did not speak of parallel concepts or ideas, but of finding parallel experiences: Jung recognized images of his visionary encounter with the soul in the writings preserved by Hippolytus. The two obvious questions that remain unanswered (and perhaps previously unasked) are: *when* did this reading of Hippolytus occur, and *what* were the specific experiences he saw mirrored in those writings?

Hippolytus' *Refutation of All Heresies* (cited by Jung using the abbreviated Greek title *Elenchos*) had only been discovered at the Mt. Athos monastery in Greece in 1842. A first published edition of the Greek text appeared in 1851, but with authorship still then tentatively attributed to Origen.[48] The work would not be firmly accredited to Hippolytus until the last decades of the nineteenth century.[49] A generally recognized value of Hippolytus' *Elenchos* is that it contains abundant quotations from second century Gnostic writings, texts that were otherwise completely lost.

By the end of 1915 Jung had acquired several books dealing with Gnosticism, and at least three of them included major excerpts from the recently discovered writings of Hippolytus.[50] Dr. Ribi notes two of these books as possible early sources used by Jung: Wolfgang Schultz, *Dokumente der Gnosis* (Jena, 1910),[51] and G. R. S. Mead, *Fragments of a Faith Forgotten* (London, 1906).[52] Both texts were indeed important to Jung, as I will explain below. But there is another book in Jung's library that should also be mentioned: Jung had Mead's *Simon Magus* (1892), which quotes all of Hippolytus' extended commentary on Simon Magus along with excerpts from his writings.[53] Since Jung subsequently recognized his guide Philemon had once been Simon Magus (I will explain further below), one surmises that he read this material with a focused personal interest.

I have examined these volumes and other related books still held in Jung's personal library.[54] Based on that study, I believe it was the work by Wolfgang Schultz—*Dokumente der Gnosis (Documents of Gnosis)*, published in 1910—that initially transformed Jung's understanding of his experiences and opened his perception to Gnostic parallels. Though he of course subsequently read widely on Gnosticism, this appears to have been a singular book that awakened his attention in 1915.

The evidence for this conclusion requires further explanation. Jung lightly added marginalia to a small number of his books; perhaps a few hundred of the over four thousand books in his library have some marginal markings. In most cases, Jung would simply make a line in the margin; more rarely he would underline a passage. Of the books that he marked, few contain more that a couple such notations.[55] But in this book, *Dokumente der Gnosis*, Jung marked or underlined passages on the vast majority of the pages. Although never previously noted, this appears to be the most heavily marked book in his library collection.[56] At the time he read it, this book clearly evoked an unusual response from him; his atypically extensive markings emphatically reflect that fact.

Dokumente der Gnosis contains a collection of excerpts from ancient records, many preserved by patristic sources—primarily Hippolytus and, to a lesser degree, Irenaeus—along with Schultz's commentary. In this collection, Schultz provides an accurate overview of classical Gnosticism's extant textual legacy. He dedicates his chapters to various schools, teachers, or source texts associated with Gnostic tradition. Jung said that reading the Gnostic texts preserved by Hippolytus was important to him. Hippolytus is the main source quoted in nine of the nineteen chapters of this volume, including the chapters on Simon Magus and Basilides.[57]

When did Jung read this book, or add the marginalia to it? Jung quotes *Dokumente der Gnosis* several times in *Psychological Types*, which he drafted during 1919, so he had surely already studied the book prior to that year.[58] Based on other evidence, one can date his reading of the book to a time before December 1915. Again, I must explain.

Schultz's book is attractively printed and includes an impressive frontispiece. [It is reproduced on the cover of this book.] That frontispiece gives a modernistic rendering of an ancient Gnostic gem—very similar in its central motif to the engraving on the Alexandrian Gnostic gem that Jung mounted on a ring and wore for the remainder of his life.[59] In December of 1915 Jung painted in his Red Book an image of Izdubar, the God from the East, whom Jung had both sickened and then nurtured to glorious rebirth.[60] The layout of the crocodile and serpentine figures surrounding Izdubar in Jung's painting are so strikingly similar to the frontispiece engraving in *Dokumente der Gnosis,* one concludes that it served as an inspiration for Jung's artwork. This line of reasoning affirms that Jung had examined the book before December 1915, when he painted the picture of Izdubar.

Grounded on the preceding construction of events, I suggest Jung studied *Dokumente der Gnosis* in 1915, and that this book opened the door to an evolving Gnostic self-identification. In Schultz's compilation of ancient sources, including key Gnostic texts reproduced by Hippolytus, Jung recognized parallels with his visionary experiences.

There were of course many other sources of which Jung availed himself. In both content and structure, Schultz had based his book on the 1900 work by G.R.S. Mead, *Fragments of a Faith Forgotten,* which contained essentially the same material but often in greater detail and with a more psychologically astute commentary. Schultz expresses his debt to Mead's work in the foreword to *Dokumente der Gnosis*; in support of his own work, he however asserts that the German translation of Mead's *Fragments of a Faith Forgotten* (*Fragmenten eines verschollenen Glaubens*, Berlin, 1902) was of inferior quality, and tainted by a Theosophical tone.

By 1915, Jung already knew about and had cited some of G.R.S. Mead's work.[61] It is likely that Jung picked up *Fragments of a Faith Forgotten* promptly after reading Schultz. Jung went on to cite Mead frequently in later years.[62] In 1931, he described *Fragments of a Faith Forgotten* as, "a standard work on Gnosticism. There is no other book that can compare with it, it is written with love and great understanding... There is nothing in German equal to this book by Mead; it is well worth reading."[63]

We now come to the next question: What were the specific Gnostic texts reported by Hippolytus that offered parallels to Jung's own visionary experience? Throughout his later writings Jung frequently cited Gnostic material preserved by Hippolytus (Jung ultimately judged

that Hippolytus must have been a Gnostic sympathizer, occultly conveying texts and teachings under the cloak of an orthodox critique).
These many references aside (and Dr. Ribi discusses several of them),
there are two key Gnostic myths related by Hippolytus that strikingly
reflected Jung's experiences up until 1915. The first is the story of
Simon Magus and his consort Helena; the second is the story of Sophia
and the demiurge. Both tales subsequently entwine themselves in the
parts of *Liber Novus* composed after 1915.

Philemon, Simon Magus and Helena

Intriguingly, at the conclusion of *Liber Novus* it is disclosed that Philemon—Jung's "ghostly guru"[64] prominently mentioned in *Memories,
Dreams, Reflections*—was the ancient Gnostic teacher Simon Magus.
While considering how Jung read Simon's history, one must keep this
strange fact in mind. In telling the story of Simon Magus, Schultz
quotes Hippolytus. Mead's *Fragments of a Faith Forgotten* and his
earlier work *Simon Magus* (all in Jung's library) include this same material; the latter work by Mead adds quotations from other ancient
sources that mention Simon Magus.

Simon Magus, "the Magician," is the first historical figure named
in ancient accounts of the Gnosis. The date of his life remains unclear;
most reports place Simon in the first century of the Christian era. Later
critics generally identified Simon Magus as the father of Gnostic "heresy." Writing in the late second century, the early orthodox apologist
Irenaeus called him, "the Samaritan Simon, from whom all the heresies
took their origin."[65] Hippolytus is, however, the most complete primary
source on Simon Magus; he recounts both Simon's history and quotes
from writings attributed to him.

Accounts of Simon's life emphasize that he had a consort named
Helena. Later critics asserted that Helena was a prostitute whom Simon
had purchased in the Phoenician port of Tyre and then liberated.
Simon told the tale differently, adding a mythic or archetypal dimension. He proclaimed that in Helena he found and liberated a deific
feminine power hidden within physical creation. Helena was a manifestation of the divine *Sophia* (Wisdom); through her mediation, Simon
had met the primal *Epinoia*. This term, *Epinoia* (imperfectly translated

by the words "thought" or "conception"), appears often in subsequent Gnostic mythologies as the title for the first feminine emanation manifest within the primordial mystery of divinity.[66]

Simon says of her: "Wisdom was the first Conception (or Thought) of My Mind, the Mother of All, by whom in the beginning I conceived in My Mind the making of the Angels and Archangels."[67] Using gender in metaphor, Simon explained that the *masculine* Mind, or Logos, was in primordial relationship with a *feminine* syzygy, which Simon named *Epinoia*—the primal first Thought of the divine Mind. G. R. S. Mead commented upon this story in his *Fragments of a Faith Forgotten*, explicitly noting its psychological nature:

> The Logos and his Thought, the World-soul, were symbolized as the Sun (Simon) and Moon (Selēnē, Helen); ...Helen was the human soul fallen into matter and Simon the mind which brings about her redemption.[68]

When Jung met this text in 1915, would he have seen a reflection of his own experience? It seems as though he did. In a vision recorded at the beginning of his imaginative journey during December of 1913 Jung had met Elijah and Salome. Upon first encountering Salome, he was shocked by her presence and questioned, "Was she not vain greed and criminal lust?" Salome nonetheless declared her love for him and wished to become his bride.[69] Jung realized he also loved Salome.[70] In the draft of *Liber Novus*, composed in 1914-15, he penned a reflection on his encounter with Salome. Therein he ponders the relationship of the masculine mind (described as Forethought, or Logos) with Salome, which he equates with Eros.[71] This commentary parallels the Logos-Epinoia relationship expounded by Simon Magus in his consideration of Helena. In the 1920s Jung wrote yet another private analysis of his encounter with Elijah and Salome and there he affirmed, "they might just as well have been called Simon Magus and Helena."[72]

Jung probably also found a more intimate mirror of the tale of Simon and Helena in his personal life. But here the details remain veiled. Like Simon with Helena, Jung's encounter with the mystery of the soul was apparently facilitated by his relationship to a woman. On 14 November 1913, Jung wrote in his journal the following comment addressed to the soul: "And I found you again only through the soul of the woman."[73] It might be surmised that he was referring to his relationship with Toni Wolff, the woman who at this complex juncture in his life apparently assisted him in his mythopoetic journey. Whatever the manner in which that relationship is conjectured, later in his psychological commentary on "Anima and Animus," Jung did state that the anima can "be realized only through a relation to a partner of the opposite sex."[74] The complex liaison with the anima played a foundational role in Jung's psychology, and Simon's consort, Helena, is often mentioned. In 1927 he wrote, "The anima-type is presented in the most succinct and pregnant form in the Gnostic legend of Simon Magus.[75]

The Universal Root

Hippolytus also supplies portions of a text attributed to Simon Magus, called the "Great Announcement" or "Great Expectation." Much later Jung quotes this "remarkable" (as he called it) text in *Mysterium Coniunctionis,* and gives it an extended commentary:

> In the gnosis of Simon Magus, Helen is *prote ennoia*, sapientia, and *epinoia*. The last designation also occurs in Hippolytus: "For Epinoia herself dwelt in Helen at that time." In his "Great Explanation", Simon says [here begins the quotation from Hippolytus]:
>
> "There are two offshoots from all the Aeons, having neither beginning nor end, from one root, and this root is a certain Power, an invisible and incomprehensible Silence. One of them appears on high and is a great power, the mind of the whole, who rules all things and is a male; the other below is a great Thought, a female giving birth to all things."[76]

Simon Magus had more to say that would have interested Jung in 1915. As reported by Hippolytus, Simon also indicates there is a "Great and Boundless Power" that has been "sealed, hidden and concealed" and placed within the Dwelling that we call humankind. "And he [Simon] says that man here below, born of blood, is the Dwelling, and that the Boundless Power dwells in him, which he says is the Universal

Root." This Power has a two-fold nature: one part is concealed inward-
ly, the other is outwardly manifest; furthermore, "the concealed (parts)
...are hidden in the manifested, and the manifested produced by the
concealed."[77] The concealed portion must be met through "imaging"
and by "art;" otherwise it will perish unknown.[78]

All of these texts roused Jung's attention, as evidenced by his use of
the material in *Mysterium Coniunctionis* many decades later.[79] But
again, the question is: did he see in them a reflection of his own experiences recorded through 1915? At the outset of *Liber Novus,* Jung
encountered contrasting realities, concealed and manifest, one reflect-
ing the other. The concealed had been revealed to him through images,
through the "art" of mythopoetic imagination. Jung gave this summary
of the revelation of the concealed:

> The world of the inner is as infinite as the world of the outer. Just
> as you become a part of the manifold essence of the world through
> your bodies, so you become a part of the manifold essence of the
> inner world through your soul. This inner world is truly infinite, in
> no way poorer than the outer one. Man lives in two worlds.[80]

In *Liber Novus,* Jung was gathering empirical evidence for a collective
foundation, or primordial rhizome, underlying consciousness; in his
scientific writings, he later termed it the "collective unconscious."
Simon Magus' "Universal Root" seems an apt analog to Jung's later
conceptualization of a collective unconscious.

Jung's relationship with Simon Magus became even more complex
and peculiar around 1916. In an episode during the summer of 1916,
recorded in his journal and recounted on the last pages of *Liber Novus,*
Jung was walking in the garden with Philemon. A figure appeared to
them; Jung identified him in the journal as Christ. Philemon addressed
Christ, "My master, my brother." Christ responded, but recognized
Philemon as Simon Magus. Philemon explained to Christ that his name
was once Simon Magus, but that now he has become Philemon.[81]

The *Septem Sermones ad Mortuos* are recorded in a more fully elaborated form in the last section of *Liber Novus,* compiled in 1917. In this
final version of the Sermons, Philemon (who was identified in 1916 as
Simon Magus) appears vested in the white robes of an Alexandrian

Gnostic priest. Resting his hand on Jung's shoulder, Philemon—not Jung or the Gnostic teacher Basilides[82]—addresses the Sermons to the dead. In this version, a homiletic dialogue between Philemon and Jung follows each sermon; Philemon therein declares to Jung that his statements in the Sermons are an expression of his knowledge, his *gnosis.*[83]

Jung painted a portrait of Philemon (or, Simon Magus?) during 1924 in his Red Book; above the picture, he inscribed in Greek an appellation: "Father of the Prophets, Beloved Philemon."[84] On the facing page, he painted an image of a veiled woman standing on an altar within a sanctuary. Above her he inscribed, *"Dei sapientia in mysterio"* ("The Wisdom of God in mystery"). These two facing portraits mark principal companions met during his visionary journey. They form a thematic conclusion to Jung's transcription of *Liber Novus* into his red leather folio volume.[85]

Around the time Jung finished these images, he had begun construction of his Tower at Bollingen. Above the door of the Tower, he carved a dedication, consecrating the place: *"Philemonis sacrum"* (Shrine of Philemon). On a bedroom wall upstairs in the Tower, in large mural format, he again painted an image of Philemon. Above that painting, he added the appellation: "Philemon, the Prophets' Primal Father."[86] Jung obviously had a formidable relationship with this figure named Philemon, who was also anciently known as Simon Magus. No less complex was his relationship with a protean feminine power met in guise of the soul. In 1924, he named her *Sapientia:* Sophia, the Wisdom of God in a mystery. Both figures apparently integrated themselves within Jung's perception of a Gnostic heritage.

Sophia, the Demiurge, and the *Septem Sermones ad Mortuos*

The published edition of *Liber Novus* includes three appendices provided as an integral part of the editorial apparatus constructed by Sonu Shamdasani. Each appendix offers a glimpse into Jung's journal accounts. These are indispensable to the understanding of the mythic framework within the sections of *Liber Novus* composed after 1915—the months during which Jung confronted his roots in the Gnostic tradition.

The first of the supplements, Appendix A, supplies a facsimile copy of a page from Black Book 5, on which Jung carefully sketched his first symbolic "mandala," the *Systema Munditotius*. Apparently done around mid-January 1916, Jung's drawing might be most aptly described not as a mandala—a term Jung would not use until several years later—but as a Gnostic aeonology.[87] This complex symbolic figure would be interpreted some two weeks later in the text Jung penned and called *Seven Sermons to the Dead*—Jung's address to the ghostly horde of Anabaptists returned from Jerusalem, who rang his doorbell in late January 1916.[88]

The third supplement, Appendix C, again reproduces the Black Book 5; this entry is dated 16 January 1916. It is an astounding text in which the feminine voice of Jung's soul reveals to him a story that will be recognized by every student of Gnosticism as the foundational myth of the tradition, the myth of Sophia and the demiurge.

In classic Gnostic mythology, Sophia (Wisdom) was a feminine aeon, a twin archetype or syzygy of the masculine Logos. She is the feminine aspect of divinity indwelling creation. Much like the *anima mundi* of alchemical myth, Sophia is present within the very tissue of cosmos and consciousness. In the Gnostic drama of creation, an abortive emanation had separated from Sophia soon after her entry into the depths of the coming cosmos. This defective child grew into a fiery cosmic force that falsely claimed to be the singular and supreme deity. As self-declared ruler of the material world, he sought to hold humanity in his thralldom. This was the demiurge. Gnostic myths gave him many different names, such as Saklas and Yaldabaoth; Jung called him Abraxas. In this ancient and oft restated Gnostic myth, Sophia was the opponent of the demiurge. She was the higher power who awakened in humankind knowledge of their intrinsic inner light and origin, thereby liberating them from the deceitful worldly lordship of the demiurge.

Over the past century, several scholars of Gnosticism have argued that absent a myth of the demiurge, a mythology should not be properly categorized as Gnostic, at least in the classical sense.[89] This subject has colored some past interpretations of the *Septem Sermones ad Mortuos*. Occasional critics have contended that Jung's Sermons do not explicitly include the story of the demiurge. Thus, it is suggested, Jung did not understand the core of Gnostic mythology, and the Sermons are not a true exemplar of a Gnostic mythologem.[90] However, it is now fully manifest that this specious critique results from a misreading and misunderstanding of the complex figure of Abraxas, who appears in the second sermon of the *Septem Sermones*.

Jung's journal entry dated 16 January 1916, reproduced as Appendix C of *Liber Novus,* removes all questions about this issue: Abraxas was the demiurge in Jung's myth. In this journal entry, Jung records the following words spoken to him by the soul, who assumes the voice of Sophia. Her address is unarguably a rendition of the primal Gnostic myth of the demiurge, here named Abraxas:

> *You should worship only one God.* The other Gods are unimportant. *Abraxas is to be feared.* Therefore it was a deliverance when he separated himself from me.

Note that the soul is taking the voice of Sophia. The separation of the demiurge from Sophia—"when he separated himself from me"—is a key part of the Gnostic myth. She continues,

> You do not need to seek him. He will find you, just like Eros. He is the God of the cosmos, extremely powerful and fearful. He is the creative drive, he is form and formation, just as much as matter and force, therefore he is above all the light and dark Gods. He tears away souls and casts them into procreation. He is the creative and created. He is the God who always renews himself in days, in months, in years, in human life, in ages, in peoples, in the living, in heavenly bodies. He compels, he is unsparing. If you worship him, you increase his power over you. Thereby it becomes unbearable. You will have dreadful trouble getting clear of him. ... So remember him, do not worship him, but also do not imagine that you can flee him since he is all around you. You must be in the middle of life, surrounded by death on all sides. Stretched out, like one crucified, you hang in him, the fearful, the overpowering.
>
> But you have in you the *one* God, the wonderfully beautiful and kind, the solitary, starlike, unmoving, he who is older and wiser than the father, he who has a safe hand, who leads you among all the darknesses and death scares of dreadful Abraxas. He gives joy

and peace, since he is beyond death and beyond what is subject to change. He is no servant and no friend of Abraxas.[91]

This journal entry unambiguously identifies the figure of Abraxas, who shortly thereafter appears in the Sermons, as the demiurge of classical Gnostic mythology. The identification of Abraxas with the demiurge is further established in the manuscript of *Liber Novus,* where in his transcription Jung substitutes the term "ruler of this world" for the name "Abraxas" original written in his Black Book journal.[92]

Jung recognized the Gnostic provenance of this January 1916 apparition. A Sophianic voice had declared to him the fundamental Gnostic assertion: "You have in you the *one* God, the wonderfully beautiful and kind, the solitary, starlike, unmoving." Jung turned to that star, and it became his life's guide.

Two years after beginning the journey of *Liber Novus,* Jung was now placing his visionary experience into an interpretive form impregnated by his reading of Gnostic mythology. In his journal entry from January of 1916, the soul speaks to him in the vocabulary of Gnostic myth; two weeks later that same vocabulary enters into the initial journal formulation of the *Seven Sermons to the Dead.* In the summer of 1916, his guide Philemon is revealed to be Simon Magus. Jung's myth had met its rhizome, and he knew it.

Of course, one should note that the basic declaration of the demiurge had already appeared in another form at the very beginning of *Liber Novus.* Jung finished this section of his manuscript text and its final calligraphic rendering into the Red Book earlier in 1915. In the preamble he penned on the first pages of Liber Primus, Jung confronts two powers: the "spirit of the time," and the "spirit of the depths." The "spirit of the time" unmistakably manifests as a demiurge, declaring—in a fashion typical of the Gnostic demiurge—that there is no other power before him.[93] The "spirit of the depths" rebuffs the demiurge's claimed sovereignty, and entreats Jung to look beyond his fabrications. What Jung encounters and records two years later, in 1916, is not a new theme. Rather, it is a metamorphosis in voice, vocabulary, and the mythological identification of his guide: in 1916, Gnostic mythology had become a symbolic vessel for expression of his visions.

In 1916 Jung had seemingly found the root of his myth and it was the myth of Gnosis. I see no evidence that this ever changed. Over the next forty years, he would proceed to construct an interpretive reading of the Gnostic tradition's occult course across the Christian aeon: in Hermeticism, alchemy, Kabbalah, and Christian mysticism. In this vast hermeneutical enterprise, Jung was building a bridge across time, leading back to the foundation stone of classical Gnosticism. The bridge that led forward toward a new and coming aeon was footed on the stone rejected by the builders two thousand years ago.

Alchemy and Gnostic Studies

Jung began his focused study of alchemy in the mid-1930s. Over the ensuing decades his detailed, extensive and very complex writings concerning alchemy have left many readers completely bewildered. In light of *Liber Novus*, Jung's mission is finally evident. The interpretive key he used to unlock the mystery of alchemy was integrally connected to his own earlier visionary experience. He entered the alchemical retort himself in 1913, and from the alembic of personal experience, he extracted a stone. Those who have spent a few years studying *Liber Novus* find there many reasons why Jung discovered in the alchemical opus a reflection of his experience. After meeting *Liber Novus*, one reads Jung's writings on alchemy with eyes wide open.

Sonu Shamdasani proposes that in considering Jung's study of alchemy, we must now understand,

> the real referent of his alchemical works to be not medieval alchemy per se but the symbolism of the individuation process. The hermeneutic key that Jung was using to read alchemical texts consisted of his own self-experimentation, as presented in *Liber Novus*....[94]

This same hermeneutic key opens the door to understanding Jung's repetitive reference to ancient Gnostic texts, documents dating to the beginnings of the Christian age. His interpretive referent remained his own experience, the event crystalized in *Liber Novus*. Other than works from the alchemical tradition, there was no categorical source Jung turned to more frequently in his major writings to illustrate the dynamics and contents of the collective unconscious and the constellation of the Self, than the ancient texts of the Gnosis. Jung is quoted in *Memories, Dreams, Reflections* as saying:

> When I began to understand alchemy I realized that it represented the historical link with Gnosticism, and that a continuity therefore existed between past and present... Alchemy formed the bridge on the one hand into the past, to Gnosticism, and on the other into the future, to the modern psychology of the unconscious. ... The possibility of a comparison with alchemy, and the uninterrupted intellectual chain back to Gnosticism, gave substance to my psychology.[95]

At Yale University in 1937 Jung asserted, "The religious or philosophical views of ancient alchemy were clearly Gnostic;" he then listed keynotes of the Gnosis that had entered into alchemical tradition, highlighting alchemy's recognition of the Sophianic "anima mundi," and the opposing demiurge.[96]

Jung saw his life's work—or his psychology, if one wishes to use that narrower category to circumscribe his expansive vision—as organically connected to a tradition with roots in the experience of Gnosis. This connection back to the Gnosis manifest at the beginning of the Christian aeon was the deep soil and bedrock that rooted his life in history. Jung's encounter with Gnostic literature—begun years before his study of the alchemical tradition—intimately entangled itself in the primary expression of his experiences in *Liber Novus*. Gnostic mythologems thereafter became for Jung a prototypical image of his individuation.

Gnosis and the New Aeon

Based on his readings of ancient texts, Jung judged that the Gnostics of the first centuries had essentially done what he had done, and seen what he also had seen. But there exists yet another, much deeper, perception behind Jung's special relationship with the Gnosis of antiquity that has not yet received wide attention. I suggest it was the most important factor Jung identified as historically uniting his experience with classical Gnosticism. It placed the ancient Gnosis in a unique temporal situation relative to all other later manifestations of the tradition, including those he recognized in alchemy, Kabbalah, and other "heretical" movements emerging during the second millennium of the current epoch.

Not only had the Gnostics met and engaged a psychic reality emerging from the depths, but they had undergone their experiences of this mythopoetic power at a uniquely transformative moment in the evolution of human consciousness: the threshold of a new aeon. And so, two thousand years later, had Carl Gustav Jung.

Jung composed the first page of his Red Book in 1915. On that introductory leaf he graphically intertwined a prophecy of the future, and the coming of a new age: an epochal turning point in human consciousness. It was, as he announced with the first words of *Liber Novus*, "The Way of What is to Come." This was the keynote of his visionary journey, and it continued to be reflected throughout the text of *Liber Novus*. The two millennia long Christian age—coincident with the astrological aeon of Pisces—was coming to an end. A new God-image was seeking constellation in human consciousness.

Although this keynote was a foundational motivation to his subsequent work, for decades Jung did not feel free to publicly disclose it.[97] Perhaps he thought it, too, would not be understood. Then in February of 1944, at age sixty-eight, Jung slipped in the snow and broke his ankle. This modest injury and associated immobilization led to the development twelve days later of a life-threatening pulmonary embolism and heart attack. For three weeks he hung between life and death. And in that twilight, he was immersed in a prolonged series of visions. They seemed the end of his journey, the conclusion to the story he had lived. "It is impossible to convey the beauty and intensity of emotion during those visions. They were the most tremendous things I have ever experienced."[98]

> I would never have imagined that any such experience was possible. It was not a product of imagination. The visions and experiences were utterly real; there was nothing subjective about them; they all had a quality of absolute objectivity.
>
> We shy away from the word "eternal," but I can describe the experience only as the ecstasy of a non-temporal state in which present, past, and future are one. Everything that happens in time had

been brought together into a concrete whole. Nothing was distributed over time, nothing could be measured by temporal concepts.[99]

This illness, these visions, and a year of convalescence—soon followed by a second serious cardiac event in November of 1946—deeply affected Jung's perspective upon his life, his story, and the task remaining to him. They marked the summation of an experience foreshadowed by *Liber Novus* and motivated formation of his last four major works, the books I have called his "Last Quartet."[100] *Aion* was the initial work composed in this period. He explained:

> Before my illness I had often asked myself if I were permitted to publish or even speak of my secret knowledge. I later set it all down in *Aion*. I realized it was my duty to communicate these thoughts, yet I doubted whether I was allowed to give expression to them. During my illness I received confirmation and I now knew that everything had meaning and that everything was perfect.[101]

The first manuscript page of Liber Novus penned by Jung in 1915—deeply considered, dense with verbal and pictorial imagery formed in response to the spirit of the depths—and the complexly crafted commentary in *Aion*, published in 1951, both declare the dawning of a new age.[102] Shortly thereafter Jung feverishly wrote *Answer to Job,* his most personal and controversial confession. He said it had erupted unbidden, even against his will. It, too, was a declaration of visionary insights underlying *Liber Novus.*

Sonu Shamdasani has described Jung's *Answer to Job* as an articulation of the theology of *Liber Novus.*[103] But this is not theology in an orthodox sense. To the contrary, it is a bold statement of Gnostic myth, spoken in a new voice for a new time. Talking with Mircea Eliade in 1952, Jung explained his *Answer to Job,* which was then rousing wrath among the theologians. He said, "The book has always been on my mind, but I waited forty years to write it."[104] Almost four decades earlier, in January 1916, the soul had given to Jung the tale that he retold in *Answer to Job:* a story of the demiurge and Sophia. It had been on his mind ever after, awaiting, and then decisively demanding, contemporary declaration.

Jung saw humanity facing an epochal task. We stand before a pivotal moment in our story, and "we also need the Sophia that Job was
seeking."[105] The prior anamnesis (remembering) of Sophia had come at
the threshold of the Christian aeon, as witnessed by the Gnostics who
heard her tale two thousand years ago. However, over the succeeding
millennia of the Christian epoch, the *experience of her* had almost been
forgotten. Now Sophia was returning. In Pope Pius XII's 1950 pro-
nouncement of the Assumption of the Virgin,[106] Jung identified a
modern dogmatic evolution that evidenced Sophia's myth awakening
to new life. For Jung, it was a sign of the times, and an independent
confirmation of his own Sophianic encounter years before.[107]

In *Aion,* Jung asserted, "For the Gnostics—and this is their real secret—the psyche existed as a source of knowledge."[108] That statement
succinctly summarizes Jung's defining perception about the nature of
Gnosis. His own experience was the foundation for his definition.
Beginning in 1913, Jung turned to the soul seeking knowledge. It came.
What he saw and heard was incredible; it stood beyond belief. He
himself could not *believe* it:

> I do not want to believe it, I do not need to believe it, nor could I
> believe it. How can one believe such? My mind would need to be
> totally confused to believe such things. Given their nature, they are
> most improbable.[109]

But what could not be believed, he now *knew*:

> not with reference to the opinions of the ancients or this or that
> authority, but because I have experienced it. It has happened thus
> in me. And it certainly happened in a way that I neither expected
> nor wished for.[110]

Jung did not use the writings of the Gnostics as sources for his psychology; he turned to Gnostic accounts seeking confirmatory *resources*
that supported his observations about the mythopoetic depths underlying consciousness. Whatever his sympathies, Jung was simply not an
ancient Gnostic, and he could not model himself in that archaic mold.
He was a modern man, perhaps even the first truly modern man. Establishing the link between the Gnosis of old and his new praxis was,

however, an undertaking with a hidden significance for Jung. In *Liber Novus*, Carl Gustav Jung received a vocation that burdened him with an epochal task:

> To give birth to the ancient in a new time is creation. This is the creation of the new, and that redeems me. Salvation is the resolution of the task. The task is to give birth to the old in a new time.[111]

To understand more than "the this and that" of C. G. Jung, it is imperative we now ponder the way he worked the redemptive task of giving birth to the old in a new time. It is a complex enterprise; it demands the conjoint consideration of old traditions and of a New Book. In the labor, many prior assumptions and obscuring accretions will need to be stripped away; the nature of Jungian studies may even be fundamentally changed. Nonetheless, by delving into the depths of Jung's relationship with Gnostic tradition, we will unearth a key that unlocks transformative perspectives on Jung's hermeneutics of creative imagination and on his vision of a coming new chapter in our human story. In *The Search for Roots: C. G. Jung and the Tradition of Gnosis*, Dr. Alfred Ribi provides us with a place to begin that task of tasks.

The Search for Roots

C. G. Jung and the Tradition of Gnosis

Chapter 1

Introduction

I owe the reader both an explanation of how this book came about and a guide to its contents.

The eminent scholar of Gnosis, Professor Gilles Quispel, invited me to write an article for a book that was to appear under his editorship, titled "Hermetic Gnosis in the Course of Time."[1] My proposed article would evaluate the contributions of Carl Gustav Jung and Marie-Louise von Franz to the understanding of Gnosis.

I applied myself to this topic with great enthusiasm, so much so that the result far exceeded the bounds of an essay. My intention was to write an extensive depth-psychological interpretation of Gnostic texts, oriented specifically to readers already possessing considerable knowledge about Gnostic tradition. The result grew into the book I published in 2001, titled *Zeitenwende ("The Turning of Time")*.[2] Of course, I realized that many potential readers were not knowledgeable about Gnosis, or C. G. Jung's relationship to the tradition. Therefore, a more basic introduction to the subject was also needed. This present volume offers that introduction.[3] This book constitutes the first and introductory volume to my opus; the second and concluding volume is *Zeitenwende*.

When Professor Quispel reviewed my initial efforts, he strongly suggested that I add to this introduction a consideration of the controversy between Martin Buber and C. G. Jung. My first reaction was to resist any such suggestion. As a Jungian analyst, doctor, and psychiatrist, I did not consider myself in a position to produce something of value about Martin Buber. I was not familiar with his work, and I was profoundly reluctant to set myself up as judge in a past dispute between two such exceptional intellects. I thus laid Quispel's letter aside for some months, until at last my scientific curiosity drove me to at least take a closer look at Martin Buber's ideas.

It then became clear to me that here, in the guise of a personal controversy, was a fundamental problem of extraordinary significance for the understanding of Gnosticism. What is it that distinguishes Gnosis from orthodox Christianity? Why, during the early centuries of Christianity, did the Church wage such a bitter struggle against Gnosis? Why does the word "gnosis" retain among theologians even today a note of disparagement? What, given the defeat of the early-Christian Gnostic movement, explains its persistent reemergence in new forms over the course of succeeding centuries (e.g., Cathars, alchemy, Kabbalah, the Hermeticism of Marsilio Ficino, Pico delle Mirandola, Jacob Boehme, Goethe's Faust, Theosophy)? The central question pressed for an answer: *what is the significance of Gnosis in our own time?* For it is without doubt that research into Gnosis is at present undergoing a renaissance.

The fundamental issues from the perspective of theology and church history have been treated by persons more qualified than I.[4] As pointed out by Georg Kretschmar in his article "Zur religionsgeschichtlichen Einordung der Gnosis,"[5] Gnosis is in principle subject to two possible descriptions: one outer, or extraverted, and the other inner, or introverted. In our culture the former is regarded as the so-called "objective method." It is the one adopted by most scholars, in that they isolate individual ideas that are typical of Gnosis and describe them in substantive and historical terms. The drawback of this otherwise valuable approach is that a recognition of the meaning of Gnosis lies beyond its capabilities. It conducts research into the historical sources from which the collection of Gnostic images and ideas stem, as if Gnosis were a more or less conscious composition, a potpourri, as it were. It is possible to hold endless debates over the precise influence of Egyptian religion on Gnosis, on the importance to it of Hellenism, on what significance should be attached to oriental and, in particular, Iranian sources. This we shall never know with certainty, for those who could have informed us about it are long since dead. Alternatively, is it perhaps possible that even the Gnostics would be unable to tell us, because it was not at all conscious to them?

From the perspective of an inner, introverted understanding of Gnosis, it reveals itself to be a spontaneous, personal event—a primordial psychic experience—that assimilated itself to emerging

Christianity. Unconscious experience provided the content, the collective Christian outlook the container. Our experience with the modern unconscious teaches us that it is a rich reserve of ideas and images, consisting in part of contemporary intellectual culture, absorbed both consciously and unconsciously, as well as constituting a spontaneous, creative phenomenon, independent of all inheritance. If Gnosis is a spontaneous, creative phenomenon—and I see no reason to dispute this—then it is always a fresh creation, a processing of material that to some extent is already known, but now newly organizing in novel ways and contexts. Individual texts may even take on the character of a homily on Biblical themes. Perhaps a comparison will make the point more clearly: what we admire in the painting of Rembrandt is not the way he adopted the stylistic techniques from his teacher, predecessors, or contemporaries, but that he took over this familiar material, placing it in his own surprising and creative context. This was the achievement of his particular genius. And this is what C. G. Jung did with the Gnostics!

Achieving an understanding from the "inside out" presupposes that one has had similar experiences. It was not merely the "Septem Sermones ad Mortuos" that earned Jung Martin Buber's reproach for being a Gnostic. It was the similarity between Jung's experiences of the collective unconscious and the corresponding statements by Gnostics. Simply noting the striking parallels to be drawn between modern dreams and Gnostic ideas certainly does not suffice to make one a Gnostic. Jung had, and had witnessed in others, the original Gnostic experience. (In the second volume of this study, *Zeitenwende,* I lay particular emphasis on the usefulness of modern dreams to illustrate Gnostic motifs.)

The weakness of working from a basis in inner understanding is the temptation it involves to attribute a general validity to one's own personal experience, and thus offer an explanation of Gnosis from a strictly subjective and limited point of view. Gnosis is a general human phenomenon, as G. Kretschmar[6] writes, but no given individual ever experiences the full range of the collective unconscious.

There are two ways of understanding Gnosis—that is to say, two approaches that are logically exclusive of each other but nevertheless complementary. I feel that my legitimate role is limited to an attempt to help illuminate the unconscious psychological preconditions behind the emergence of Gnosis and Gnosticism. No agreement now exists on even the basic conceptual definitions of Gnosis and Gnosticism.[7] As a layperson in this area, I am obliged to confine myself to issues covered by my own area of expertise. Nevertheless, it is my view that Jungian psychology is capable of prodding specialists in Gnosis or church history toward a better understanding of their own fields. Gilles Quispel— who inspired this present work—has garnered a great deal of recognition for his research in the area of Gnosis. He has spent his life pursuing indications provided by C. G. Jung about gaining an understanding of Gnosis from the inside.[8] Quispel's attempt to mediate between the two complementary approaches I am here describing is evident from his list of publications.[9] The extent to which, as a classical philologist, he has managed to work his way into the experiential and intellectual world of depth psychology is remarkable. This accomplishment is not to be under-estimated.

The empirical experience of the psyche, which led C. G. Jung to his own particular conceptualization of Gnosis, is not immediately available to the scholar. People who lack Jung's experience speak of his theory as if it were mere speculative philosophy. Yet, Jung himself emphasized to his critics time and again his reliance on his experience as a doctor of psychiatry. It was thus not a matter of applying a theory to Gnosis, but on the contrary, of taking note of the surprising parallels to be found between Gnosis and material drawn from depth psychology.

Jung's approach should spark the interest of scholarly specialists in Gnosis. It would ground their research in life, provide it with a firm foundation, and at the same time expand their discipline. I regard it as the task of this book to build these bridges, thus supplementing Quispel's work. Those with no personal experience of dreams, fantasies, or delusional ideation—as they come to light either in one's own analysis or in clinical psychiatric work—understandably doubt the empirical verifiability of Gnostic intellectual phenomena. It is impossible, in the following discussion, for me to simply produce examples of the appropriate "proof" dreams. Dreams always appear in personal garb. Thus, is it necessary to extract the basic structure of the dreams from the personal cloak in which they are wrapped before it is possible to recognize in them the Gnostic kernel they contain—a kernel that is present independent of all historical transmissions.

C. G. Jung's students never really attended to the historical references he made to Gnostic motifs. The reason behind this lack of attention perhaps rests in the assumption that Gnostic motifs, as products of the psyche, were apt to appear at any time, anywhere, and independently of tradition. Jung observed that in the objective psyche there exist potential fundamental ideas that continually recur. He called these "archetypes." This potential is not about "inborn ideas," but relates to a kind of matrix capable of producing generally similar ideas—though they are modified by conditions as they present themselves in different cultures and time periods. It takes years of experience with the material presented by the collective unconscious—and with the comparative history of religion, mythology, or fairy tales—to be able to recognize the archetypal core that such material contains. This is such a daunting task that these days even many so-called "Jungians" have abandoned it in favor of a return to their own personal conceptualization of the unconscious.

It is legitimate to ask, in all seriousness, why anyone should continue to insist on Jung's concept of the archetypes. The answer is quite clear: the archetypes or archetypal ideas represent the objective psyche, the source of all religious statements.[10] This raises a further question: why should analytic psychology overreach, as it might seem, into the arena of theology, and concern itself with religious statements? My response is that the primary issue for psychology is not the truth-content of religious assertions, but the eminently significant fact that the soul (psyche) does spontaneously make statements of this sort, and that they are accompanied by feelings of supreme numinosity. These numinous feelings point to the importance of religious expression for the individual.

Experientially, the archetypes are the interface in the psyche where the mental and the physical meet, and where emotions and libido originate. For this reason, Jung designated the archetypes not as psychic, but as *psychoid*—as a bridge between psychic and material realms.[11] The psychoid nature of the archetype forwarded by Jung might strike many as a mystical concept; indeed, it is a mysterious link between the inner and outer realms of human relationship. Buber did not understand this concept. He apparently thought that, like Freud, Jung had understood the unconscious in a purely materialistic manner and isolated it entirely within the individual. The result, in Buber's view, was that the foundation of human reality and relationship was regarded as intrapsychic. This entailed the psychologization and isolating interiorization of human relationships.[12]

Contrary to Buber's understanding, the psychoid nature of the archetype manifests itself precisely in human relationships. Falling in love, for example, might occasion any number of synchronicities—meaningful actions and events that materialize as exterior manifestations of the relationship's power both on the individuals and their environment. The psychoid nature of the archetypes is also responsible for some so-called psychosomatic illnesses, in which a problem of the psyche comes to expression as very real physical illness.

I am quite aware of the difficulties people can have comprehending the conclusions drawn by Jung, especially when they are not accustomed to attending in their daily lives to the corresponding manifestations of the evidence for those conclusions. Jung never tired of pointing to experience as the foundation of his views. Those who do not share in this experience will have a certain amount of difficulty understanding his findings—but this is no warrant for simply rejecting them as false!

Psychology was once a sub-discipline of philosophy, and thereby was primarily a psychology of conscious processes. Over the course of the last century, psychology has cast off these childhood shoes and established itself in a variety of ways as an empirical science.[13] A philosopher such as Martin Buber—one of Jung's many critics—faced the difficulty of not having had the requisite empirical experience foundational to an understanding of the field. Of course, on the other hand, many psychiatrists themselves often fail to put in the effort required to explore in adequate depth the unconscious interconnections presented by their patients.[14]

Chapter 2

Martin Buber versus Carl Gustav Jung

Whenever stark differences appear between two contemporary thinkers who both have exercised enormous influence, we are justified to assume from a psychological viewpoint that the differences between them are not merely personal, but *fundamental*. The dispute between Buber and Jung thus acquires a collective aspect, lending to it a significance that makes a more detailed investigation of their respective views worthwhile.

The basic fact that I am a Jungian analyst amply witnesses my inability to depict the conflict as a nonpartisan observer. My background necessitates that my understanding of Buber's views can only be psychological. Furthermore, Martin Buber—by resort to a sophism—essentially secured his system against criticism by anyone who has not already accepted it. In his terminology, his critics occupy an "I-It" relation to the material being judged: they understand it merely as an object, and from a distance. Thus, according to Buber, anyone who would seek to gain an adequate understanding of his thought must adopt an "I-Thou" relation toward it—that is, one must passionately embrace with his whole being the very views under consideration and critique.

Little do I imagine that my insights will influence an adherent of Buber's system. Nor is that my intention. Nevertheless, nonpartisan readers may perhaps discover in the following discussion certain insights into psychological matters. Of course, Buber ruled out in advance the possibility of being understood in this fashion; he dismissed any such approach as "psychologizing."

By "psychologism"—the charge with which Buber reproaches Jung—Buber understands the tendency to divide manifest reality into two parts: On the one hand is the external world to which we adapt ourselves, and on the other is the internal reality into which we force the world to fit. His doctrine of the I-Thou relation allows no psychology in our sense of the term, for the latter is capable only of generating knowledge of the inferior I-It form. Psychology, because it turns the psyche into an object of knowledge, is in Buber's view capable neither of understanding the psyche nor apprehending its true meaning.[1]

Martin Buber

Mordecai Martin Buber was born in Vienna in 1878. As a child of three something terrible happened to him: his mother suddenly disappeared without a trace. The boy was sent to live with his paternal grandparents in Lemberg (Lvov), the capital of Galicia. The child hoped to be reunited quickly with his mother, yet no one explained to him what had taken place. Only when he was four did a girl a few years older, who was looking after him, finally tell him: "No, she [his mother] will never come back." This hard fact settled more firmly into his heart from year to year, until he coined the term "mismeeting" (Vergegnung) to express the failure of a genuine meeting to take place between people. When he saw his mother again twenty years later—she had moved to Russia and remarried—he "could not gaze into her still astonishingly beautiful eyes without hearing from somewhere the word 'Vergegnung' as a word spoken to me." "I suspect," writes Buber in his Autobiographical Fragments, "that all that I have learned about genuine meeting in the course of my life had its first origin in that hour on the balcony" of his grandparents' house.[2]

Buber's entire life was overshadowed by this tragic experience he had as a child, without his ever having become fully conscious of it. Already as a boy he had learned that it was not to be spoken about. Neither his father nor his grandparents gave him the information he needed. He spent his whole life searching for "the mother." This much is evident from a report of an encounter with his wife-to-be, Paula Winkler, whom he met in Zurich in 1899.[3] She evidently possessed an extremely strong personality, as well as remarkable intellectual gifts, and she was no doubt more mature and stronger than he. In a 1902 document signed "For you" (and described by Grete Schaeder as "monstrous"[4]) Buber wrote: "Before you, I was but a dream and a golem. But finding you, I found my soul. You came and gave me my soul. Is my soul not therefore your child? So must you love it..." Buber gained courage and confidence from his wife, Paula Winkler; he became stronger and more well defined. This was the decisive relationship of his life.

The mother provides not only a physical but also a psychological foundation for the child. Physically, the young Buber was looked after by his grandmother Adele, who left a lasting intellectual impression on him. Buber writes in Autobiographical Fragments, "My grandmother's love for the genuine word affected me even more strongly than [my grandfather's]: because this love was so direct and so devoted."[5] In Paula Winkler, the stronger personality, he found to some extent a replacement for his lost mother. Yet no other woman could truly replace the mother and help him overcome the shock of his sudden loss. He projected his soul, the ground of consciousness, onto Paula Winkler, which explains why he could not accept psychology. He did not want to be reminded of this "sore spot" in his soul, and therefore eliminated all trace of "psychological brooding" from his life.

At the same time he sublimated his search for the mother in the form of his I-Thou philosophy, composed just after the midpoint of his life (1923). Under the influence of his reading of Johann Jakob Bachhofen's *Mutterrecht*, Buber writes:

> Every child that is coming into being rests, like all life that is coming into being, in the womb of the great mother, the undivided primal world that precedes form. From her, too, we are separated, and enter into personal life, slipping free only in the dark hours to be close to her again; night-by-night this happens to the healthy man. But this separation does not occur suddenly and catastrophically like the separation from the bodily mother; time is granted for the child to exchange a spiritual connexion, that is, relation, for the natural connexion with the world that he gradually loses. He has stepped out of the glowing darkness of chaos into the cool light of creation.[6]

Here once again it becomes clear how sudden and catastrophic for the young Buber the separation from his mother must have been. He senses that a great mother, namely, the unconscious, takes her place. And he must *separate himself from her too*, as the "glowing darkness of chaos" — the "mother-dragon," as Jung has described it in his *Symbols of Transformation.*[7] For in disentangling itself from her, consciousness creates the world, and enters, as Buber terms it, into "the cool light of creation," in which his resistance to having been born into this world of good and evil comes to clear expression. Nevertheless, he is not—as in Sartre—simply abandoned into the world; he is given time to construct an intellectual or psychological connection to it, in place of the natural, dependent one.

The Glowing Darkness of Chaos

In my book *Anthropos*[8] I offer a detailed mythologemic description of the creation of the world through the sacrifice of the cosmic giant, in this case the great mother. The relation is the umbilical cord that connects emerging consciousness with the glowing maternal soil from which it grows, and into which it resubmerges night after night in order to be regenerated. Buber was strangely incapable of ever overcoming the loss of his personal mother and finding in her place a relation to this greater mother, that is, to his unconscious. In my analysis, rather than undertaking the necessary psychological work on the problem, Buber forced it into his own specific philosophical form, as is evident from a recurring dream that he reports.

A dream recurs when consciousness is *unable to understand it* and transform it into action. The dream does not offer something already known to consciousness—or does so only when consciousness finds itself in a state of insecurity. Buber conceptualizes this dream incorrectly as providing confirmation for his theory, which is why we have it in published form. His own version is presented in such a fog of verbiage that I reproduce it here reduced to the essentials:

> I find myself in a vast cave...or in a mud building...or on the fringe of a gigantic forest whose like I cannot remember having seen. The dream begins in very different ways, but always with something extraordinary happening to me, for instance, with a small animal resembling a lion-cub (whose name I know in the dream but not when I awake) tearing the flesh from my arm and being forced only

with an effort to loose its hold.... I stand there and cry out.... Each
time it is the same cry, inarticulate but in strict rhythm, rising and
falling, swelling to a fullness which my throat could not endure
were I awake, long and slow, quiet, quite slow and very long, a cry
that is a song. When it ends my heart stops beating. But then,
somewhere, far away, another cry moves towards me, another
which is the same, the same cry uttered or sung by another voice.
Yet it is not the same cry, certainly no "echo" of my cry but rather
its true rejoinder.... Each time the voice is new. But now, as the reply ends, in the first moment after its dying fall, a certitude, true
dream certitude comes to me that now it has happened. Nothing
more. Just this, and in this way - now it has happened.... After this
manner the dream has recurred each time - till once, the last time,
now two years ago [1930]. At first it was as usual (it was the dream
with the animal), my cry died away, again my heart stood still. But
then there was quiet. There came no answering call.... As though I
had till now had no other access from the world to sensation save
that of the ear and now discovered myself as a being simply
equipped with sense... And then, not from a distance but from the
air round about me, noiselessly, came the answer... If I were to report with what I heard it I should have to say "with every pore of
my body." ...When I had reached an end of receiving it, I felt again
that certainty, pealing out more than ever, that now it has happened.[9]

Martin Buber understood this dream as confirmation of his conception of the I-Thou dialogue. However, if one were to interpret the
dream more objectively, it would be apparent that it was trying to
convey a completely different message—a new message not at all the
same as his nonsensical insistence on his theory. Already in the dream's
"exposition"[10] he is led away from the artificiality of his theory into the
maternal environs of a great cave (which could have to do with birth or
security), or into a simple mud building of the type lived in by the
fellahin. He is led to a natural environment, to the simple life on the
edge of the boundless expanse of a forest, symbolizing the unfathomable physical unconscious.[11] At this initial point, the dreamer is already
relocated to the ground of the mother, in which he is in reality rooted.

In the ensuing development of the dream, something unexpected happens: he is scarcely capable of defending himself even against a young lion-like animal that threatens to tear the flesh from his arm. In my experience, unpleasant little animals of this sort refer to complexes, which unsettle the dreamer for the purpose of being noted and consciously evaluated. The lion here is a relatively harmless baby, but as a fully-grown animal, when the unresolved complex achieves its full strength, it becomes a predator, something ravenous that rules the life of the dreamer. At the climax of the dream, the "peripeteia," he calls out. We do not know to whom he calls—yet in the face of all the dangers of life, the name "mother" is foremost in our mind. As "mistress of the animals," it is she who should free him from this aggressive little beast. That seems to him to be the simplest solution. But the self offers him a less childish solution, or "lysis." The unknown answers him, the "true mother-father" of all people, namely, God—or in more neutral terms, the self. Buber failed to understand this call,[12] instead putting himself—his ego—in the place of the self and attempting to play the role of the Wise Old Man. The final repetition of the dream tells him quite clearly: He should listen; he should turn himself into a receptive organ, and a very sensitive one. Then the call would penetrate soundlessly into him. This Buber never understood as long as he lived. His lion, his greed for recognition and power, always had the upper hand, because he never managed to achieve that passivity, that ability to wait attentively, until an answer comes from beyond.

Buber characterized himself as a "religious thinker."[13] This raises the fundamental question motivating our consideration of the "Buber versus Jung" opposition: What does it mean to have a religious attitude? Buber's dream, as the voice of the self, attempted to convey to him what a religious orientation might be. To God belongs the word, and the human being—including "the thinker"—is allotted a secondary role. The human must first become receptive, he must become a single organ of perception; only afterward will he understand and become capable of realizing the message in his life.

This Buber could not do. He was closed to revelation, for God, having spoken once, "will not do so again" (Job 39:35). Jung saw that having a religious attitude entails "a careful and scrupulous observation of...the numinosum, that is, a dynamic agency or effect not caused by an arbitrary act of will."[14] Religion does not simply mean a profession of faith, which we designate as a confession. Confessions refer to the forms taken by primal religious experiences that have been codified and rendered dogmatic, whereas the primal experiences themselves relate to the transformative power of the numinous, which is capable of seizing hold of a personality and transforming it. The conversion of Saul on the road to Damascus into Paul is an example of this kind of experience. The religious attitude is the orientation of consciousness that is open to such experience.

I can well-imagine that Martin Buber or his followers would correct my statements; this is particularly apparent when I read Buber's replies to his critics presented at the end of the volume, *The Philosophy of Martin Buber*.[15] Therein he dismisses practically every interpretation of his doctrine as being inapplicable. But the essential factor for me is not what Buber's tries to make credible to his public in so many and such beautiful words, but his core nature. None of us are the heroes we would like the world to imagine us being. We all have our frailties and our problems, which we would like to conceal from the world under a thousand beautiful words. If I attempt here to uncover the real Martin Buber—the core behind his outpouring of words—the purpose is not to disparage him or to minimize his greatness, but to check whether his statements correspond to his own reality. Buber reassures the reader:

> Since, however, I have received no message which might be passed on in such a manner, but have only had the experiences and attained the insights, my communication had to be a philosophical one. It had to relate the unique and the particular to the "general," to what is most discoverable by everyman in his existence. It had to express what is by its nature incomprehensible [cf. the glowing darkness of the chaos] in concepts that could be used and communicated [namely, the cool light of creation].[16]

Under the Magnifying Glass

At the time I was beginning my study of Martin Buber's writings, I had the following dream of my own:

I am watching a surgeon perform an operation on a "brain tumor."
He cuts off pieces of the brain in various slices. I put these in pre-
serving fluid for microscope tissue examination (histology). I am
amazed at the way the surgeon is able, with his steady hand, to distinguish between healthy and diseased brain tissue, although from
the outside there is no difference to be seen between them.

At first I must understand this dream as a message being sent to me
from the self: namely, that for me, as a thinking type, there exists the
danger of a kind of over-thinking. In strict medical terms there is no
such thing as cancer of the brain tissue, a fact of which my unconscious
is obviously aware. It uses this image, however, in an effort to represent
a pathological growth of the thinking function. The surgeon is a function in me, endowed with the marvelous gift of being able to recognize
the difference between thinking that is healthy and necessary, and
thinking that is excessive and pathological. It will be necessary later on
to reexamine the case more precisely by putting it "under the magnify-
ing glass" (histology). The surgeon is another function (the knife!),
namely, the feeling that evaluates what something is worth. Pure
thought, the primary function, must be restricted from the inferior
function.[17] The same applies not only on the subjective,[18] but also on
the objective level[19] of dream interpretation.

I noticed in Buber's work how in certain passages he is gripped
with feeling. Then he shifts into a more elevated language. The poet
displaces the philosopher, and the concepts become flowery and impre-
cise. Had he been able to acknowledge the way he was being gripped by
the numinous, there would be no objection whatever to be made in this
regard. But he tries stubbornly to maintain his philosophical-rational
line of argument and to make a theory out of his emotional investment.
This leads in turn to a variety of pathological or neurotic contortions.

The central issue is Buber's conceptualization of the I-Thou relationship, which, as we have seen, is rooted in a mother complex. Thus
the meaning of relationship for Buber is not what the average person
understands by the word "relationship", but an act of "imagining the
real," that is, mutual "inclusion" [Umfassung].[20] For Buber, "inclusion"
is a technical term, and as such calls for special attention. It stems from
the early mother-child relationship, in which psychically the child has

not yet been fully born, remaining part of the maternal psyche. According to Buber, "inclusion" is "the quite concrete imagining, through the most intense action of one's being and bold swinging to the other, of what the other person is feeling, thinking, and willing."[21] In another passage "inclusion" is presented, in opposition to empathy and identification, as...

> a bold imaginative swinging "with the intensest stirring of one's being" into the life of the other so that one can, to some extent, concretely imagine what the other person is thinking, willing, and feeling and so that ones adds something of one's own will to what is apprehended.[22]

What is being expressed here—in convoluted sentences—I would designate symbiosis, or more precisely, the participation mystique of Lévy-Brühl. It characterizes the infantile mental condition, as it normally exists between mother and child, and signifies—because it is unconscious—a compulsive mutual dependency. It is the exact opposite of a free relationship. Buber, acting out his early childhood trauma, seeks reassurance in every encounter, in order not to be disappointed again. This is the same pathological desire to appropriate, to hold on tightly and cling to what he is incapable of surrendering in trust, which we have already encountered in his recurring dream. Because Buber fails to acknowledge his early childhood trauma—from which he would then suffer, and through this suffering heal the wound—he loses himself more and more in thought. The more he distances himself from his primary experience, the more he represses it, and the more threatening are the forms it takes on.

That is the real reason Buber must deny psychology as such and keep it away. For Buber what is essential in a relationship takes place not in the two psychic systems (as it does for Jung) but in the area "between" the two partners—which he designates the "dialogical." The psychological, which takes place in the soul of each individual, is only the secret accompaniment of the dialogical. He demands that the distinction between the "'dialogical' and the 'psychological' constitutes a radical attack on the psychologism of our age."[23] For one who has lost his soul there can be no psychology, but only the airy space of the in-between. With his soul projected entirely into the world, he is bereft of innerness. Thus does Buber write in "Events and Meetings":[24]

> But I am enormously concerned with just this world, this painful and precious fullness of all that I see, hear, taste. I cannot wish away any part of its reality. I can only wish that I might heighten this reality.... And the reality of the experienced world is so much the more powerful the more powerfully I experience it and realize it. Reality is no fixed condition, but a quantity which can be heightened. Its magnitude is functionally dependent upon the intensity of our experiencing. There is an ordinary reality which suffices as a common denominator for the comparison and ordering of things. But the great reality is another. And how can I give this reality to my world except by seeing the seen with all the strength of my life, hearing the heard with all the strength of my life, tasting the tasted with all the strength of my life? Except by bending over the experienced thing with fervour and power...until the confronting, the shaping, the bestowing side of things springs up to meet me and embraces me so that I know the world in it? The actual world is the manifest, the known world. And the world cannot be known otherwise than through the response to things by the active sense-spirit of the loving man.

The unhealable wound Buber carries inside causes him to adopt a radically extraverted attitude, oriented solely by the external realities of the sense organs. This opens a chasm that separates him from the psychological attitude, which affirms inner reality as primary, and as a way of receiving information about the external world in the first place. Buber transformed this issue into a fundamental philosophical question—which it by no means is.

Misencounters

At issue is not whether Jung or Buber is correct; from a psychological perspective it is easy to see how Buber would ultimately arrive at the understanding that is typical of him. One always speaks the most about what is problematic; or to put it scientifically, the complex causes the individual to attend constantly to it. On account of his "misencounter" in early childhood, encounters with other human beings in the genuine sense posed a lifelong problem for Buber, and he had to speak about it. And because in our time many people suffer from narcissistic disturbances, he found broad resonance. This is what is universally valid in his teaching.

Buber's fear of the inner world appears clearly in an excerpt from his I-Thou work, where he expresses his position on psychosis: "If a man does not represent the a priori of relation in his living with the world, if he does not work and realize the inborn Thou on what meets it, then it strikes inwards." The result is that the confrontation with the other person takes place inside oneself, which entails an inner contradiction—the horror of an interior double. "Here is the verge of life, flight of an unfulfilled life to the senseless semblance of fulfillment, and its groping in a maze and losing itself ever more profoundly."[25]

This is not the first time schizophrenia has been designated a psychosis of introversion, but it is not necessary to imply, as the above quotation seems to do, that all introversion is necessarily in some sense pathological. Given a personal bias in regard to the unreliability of the mother, who simply abandoned the three-year old child, the inner world seems to him a maze in which he can only get lost. Precisely in regard to this point, the recurring dream was an attempt to facilitate assistance in the form of a trust-inspiring answer from within. "But the unconscious is also feared by those whose conscious attitude is at odds with their true nature," writes Jung:[26]

Naturally their dreams will then assume an unpleasant and threatening form, for if nature is violated she takes her revenge. In itself the unconscious is neutral, and its normal function is to compensate the conscious position. In it the opposites slumber side by side; they are wrenched apart only by the activity of the conscious mind, and the more one-sided and cramped the conscious standpoint is, the more painful or dangerous will be the unconscious reaction. There is no danger from this sphere if conscious life has a solid foundation. But if consciousness is cramped and obstinately one-sided, and there is also a weakness of judgment, then the approach or invasion of the unconscious can cause confusion and panic or a dangerous inflation, for one of the most obvious dangers is that of identifying with the figures in the unconscious. For anyone with an unstable disposition this may amount to a psychosis.

Because of his negative experience with his mother, Buber has a fear of the unconscious and comes increasingly into opposition with it. He may speak of the unconscious, but he does so in a quite specific way. At a seminar on the unconscious and dreams at the Washington School of Psychotherapy in 1957, he said,

> The unconscious should have, may have, and indeed will have more influence in the interhuman than the conscious. In shaking hands, for example, if there is a real desire to be in touch, the contact is not bodily or psychical, but a unity of one and the other. There is a direct contact between persons in their wholeness, of which the unconscious is the guardian.[27]

Buber uses the concept of the unconscious in two different ways: sometimes referring to the totality of the person prior to the physical and psychic form; and sometimes more in a Freudian sense of an unknown sphere that can only be accessed through the effects it has on conscious life. The first corresponds to the prenatal unconscious totality of the individual, his or her self, which plays such a large role in Zen Buddhism. Therefore Buber is able to maintain that the unconscious is our worldly being (Dasein) itself in its totality. This is what the Gnostics would term the pleroma, namely, a plenitude of possibilities. He maintains further that the unconscious is not phenomenal. It is that which it is taken to be by modern psychology—a dynamic that makes itself felt through its effects. In this sense we can say nothing about the unconscious as such, for it is never given to us.[28]

Jung, in various places in his work, states emphatically that the unconscious is a hypothesis, because as the name suggests, it lies beyond observation. It can only be revealed through its effects. And yet, in as much as it has real effects, is it real. It is typical of Buber that, while indeed recognizing the energetic aspect of the unconscious, he does so only in terms of its external effects, and not the internal ones—those consisting of notions, ideas, images, emotions, motivations, and the disturbances to which all of these are subject. The nature of the unconscious cannot be specified at all, because it is known to consciousness only through its evident influences. Our psychic system is the instrument by which the influences are received and transformed into contents accessible to consciousness.

Intuition is the conscious function that perceives via the unconscious. People with good intuition, especially if they are also introverts, have easy access to the unconscious and therefore understand Jung's psychology quite naturally. For Buber, who is unable to understand intuition in its introverted form, its role instead is to,

> bind us as persons with the world which is over against us, binds us to it without being able to make us one with it, through a vision that cannot be absolute. This vision is a limited one, like all our perceptions, our universal-human ones and our personal ones. Yet it affords us a glimpse in unspeakable intimacy into hidden depths.[29]

He identifies intuition—described in such a way as not to raise objections from a Jungian standpoint—with "imagining the real" and "inclusion," which aroused some suspicion when it came up in the discussion above. Nor is our mistrust lessened when Buber assures us of his own profound mistrust of intuition, in the sense of believing in the possibility of peering into another's heart and saying, "These are the reasons for your action." Intuition here, in Buber's view, involves not viewing the relationship with the eyes of the other and thus fails to imagine his reality. This form of intuition he regards as dangerous and destructive of human relationships, and in his view is only all too frequently used by therapists, gurus, teachers, ministers, and friends.[30] Like all functions of consciousness, intuition can be differentiated or undifferentiated, and it can be used correctly and incorrectly, which says nothing about the value of the function as such. Intuition is all but indispensable for understanding the products of the unconscious. The Gnostics made great use of it in an introverted sense.

In the seminars at the Washington School of Psychiatry, Buber acknowledged that the meaning of dreams can be interpreted according to the doctrine of some specific school. His personal preference, however, was to adopt a more musical, free-floating relation to dreams, in which each one is approached like a poem, to be understood according to one's own concepts.[31] In the second volume of this opus, *Zeitenwende*,[32] I shall demonstrate that the products of the unconscious cannot be interpreted from within the unconscious itself, but that an objective standpoint outside the unconscious is needed. This objective standpoint is knowledge of the soul. Lacking such knowledge, all interpretation is subject to arbitrary intuition. The objectivity of an interpretation derives from a number of characteristics, among them amplification,[33] which is to say, enriching an idea with other comparable ideas, and understanding the symbol[34] as, intuitively speaking, the best form available for a given instance of unconscious content. As long as we know only the conscious meaning of an image, we can never recognize its sense. As indicated in the quotations cited above, Buber clings so desperately to the external world as it is given to perception that it renders symbolic interpretation impossible. He thus could only misunderstand the true concern of Jungian psychology, dismissing it as modern psychologism. He states,

> What is new about today's Psychological Man is that the psyche is now converted into the more impersonal "mind," that its main determinants are seen as residing in an impersonal and largely repressed "unconscious" mind, and that individuals, thus relatively depersonalized, are seen as existing, in the real sense of the term, not in their relation to the environment or to other people or to the world, but in their minds.[35]

Whoever had experience with the "redeeming" (in a literal sense) effect that an archetypical dream can have on a dreamer when it is correctly understood, would never make such a statement. Lacking such experience—which admittedly is more likely to be the special domain of the analyst—Buber transforms inner psychic experience into psychologism, which for him entails an improper use of psychology, usually made in the service of a power complex. He continues:

> If psychologism be defined as the tendency to convert events that happen between oneself and others into psychological happenings or categories, then we must say that all modern psychology, psy-

chotherapy, and psychoanalysis run the risk of falling into precisely this. The very attempt to look at the person in abstraction from his or her relations to others, as a more or less isolated psyche, means this.[36]

Martin Buber thus utters his divine word, denying the right to existence of any form of objective engagement with the soul. Given such an attitude, the only possible understanding of Gnosis is negative and it must be rejected. This brings us to the general and fundamental aspect of the conflict between Buber and Jung.

It is possible that someone who knew Martin Buber would not recognize him in my description. The reason for this is that I am attempting to represent him from within and not as the brilliant, worldly, powerfully eloquent prophet-like man whom the world knows and values. My description might make some of his essential contradictions understandable—for example, that he himself was originally somewhat Gnostic in his orientation, while he later reproached Jung for the same thing. The widespread recognition that Buber achieved shows that the world was unaware of this aspect of his being. The individual consists of contradictory character aspects, which, if not integrated consciously, will make their appearance in projected form as characteristics of the environment.

In summary, let us look back once more at the personal circumstances responsible for bringing Buber to his very one-sided understanding. The key experience, the tragedy that completely overshadowed his life, was the sudden disappearance of this mother when Buber was three years old. Had she died, it would still have been a great shock, but one that could be mitigated by the process of mourning. As it was, the young boy spent a year hoping that she would return and take him into her embrace. Then came the critical moment of certainty, conveyed by the older girl: she was never coming back. Aggravating the blow, his closest relatives were unable to empathize with the boy and provide him with information about what had happened. The disappearance remained a dark, unspeakable secret.

Later on, the soul became another such secret; it could be turned into an object of scientific curiosity only at the risk of the scientist losing his way in the maze. And, at that point, there emerges the danger of losing the world. Thus did Buber align himself fully with visible reality, and as a rationalistic natural scientist he would probably have ended up committed to a crude materialism. He was probably spared this fate by the spirituality of his Jewish heritage, even while his pronounced rationality provided him with an adequate defense against the "glowing darkness of chaos." This one-sidedness in his view of the world, brought about by unfavorable life circumstances, has a tragic aspect: it hindered the development of latent potentialities.

This, in my view, is what motivates Buber's enraged attacks on C.G. Jung. People experience rage only in relation to things that have some meaning for them, things with which they have an unconscious connection. Buber's interest in the psychological, which makes its ashamed appearance repeatedly in his work, could have opened a path toward healing, had he possessed the humility to heed the call from the other side. For the divine often conceals itself in neurotic symptoms—though frequently, to be sure, in unrecognizable or unrecognized form. Instead of turning his attention to this unknown god (the "agnostos theos" of Acts 17:23), he preferred dealing with the more concrete JHWH of archaic scripture. At the same time, he dismissed as psychologism any other encounter with an unknown god, or with Gnosis. Thus did his view of the world necessarily remain one-sided, and his life fragmented.

Chapter 3

Devotio versus Gnosis

Gilles Quispel drew my attention to the tremendous resonance Martin Buber met with his book, *Eclipse of God*,[1] in which he gave expression to a widespread cultural feeling of malaise. We find ourselves before a threshold in intellectual history similar to that which characterized late antiquity. In that epoch, the old gods had become formulaic and lifeless, as they have now. The educated class turned to philosophy (for example, Seneca), seeking a replacement for what had been lost. On these derelict foundations, foreign cults of every conceivable description (such as Isis worship, and the cult of the Great Mother) gained an enthusiastic reception. Not the least effect of the decline of the old gods was the preparing of the soil for the rise of an eastern religion of revelation, which in time developed into Christianity.

Revelation, the direct reception of the substance of a religion from a divine source, was foreign to the religions of Rome and Greece.[2] All the more eager, then, was the welcome accorded to the miracle of a god communicating directly with his people, and later sending his "only begotten son" for redemption. Philosophy represented but a distant echo of this sort of direct self-revelation of the numinous, in which contact with the godhead was so much more direct than it had been in traditional worship. This central relationship of all religion was given an entirely new dimension. The godhead as represented in philosophy was an idea—a real one, to be sure, but still rather lukewarm. This new religion, on the contrary, held out in the form of the resurrection a mysterious occurrence that seemed impossible from the point of view of philosophy, but which held extraordinary appeal for precisely that reason. Philosophy, however much it might offer certain assistance in coming to terms with life, was lacking in the element of the irrational.

In our own time, the rational and the irrational have been cut off from each other in separate spheres. A great many people conduct their daily lives in exclusively rational terms, while allowing the irrational a circumscribed role on Sunday, whether by attending church or sojourning in nature. The result, to the extent of this separation, is a neurotic split; the two spheres exist side by side without any connection. Even more dangerous is the disconnected combination of a highly developed rationality in one's professional life along with an inferior form of irrationality indulged, as it were, in secret. The tendency toward the esoteric is unmistakable in our time—though unacknowledged by the dominant form of consciousness. We fail to notice that the two are meant to be treated as complementary aspects of a single phenomenon.

Protestantism is in danger of deteriorating into a one-sided rationalism, because it has become completely bereft of "mysteria." Catholicism runs the risk that its "symbola" will no longer be understood, ossifying as a result into mere formulas. For many people, in neither denomination of Christianity do they find the numinous any longer adequately represented. For this reason, many people have either abandoned the church altogether, or turned to fundamentalism of one sort or another. Where traditional denominations no longer know how to proceed, they insist on belief. And there lies the chief difficulty, for theologians as well as the laity.

Conscious rationality cannot do away with the irrational. The dogma of Mary's virginal conception by the Holy Spirit, for example, cannot be explained biologically nor as a miracle—the latter would be no explanation, for a "miracle" is precisely that which cannot be explained scientifically. Thus, for people who cannot simply accept such statements on faith, doctrines simply no longer makes sense. And that signifies spiritual impoverishment.

The effect of all this in the psyche is like a vitamin shortage in the body: atrophy and illness. Collectively, it is manifest in the emulation of false ideals and the cultivation of bad taste. The irrational is celebrated in perverted form. Considering the amount of intelligence, time, and money that was spent in the early twentieth century to eradicate diseases caused by vitamin deficiencies, the efforts devoted to overcoming our spiritual impoverishment seem ridiculously meager. Martin Buber's book was intended to take up this point and offer assistance. Yet, as welcome as his efforts may have been, they took such a one-sided and exclusive form that the book turned into a polemic against Jung. Had

Buber not, in rather authoritarian fashion, claimed a monopoly on the single effective remedy against the widespread sense of the eclipse of God, he would have been able to recognize in Jung a possible ally—one who was approaching the problem from the other direction.

Buber's text, which I take here to be characteristic of *devotio* (a word taken from Buber himself), offers for some people a remedy for the eclipse of God. For the more or less sizeable population left over, the path charted in the text is effectively impassable. Such people instead require *Gnosis* (knowledge)—precisely that thing Buber reproaches in Jung. I do not want to rehearse here the polemic that took place between the two thinkers. It is readily available in published texts, for those who want to read it.[3] My goal, rather, is to present the underlying general problematic of two fundamentally different approaches to the numinous. Different people, according to their individual temperaments, feel themselves to be addressed more effectively by one approach or the other. Buber's conceptualization entails a reawakening of the dormant capacity for belief; Jung's entails the further development of consciousness.

For Jung—as he made clear in a late exchange of letters[4]—belief is the private affair of every individual. Gnosis, in the sense we are using it here, denotes in contrast an expansion of consciousness. In all those areas in which people are confronted with unanswerable questions, they must pursue on their own whatever understanding they find persuasive. When the result is effective and valid, it offers genuine assistance in life. A female analysand once asked Jung about his view on life after death. Jung reportedly said to her: "What good is it to you in *conspectu mortis*, to know what Jung thinks about it?"

"Unfortunately, the mythic side of man is given short shrift nowadays," writes Jung,[5]

> He can no longer create fables. As a result a great deal escapes him; for it is important and salutary to speak also of incomprehensible things... What the myths or stories about a life after death really mean, or what kind of reality lies behind them, we certainly do not know. We cannot tell whether they possess any validity beyond their indubitable value as anthropomorphic projections. Rather,

we must hold clearly in mind that there is no possible way for us to attain certainty concerning things which pass our understanding.

Each individual can search for his own myth,[6] as it emerges from the products of the unconscious and his life circumstances, in order to live a meaningful life. This is a very personal task, which in great individuals such as C. G. Jung entails a claim to general validity.[7] The rest of us must be more modest, not mistaking our own truth for "the truth." Nevertheless, it is of paramount importance that people search for their truth in life. It is a transcendent truth, not one simply cobbled together by our consciousness. (I explain further in the next volume of this work, using as basis Gnostic and alchemical texts.) It consists of all of the factors that go into determining what in a life has value, as well as what has none.

In a "Face-to-Face" interview with John Freeman,[8] Jung was asked whether he believed in God. He hesitated a moment in perplexity, and then said: "I know. I don't need to believe. I know." In responding like this, he was not saying that he had no sense of inner conviction on the matter, but that sufficient evidence had come to him from the unconscious for him to have experience of the invisible. If someone experiences something, there is no further need to believe in it. Belief always contains a moment of doubt. We encounter a great many things in our daily life that we simply believe, because we cannot prove them—take, for example, the distance between Earth and the Sun. This kind of "belief" we are always willing to correct as soon as more precise information comes along. There is not even any need to doubt, because we are profoundly convinced of the provisional nature of all of our knowledge.

But for what we term "belief" as such, it seems that doubt is not only not permitted, but positively objectionable. I have frequently observed in analytical sessions how, once the initial objection is overcome, some conventional childish belief gives way to a much more mature conviction that is more in line with the facts of life. "Either I know a thing, and then I don't need to believe it," writes Jung to H. L. Philp,[9] "or I believe it, because I'm not sure that I know it."

This split between knowledge and belief had already opened up in the first centuries of the current era: for the established church it was enough for someone to swear by a certain credo to be a member. For the Gnostics certain matters of revelation provided the point of departure for their own inner experience. This experience was the source of their conviction; and establishing the canon did not spell the end of revelation. Many of the texts from Nag Hammadi operate on the assumption that, prior to the ascension, the resurrected Christ revealed certain special things to a narrow circle of disciples. In psychological terms we interpret this to mean that the recorded words and deeds of Christ did not make up the whole of revelation. Those who find such a conclusion objectionable might want to recall that the "intuitions" of Paul, who had no personal experience of the living God-man, have been accepted as part of the canon.

Anything we might say about God, in any case, is human and inadequate. "I am far from making statements about God himself," writes Jung to Philp.[10] "I am talking about images, which it is very important to think and talk about, and to criticize, because so much depends upon the nature of our dominant ideas." That the Gnostics did not merely recognize the Christian myth as a belief, but sought instead to bring to consciousness their unconscious reactions to it, shows how important it was to them. Through the interpretation and assimilation of the myth, they are led inside themselves. Without this inner journey, there is the danger that "God remains all outside" (Meister Eckhart). "A religion that can no longer assimilate myths is forgetting its proper function," writes Jung.[11]

> But its spiritual vitality depends on the continuity of myth, and this can be preserved only if each age translates the myth into its own language and makes it an essential content of its view of the world. The Sapientia Dei which reveals itself through the archetypes always ensures that the wildest deviations shall return to the middle position.

The church fathers practiced theology only in a minor way, but they were heavily involved in hermeneutics, which is why the early centuries were so fruitful and lively. Their aim was not so much to build up the church in the sense of an organization, but the development of the *ecclesia spiritualis*. This was also the goal of the Gnostics, who were mindful of the fact that the alpha and omega of every religion is the subjective experience of the individual. "I have Gnosis," writes Jung, "so far as I have immediate experience."[12] "Instead of basing themselves upon immediate experience they [the faithful] believe in words for want of something better. The sacrificium intellectus is a sweet drug for man's all-embracing spiritual laziness and inertia."[13] Belief is responsible, specifically, for maintaining the conviction that the projection represents a reality.[14] The *word* remains for us a fetish, and we presuppose that it will produce the thing of which it is merely a sign. Moreover, our childish belief in the almighty word is a genuine obstacle to thinking.[15]

The shocking contradictions of Christianity inspired the Gnostics to devote themselves to hermeneutics; for many people today those contradictions instead motivate rational critique and atheism. It becomes increasingly difficult to convince educated lay people that theology *has nothing to do* with psychological experience.[16] Thus Jung says[17] that he can experience genuine community,

> only with those who have had the same or similar religious experience, but not with believers in the Word, who have never even taken the trouble to understand its implications and expose themselves to the divine will unreservedly. They use the Word to protect themselves against the will of God... An act of introjection is needed, i.e., the realization that the self lives in you and not in an external figure separated and different from yourself.

Buber's Attack on Gnosis

The above comments were a necessary introduction for readers desiring not only to understand the core meaning of Martin Buber's polemic against C. G. Jung, but also the basic attitudes toward the numinous that underlay it. This understanding should in turn make it possible to understand the pivotal status of human relationship to transcendence and the extent to which it is the reason for the "eclipse of God."

Now, however, it is necessary for the two adversaries to be given the chance to present the problem from their respective points of view. The major point in dispute concerns Martin Buber's claim that Gnosis in its modern form is "a psychological doctrine which deals with mysteries without knowing the attitude of faith toward mystery." Buber continues, "Gnosis is not to be understood as only a historical category, but as a universal one," a point with which I am in full agreement.[18]

> It [Gnosis]—and not atheism, which annihilates God because it must reject the hitherto existing images of God—is the real antagonist of the reality of faith. Its modern manifestation concerns me specifically not only because of its massive pretensions, but also in particular because of its resumption of the Carpocratian motif. This motif, which it teaches as psychotherapy, is that of mystically deifying the instincts instead of hallowing them in faith. That we must see C. G. Jung in connection with this modern manifestation of Gnosis I have proved from his statements and can do so in addition far more abundantly.

In 1951 Buber remarked to Maurice Friedman[19] that he regarded Jung as yet more dangerous than Heidegger for the simple reason that Jung's "Gnostic transformation of faith seemed...to contribute far more in actuality to the human responsibility for the 'eclipse of God' than Heidegger's thought-magic." The aspect of Heidegger's thought that dealt with the coming appearance of the divine Buber took to be less influential, in fact, than the aspect of Jung's thought that transformed belief into Gnosis—which in his view was central to Jung's extremely popular philosophy of individuation.

From these statements, it is clear that Buber feels personally threatened specifically by Jungian psychology, which in his mind is a philosophy (although, as noted above, it is not). But more is at stake for Buber in this dispute than a philosophical point of contention. As an elderly man, he clarified his standpoint once again:[20]

> I am against Gnosis because and insofar as it alleges that it can report events and processes within the divinity. I am against it because and insofar as it makes God into an object in whose nature and history one knows one's way about. I am against it because in the place of the personal relation of the human person to God it sets a communion-rich wandering through an upper world, through a multiplicity of more or less divine spheres.

...When I have talked of devotion, I mean by that exclusively life as personal service of God. The reverence that a man pays to the "truth," his faithfulness toward "knowledge" I respect completely. But they have something to do with the devoted immediacy to God, that I mean, only if they proceed from it and are determined by it.

I do not hold it to be a trait common to all Gnostics that they presume to find the absolute in the depths of their own soul; but from Simon Magus, who identified himself with the "Great Power of God," to certain modern manifestations, characteristic expressions of the sort have not been lacking.[21] Bergman [to whose essay, "Martin Buber and Mysticism,"[22] he is responding] points, in opposition, to the turning away from one's ego also postulated by some Gnostics. What this demand is founded upon, however, is precisely the distinction between the I, as that which is to be stripped away, and the Self, as that in whose depths the Godhead is to be discovered.

Here we have hit upon something fundamental and general: the relation between the individual and God and the relation between God and the individual. "I have written a book," writes Buber in the "Replies to my Critics,"[23]

That I call Eclipse of God because it discusses the obscuring of the divine light through something that has stepped between it and us. One has misunderstood it as thereby introducing an "almost Gnostic" conception of a strange and hindering element. Nothing of the sort is meant. I thought that I have made what was meant clear enough when I wrote in the conclusion of the book:[24] "The I-It relation, gigantically swollen, has usurped, practically uncontested, the mastery and the rule... It steps in between and shuts off from us the light of heaven." Note well, not the I-It relationship itself, without which no earthly persistence of human existence is conceivable, but its hybris overstriding all measure is meant. And thus we ourselves are meant. No demonic power works here that we have not reared ourselves.

That is the side of the event known to us. The other, the divine side, is called in the holy books of Israel the hiding of God, the veiling of the divine countenance. Nothing more than such an anthropomorphic image seems to be granted us.

One may also call what is meant here a silence of God's or rather, since I cannot conceive of any interruption of the divine revelation, a condition that works on us as a silence of God. One is the right to see here a "most troubling question."[25] These last years in a great searching and questioning, seized ever anew by the shudder of the now, I have arrived no further than that I now distinguish a revelation through the hiding of the face, a speaking through the silence. The eclipse of God can be seen with one's eyes, it will be seen.

As already noted, Buber and Jung agree that we find ourselves today in a religious crisis. The empty houses of worship and the increasing numbers of people abandoning the church every year are merely the visible signs of a more fundamental loss of orientation. But on the question of where the evil is rooted, their views diverge. In Fackenheim's presentation[26] of Buber's conceptualization, God, in addressing us, forces us to listen and to freely give our answer. An eclipse of God would come from our inability to hear what is there to be listened to, while in other times it could be because God has fallen silent. The relation between the divine address and the human response is an antinomy that cannot be resolved by thought.

In speaking to me the Infinite Thou makes me His listening I; yet unless I make myself His listening I neither shall I be His Thou nor He mine.

We recall in light of these statements that Buber has reported a *recurring* dream, which he himself understood as a confirmation of this dialog between God and the individual. As I earlier noted, dreams that have been understood—had their meaning realized—do not recur. Thus, we are obliged to contradict Buber; the "eclipse of God" originates in Buber himself, because he has failed to understand the appeal from the realm beyond consciousness. The recurring dream is the thing he has not understood; it is where he would have found the new, still unknown message—the message that was yet to be deciphered with his understanding and his heart. Instead, he calls on the holy writ in which JHWH is revealed. Then he further assures us, God's revelation is not closed. Yet, as he also says,[27] while he might *believe* in divine revelation, he is *incapable of understanding any specific instance of it* in the sense of divine content being poured into an empty human vessel.

> The actual revelation signifies to me the breaking of the eternal divine light into the human manifoldness, i.e., the breaking of the unity into contradiction. I know no other revelation than that of the meeting of the divine and the human in which the human takes part just as well as the divine. The divine appears to me like a fire that melts the human ore, but what results is not in the nature of fire... In other words, I possess no security against the necessity to live in fear and trembling; I have nothing but the certainty that we share in the revelation.

This is one of those passages, as I have already noted, in which Buber takes leave of his philosophical language, falling into a more imagistic—in this case alchemical—mode of expression. Dialogue can only make sense if the interlocutor is understood. "This question," as E. L. Fackenheim ventures to maintain,[28]

> cannot even be raised, let alone be answered, by a biographical account, that is, the kind of account which explains an author's teachings in terms of his personal experience.

As noted previously, Buber would be unique among human beings if his specific understandings had not crystallized out of his own individual experiences. In this point Buber falls into the trap set by his own philosophy. It is nothing more than pure I-It philosophizing, because of the way it proceeds in a detached rather than connected fashion. Nevertheless, it must transcend the realm of the I-It if it is to refer to a personal encounter with the divine. As he himself writes in *Eclipse of God*:[29]

For the philosopher, if he were really to wish to turn his back on that God, would be compelled to renounce the attempt to include God in his system in any conceptual form. Instead of including God as one theme among others, that is, as the highest theme of all, his philosophy both wholly and in part would be compelled to point toward God, without actually dealing with him. This means that the philosopher would be compelled to recognize and admit the fact that his idea of the Absolute was dissolving at the point where the Absolute is loved; because at that point the Absolute is no longer the "Absolute" about which one may philosophize, but God.

This is the old dilemma between believing and knowing, which has been posed again in our time by the natural sciences and technology. Many people have sought recourse in fundamentalism because, aside from atheism, they see no other way out of this dilemma. Many, like Buber, let the dilemma stand, speaking now from this vantage, now from that. Behind this is yet another dilemma, namely, the one between thinking and believing. Are we to take belief to be a blind, thoughtless acceptance of something that cannot be understood, in which thinking has no place? "Buber's own commitment, and the commitment he asks of his reader," as Fackenheim[30] states in his summary,

> would simply rest on the ancient and irrefutable faith that God can speak even though He may be silent; that He can speak at least to those who listen to His voice with all their hearts.

This only evades our question, which concerns how and where he makes himself heard. The matter is equally lacking in clarity when H. Bergmann[31] writes,

> It is the responsibility of man to reunite the world with God; the Christian language for this would be to prepare the way for the incarnation of God in the world. Buber does not use this terminology but that of "unification" which is derived from Jewish mysticism. But this unification does not refer to that of the soul with God but rather to the unification of God with the world and the penetration of the world by God. In the language of the Kabba-

lah this would be the unification of God with the Schechinah, i.e., with His "radiant Presence" which informs the world.

Readers familiar with Jung will have noticed how close Buber comes to Jung in many of his ideas, and yet how fundamentally different the two remain as soon as we probe a bit deeper. The reason for Buber's angry attack on Jung most likely lies in his own sense of something in him leading in the same direction as Jung, but which he was incapable of following. In Jung (as Buber understood him) he had met another side of himself, with every bit as much right to existence as the self of his official conceptualization. Indeed, does he not himself, at every turn, encounter the paradoxically of all statements about God in which revelation culminates in silence? As a coincidentia oppositorum God cannot be grasped except in oppositions, and at this point philosophy comes to an end, at least to the extent that it insists on deliberately avoiding ambiguity. It is tragic to watch Buber battling Jung on precisely the issues that would have lifted him to a more complete view. Thus he remained mired in one-sidedness and artificiality, while the "baby lion" grew up into an immense and imperious beast of prey.

Hans Trüb, Jung and Buber

Buber's attack on C. G. Jung may strike readers as odd, given the similarities between their positions. They might, with justice, suspect the presence of a very personal underlying motive: *the problem of power.* Precisely such an explanation was provided through the example of Hans Trüb (1889-1949), a psychiatrist from whom we have a partial description of private events.[32] Trüb was a brother-in-law of Jung's close associate, Toni Wolff; it was probably also Trüb who eventually gave Buber a copy of Jung's privately printed *Septem Sermones ad Mortuos.*

Trüb explains that he was in analysis with C. G. Jung from 1913 to 1922. During this period something happened to him, which he characterized as "my catastrophe, my downfall." It is not possible, from his very vague and general descriptions, to infer the cause of the problem. It seems to have been a disappointment, something that frequently occurs wherever an intense projection falls away. Trüb had projected his father image onto Jung—indeed, he had projected even his self—having surrendered "to his [Jung's] spiritual guidance for a period of many years." Since transference is an illusionary relationship, disillusionment of this sort does occur, and it serves to put the relationship on a real foundation. In the case of Hans Trüb, the ego was clearly not strong enough to withstand the shock involved. The entire system of his projections, as he put it himself, collapsed in on "itself." "I appeared to myself to be his [Jung's] victim and held him responsible for it."[33] He characterized Jung's attitude as "psychologistic," and, he wrote, "I used this reproach to separate myself from him." Henceforth, he rolled up in a ball like a hedgehog, impaling all Jungian concepts on his quills. This is a typical reaction of wounded feelings. The last time they met, on September 25, 1922, Jung spoke of a "causus belli"—the real reason for which Trüb kept secret!

The collapse had led him to his own guilt. Cryptic statements make it possible to conclude that the break was occasioned by something external: "It became incumbent on me to make an absolute break, because at the bottom of it all was an absolutely legitimate claim."[34] "I stand here as the guilty party. As the guilty one, I want to answer for my guilt, take responsibility."[35] "As high as I had risen before, that's how far down I fell. With broken wings, I lay at the very bottom."[36] With this tale went a dream he related; it allows us to get a small peak behind the scenes:[37]

He awakens in the morning at the very peak of a mountain. It is a small platform, just big enough for one person. He is alone, and rising from a squatting position, a dark veil falls from him, leaving him naked. All around from the misty depths rise countless mountain peaks. On each one he discovers a single person. A fathomless sorrow wells up in him because they are all separated. He awakens from his impulse to hurl himself into the depths.

The dream shows clearly that the poor man had overextended himself and was left isolated in the thin air. He had failed to notice that the tree of the analytic process has to grow roots just as deep as its crown grows into the air, lest it be uprooted by the first storm to come along. Thus the dreamer's inclination to throw himself into the depths must be understood as compensation. As an individual, the person is the "lonely peak"; his shadow, in contrast, is the collective person, the "human, all-too-human." His guilt probably consists in his not knowing his generic man. This is why, in his commentary on the dream, he quotes God's cry after the fall from grace: "Adam, where are you?" (Genesis 3:9). Recognizing the shadow robs the individual of the innocence of paradise, which entails the loss of childhood innocence. "In somnambulistic trance," in Trüb's own interpretation of the dream,[38] "I was led up here out of the depths of the unconscious by the hand of logos. It is dawn. I awaken and stand up. Far below me the world (!). I up here all alone. This is the individuality that results from individuation and at the same time as the potential for the fall, the surrender, the decision." He himself concedes that, under the aegis of logos (Jung), he experienced the emergence of an apparent subject of conscious development.

"Ever since I, as conscious subject, accepted the guilt, since, namely, this guilty person Hans Trüb has been identified, psychology is no longer my business, nor has it any meaning for me."[39] Trüb continues, "In 1923 I made the acquaintance of Buber, through whose personality a new image of human existence has been awakened."[40] Around that time, at the Psychological Club in Zurich, which was founded with the support of C. G. Jung, Martin Buber delivered a lecture on the topic "Von der Verseelung der Welt" ("The Psychologizing of the World").[41] It is likely that it was on this occasion that Hans Trüb met him. In his "blind opposition to Jung's individuality and to his works,"[42] Trüb states he found in Buber the foundation for "a reality that could renew human life."[43] The ensuing friendship between the two men entailed Trüb's acceptance of Buber's doctrine, which the Buber movement used as a trump card against Jung. Buber met Jung several times at the Eranos meetings in Ascona, where he became aware with growing envy of Jung's popularity. Many of the negative assessments in his polemic seem to have a very personal origin.

Jung and Gnosis

With Buber's position established, we turn now from the polemic to a clarification of Jung's point of view. The first task is to provide an introduction to Jung's psychology, which will then serve in the next volume of my work (*Zeitenwende*) as a basis for an interpretation of Gnosis.

According to Friedman,[44] Jung focuses on the internal in such a way that the external becomes either an obstacle standing in the way or a function of the internal. Thus is Jung charged with psychologism and, indeed, in a double sense: first, because self-development is the goal and, second, because it can only be achieved by means of a consistent introversion. A person whose orientation is defined in terms of an internal process runs the risk of consciously or unconsciously subordinating everything and everyone else to the goal of individuation or integration, which turns them into mere functions of the process itself. As a matter of fact, Jung did put more emphasis on introversion, in compensation for our primarily extroverted culture.[45] This cultural condition stems to a significant degree from people's unconscious tendency to perceive their own problems in others. This is termed "projection."

In the context of psychological development, projection corresponds to an earlier stage in the development of both culture and the individual. In antiquity the gods were projected outward and worshiped as external objects. Christ represented the completion of a revolutionary transformation, in that here a prophet had emerged who claimed that the transcendent God and the immanent God manifest in himself were one (John 10:30). It will probably not occur to anyone to accuse Jesus of megalomania, a charge levied by Buber against Simon Magus (Acts 8:9) for claiming of himself, "this is the power of God, which is called great."[46] What is the difference between the two cases? Our belief is that Jesus, through his word and his martyrdom, gained recognition as the Christ, while in the Acts of the Apostles, Simon Magus is depicted as a pitiable character. Aside from the persistence of this belief over millennia, there is no reason why someone else should not also designate himself the power of God.[47] Simon Magus was not the only one to do so. Many Gnostics declared themselves in these terms, and quite possibly a number of other prophets of whom we no longer have any knowledge.

Buber is expressing an idea that is widespread in theological circles, namely, that humans are capable of arrogating divinity to themselves. Precisely because of the extraverted attitude that has been characteristic of the culture since antiquity, our psychic development has been left lagging, and we are indeed in danger of identifying our ego with the divinity that is within us. It is no surprise that Jung was able to find no adequate expression in our culture for the greater human individual, but found it necessary to borrow the concept of the "self" from the East—a concept that comes from the Upanishads. In the Upanishads a distinction is drawn between the cosmic Atmân and the corresponding individual atmân. The closest our culture comes to this is the idea that "Christ is in you" (Romans 8:10, which in any case is frequently done away with by the translators.) The Gnostics, as we have seen, apparently understood themselves to be involved in theology rather than psychology. But many of them fell prey to precisely this psychological danger of identifying the ego with the indwelling divinity. From this blending of the ego with the self came their sometimes unbearably inflated language and self-arrogated divinity. This sort of language prompted Buber to accuse the Gnostics of having drawn "the map of the seventh heaven,"[48] just as he said of the Kabbalah that it made "a map of the primal mysteries." As a result of this misunderstanding, in Buber's view, the Gnostic mistook his self for the divine self and was incapable of serving God.

Jung takes every opportunity to emphasize the distinction between the ego and the self. He writes about the self:

This "something" is strange to us and yet so near, wholly ourselves and yet unknowable, a virtual centre of so mysterious a constitution that it can claim anything—kinship with beasts and gods, with crystals and with stars—without moving us to wonder, without even exciting our disapprobation. This "something" claims all that and more, and having nothing in our hands that could fairly be opposed to these claims, it is surely wiser to listen to this voice. I have called this centre the self... It might equally well be called the "God within us." The beginnings of our whole psychic life seem to be inextricably rooted in this point, and all our highest and ultimate purposes seem to be striving towards it... What is beyond our understanding is in any case beyond its reach. When, therefore, we make use of the concept of a God we are simply formulating a definite psychological fact, namely, the independence and sovereignty of certain psychic contents which express themselves by their power to thwart our will, to obsess our consciousness and to influence our moods and actions.[49]

In *Eclipse of God*[50] Buber criticizes Jung because in his treatment of religious phenomena, "he oversteps with sovereign license the boundaries of psychology in its most essential point. For the most part, however, he does not note it and still less account for it." Maurice Friedman[51] has the same aim in view in arguing that Jung subscribes to a simplistic neo-Kantian epistemology, according to which, as the necessary result of knowing, the psyche is raised to the status of the creator of all that is knowable, including even the supreme reality. On this he quotes Jung's statement from his memoirs:[52]

Man is indispensable for the completion of creation... in fact, he himself is the second creator of the world, who alone has given to the world its objective existence, without which, unheard, unseen, silently eating, giving birth, dying, heads nodding through hundreds of millions of years, it would have gone on in the profoundest night of non-being down to its unknown end.

These two remarks lead us to the fundamental question: *what distinguishes genuine psychology from psychologism?* In an extraverted culture like ours, so-called objective knowledge poses no difficulty. The object is made into the target of our scientific investigation; it is described or subjected to experiment in order for us to draw conclusions about its nature from the reactions it undergoes. Indeed, in science and technology, this approach to epistemology is responsible for magnificent achievements. The issue becomes difficult as soon as the object of understanding and the instrument of understanding are one and the same, as is the case in psychology. It is possible in this area as well to regard the psyche as an object and subject it to experiment, as, for example, in association tests. The fundamental problem arises only with interpretation, in which another psyche issues statements about the one under investigation, because the former lacks any external neutral standpoint from which to speak.

Psychiatry is faced with this problem: the psychiatrist is expected to make judgments about another psychic system in terms of whether it is working normally or pathologically. Buber designates this an I-It relationship, characterizing the knowledge that is won from it as inferior. He believes that by exercising "empathy" for the object it is possible to come to a judgment that is more faithful to reality. According to Buber himself, his means of orientation in the world is extraverted perception; empathy, then, as an introjected feeling, must correspond to a second auxiliary function. Feeling, because of its connection to the unconscious, has a numinous quality; this is the reason Buber believes this function to be capable of more than it would be accorded by Kantian epistemology. This occurs not only to Buber, but for many people who believe that by means of an inferior function they become able to leap over the bounds of their own knowledge. The relationship to the unconscious gives them apparently "supernatural" abilities, exceeding those of the conscious. Buber characterized this as "bold swinging...into the life of the other," which, if only because of the stilted way he has of putting it, reveals something of his being touched by the numinous.

Jung studied Kant[53] and in his works he adheres strictly to a Kantian epistemology. In Buber's approach we encounter once again, in modern form, the old scholastic problem of "universals," and of whether general and categorical concepts are substantial (*esse in re*) or are mere abstractions (*esse in intellectu*). For the extraverted attitude, universals represent merely a subsequent abstraction, because this attitude regards external appearances as the ultimate reality.[54] "One always talks of 'reality' as though it were the only one," writes Jung.[55]

> Reality is simply what works in a human soul and now what is assumed by certain people to work there, and about which prejudiced generalizations are wont to be made. Even when this is done in a scientific spirit, it should not be forgotten that science is not the summa of life, that it is actually only one of the psychological attitudes, only one of the forms of human thought.

It is possible to legitimately make a statement with a claim to universality only with the prior knowledge of one's own psychological presuppositions.

Modern depth psychology has been able to clarify the old dispute about universals: for logic, there exists only a relation of either/or between res (thing) and intellectus (understanding). No third or intermediate possibility exists because the "either/or" corresponds to a priori stances of the principle toward the world.[56] Both are one-sided and neither is universally valid. The unification of these two opposed stances can take place only in the intermediary "esse in anima" ("being in the psyche"), because in both cases psychological as opposed to logical statements are at work.

This issue assumes great importance in the interpretation of dreams. We speak of an interpretation on the "object level" when the dream is understood as a reference to an external reality. At the beginning of an analysis, before a relationship to the interior reality has been established, this is the form best understood by the analysand. By contrast, an interpretation of the dream on the "subject level" understands the entire scenario as an internal reality. "I can really think of no valid objection," writes Jung,[57] "to the theoretical probability of a subjective level. But the second problem is considerably more difficult. For just as the image of an object is composed subjectively on the one side, it is conditioned objectively on the other side. When I reproduce it in myself, I am producing something that is determined as much subjectively as objectively."

An understanding on the level of the subject has the considerable advantage of freeing the subject from the coercive embrace of the object. Perhaps on account of his early childhood experience, Buber never wanted to break loose from the object. This meant that Jung's conception of the reality of the psychic remained beyond his reach. From the standpoint of Buber's conscious philosophical position, only that which is palpable to perception is real for him. In contrast to this is his intensive involvement with Jewish mysticism. In the encounter with the divine, Buber regards God as "Thou." Jung, on the other hand, regards the divine as the unknown as such, as it manifests to us in all manner of—even shocking—forms. The key criterion in regard to issues of the divine is its autonomy, its numinosity, its compelling force, its independence and frequently contradictory appearance to human consciousness, and—in any case—its alienness.

This delimitation is especially important in relation to statements about God. And in this Buber was altogether incapable of understanding Jung. In his extraverted attitude, "true religiousness" counted for him as "an activity."[58] On the one hand, Jung writes,[59]

> The datum which is called "God" and is formulated as the "highest good" signifies, as the term itself shows, the supreme psychic value. In other words, it is a concept upon which is conferred, or is actually endowed with, the highest and most general significance in determining our thoughts and actions,

Furthermore, Jung explains,

> In the language of analytical psychology, the God-concept coincides with the particular ideation complex which, in accordance with the foregoing definition, concentrates in itself the maximum amount of libido, or psychic energy.[60] Accordingly, the actual God-concept is, psychologically, completely different in different people, as experience testifies. Even as an idea God is not a single, constant being, and still less so in reality. For, as we know, the highest value operative in a human soul is variously located. There are men "whose God is the belly" (Philippians 3:19), and others for whom God is money, science, power, sex, etc. The whole psychology of the individual, at least in its essential aspects, varies according to the localization of the highest good, so that a psychological theory based exclusively on one fundamental instinct, such as power or sex, can explain no more than secondary features when applied to an individual with a different orientation.

The question arises as to whether, from this point of view, theology remains possible today in terms of statements about God. If it is not to become "l'art pour l'art," then theology must bear on the supreme reality, namely, the problem of the relation between the individual and theology and the world, as it is newly posed on a daily basis. "Esse in intellectu lacks tangible reality, esse in re lacks mind," writes Jung.[61]

> What would the idea amount to if the psyche did not provide its living value? What would the thing be worth if the psyche withheld from it the determining force of the sense impression? What indeed is reality if it is not a reality in ourselves, an esse in anima?

Living reality is the product neither of the actual, objective behaviour of things nor of the formulated idea exclusively, but rather of the combination of both in the living psychological process, through esse in anima. Only through the specific vital activity of the psyche does the sense impression attain that intensity, and the idea that effective force, which are the two indispensable constituents of living reality.

This autonomous activity of the psyche, which can be explained neither as a reflex action to sensory stimuli nor as the executive organ of eternal ideas, is, like every vital process, a continually creative act.

The cosmic creative significance of consciousness is not an abstract problem for Jung. It became an overwhelming experience for him when he traveled from Nairobi to the great wildlife reserve at Athi Plains, and saw the herds of many thousands of animals grazing in unbroken silence, as they had been doing for unimaginable stretches of time.

This was the stillness of the eternal beginning, the world as it had always been, in the state of non-being... There I was now, the first human being to recognize that this was the world, but who did not know that in this moment he had first really created it.[62]

Psychology is not philosophy, but an empirical science that attempts to understand experiences and arrange them in terms of a larger context. Psychologism, in contrast, attempts to subordinate reality to an a priori theory. Life is so contradictory, it is unlikely in the foreseeable future that an idea will be found in which it is subsumed without contradiction. For this reason Jung emphasizes repeatedly that a psychological truth is true only when it is also possible for it to be reversed—this is a truth that is of benefit only to those possessed of the moral force it requires.

With increasing age, it becomes overwhelmingly clear to me how my perspective on the world changes to the extent that I become internally more mature and my experience of external life deepens the understanding of psychological interconnections. External and internal are really only mirror-image symmetries of the "unus mundus,"[63] the one holistic reality of lived experience. The more conscious I become, the more comprehensive becomes my perspective on external reality, and the more experience I have of external life, the more I am able to understand my internal world as I encounter it in dreams and fantasies. "The psyche creates reality every day," writes Jung.[64]

> The only expression I can use for this activity is fantasy. Fantasy is just as much feeling as thinking; as much intuition as sensation. There is no psychic function that, through fantasy, is not inextricably bound up with the other psychic functions. Sometimes it appears in primordial form, sometimes it is the ultimate and boldest product of all our faculties combined. Fantasy, therefore, seems to me the clearest expression of the specific activity of the psyche. It is, pre-eminently, the creative activity from which the answers to all answerable questions come; it is the mother of all possibilities, where, like all psychological antitheses, the inner and outer worlds are joined together in living union. Fantasy it was and ever is which fashions the bridge between the irreconcilable claims of subject and object, introversion and extraversion. In fantasy alone both mechanisms are united.

Fantasy or "imaginative activity" is not recognized in the realm of science—no more than is feeling—and this raises a major difficulty. It is easy to forget that every scientific discovery begins with a creative idea. Fantasy alone lifts us out of the deadly routine of daily life. Yet fantasy is primarily a product of the unconscious, and it is essentially involuntary. Although undoubtedly containing conscious parts, it is actually alien to consciousness. It resembles much more a dream, although dreams are involuntary and even more alien than fantasy. Thus, an individual's relation to fantasy in general depends very much on his relation to the unconscious. Rationalism, which denies that the unconscious is the matrix of all creative activity, is a child of the Enlightenment. Jung continues,[65]

> Christianity, like every closed system of religion has an undoubted tendency to suppress the unconscious in the individual as much as possible, thus paralyzing his fantasy activity. Instead, religion offers

stereotyped symbolic concepts that are meant to take the place of his unconscious once and for all. The symbolic concepts of all religions are recreations of unconscious processes in a typical, universally binding form. Religious teaching supplies, as it were, the final information about the "last things" and the world beyond human consciousness. Wherever we can observe a religion being born, we see how the doctrinal figures flow into the founder himself as revelations, in other words as concretizations of his unconscious fantasy. The forms welling up from his unconscious are declared to be universally valid and thus replace the individual fantasies of others.

This is the beginning of orthodoxy, which claims to be unique in its possession of the truth and which labels all other truths heretical or Gnostic.

Orthodoxy versus Gnosis

This same thing happened in early Christianity. The history of the beginnings of the Christian church[66] is filled with battles over orthodoxy. It is remarkable that even modern treatments, such as the one by Carl Andresen[67], operate on the unconscious assumption that there exists the single correct version, and everything that diverges from it is heterodoxy. What we are dealing with here, in my judgment, is much more the conflict between a simple form of belief (devotio) and alternative creative tendencies that do not regard revelation as closed (Gnosis). Ultimately, both of these orientations have their origin in psychology: a more extraverted attitude takes the revelation of its founder as a point of departure and established fact, and on that basis begins to elaborate a doctrine and build an organization, that is, a church. A more introverted attitude will regard the creative activity of the unconscious as the conditio sine qua non of all the further development of a religion, expanding the original revelation as appropriate on the basis of further exercises of fantasy. The extraverted attitude has as its major advantage that it pulls together a community of the faithful and builds a strong organization. The issue from this point of view has relatively little bearing on the inner quality of the experience. Legitimacy as a member is guaranteed by the recitation of a creed. The major advantage of the introverted attitude is that in it the creative spirit, that which was responsible for the revelation of the founder, is still at work.

The conflict between these two orientations is visible in the early period of Christianity. Historically, the extraverted tendency prevailed, by virtue of its powerful organization, while the introverted current succumbed to fragmentation into numerous schools. The young church elaborated its doctrine into an imposing edifice, systematically suppressing all views that diverged from it. But it could not avoid succumbing to the corruption of power. Wherever an organization is growing, the symptoms of power appear, suppressing the animating spirit that inspired both the founder and the initial followers of the cause.

Corresponding to this distinction in principle between the orientations underlying religious development, there are two types of adherents to religious movements. Those with an extraverted attitude are satisfied with a doctrine and a faith that they can adopt and develop further. From this point of view, God is entirely external, and it is possible to hold arguments about him. This is the situation of contemporary theology. Theologians write multivolume works of dogmatics about the object of their research, which they believe they come to know like the object of any other science. They base their work on the holy writ in which God once revealed himself, constantly reinterpreting it anew. And thus they construct an imposing edifice of scholarship. The individual believers marvel at this construction and—as in the *Shepherd of Hermas*—at the stone from which the church is built. The sacred is venerated here as an external object. This is devotion, which Martin Buber regarded as the only valid religious attitude.

Since God is the idea or object with the greatest amount of libido, the worship service is capable of mounting impressive ceremonies, for example, when thousands throng together for a visit by the pope. The Catholic Church, with a markedly sensuous bent, is actually most capable of satisfying this external orientation. Magnificent processions, glittering gold statues, the heart-rending stations of the cross, ecstatic Madonna worship, dramatic miracle cures, mystical raptures, worshipful choirs, and heavenly music should not be underestimated as sensuous experiences to which the faithful can cling. The Protestant church, which was radically introverted at its beginnings, no more avoids becoming ensnared in the external institutional aspects of the church. It is actually too little introverted. Insofar as a more archaic (but nonetheless culturally predominate) mentality focuses on the external, many people today feel insufficiently uplifted in an overly introverted church. They need the objects of cult worship, as well as the cult itself. Cultic religious practice makes an unmistakable impression; it sweeps people along and evokes feelings of community. This is why community receives such heavy emphasis in the Christian church. It conducts the individual out of his isolation, thus exercising a therapeutic effect that is not to be overlooked. Jung comments,[68]

> Not only Christianity with its symbols of salvation, but all religions, including the primitive with their magical rituals, are forms of psychotherapy which treat and heal the suffering of the soul, and the suffering of the body caused by the soul...

He adds, "How much in modern medicine is still suggestion therapy is not for me to say." And elsewhere, he continues the thought:[69]

> Freud has unfortunately overlooked the fact that man has never yet been able single-handedly to hold his own against the powers of darkness[70]—that is of the unconscious. Man has always stood in need of the spiritual help which his particular religion held out to him. The opening up of the unconscious always means the outbreak of intense spiritual suffering; it is as when a flourishing civilization is abandoned to invading hordes of barbarians, or when fertile fields are exposed by the bursting of a dam to a raging torrent. The World War was such an invasion which showed, as nothing else could, how thin are the walls which separate a well-ordered world from lurking chaos. But it is the same with the individual and his rationally ordered world. Seeking revenge for the violence his reason has done to her, outraged Nature only awaits the moment when the partition falls so as to overwhelm the conscious life with destruction. Man has been aware of this danger to the psyche since the earliest times, even in the most primitive stages of culture. It was to arm himself against this threat and to heal the damage done that he developed religious and magical practices.

This is why the medicine-man is also the priest; he is the saviour of the soul as well as of the body, and religions are systems of healing for psychic illness. This is especially true of the two greatest religions of humanity, Christianity and Buddhism. Man is never helped in his suffering by what he thinks of for himself; only suprahuman, revealed truth lifts him out of his distress.

Today the tide of destruction has already reached us and the psyche has suffered damage. That is why patients force the psychotherapist into the role of the priest and expect and demand of him that he shall free them from their suffering. That is why we psychotherapists must occupy ourselves with problems which, strictly speaking, belong to the theologian. But we cannot leave these questions for theology to answer; challenged by the urgent psychic needs of our patients, we are directly confronted with them every day.

We see today more clearly than ever how people whose psyches are endangered join the fundamentalist movements within their denominations. In their fragile psychological condition, all manner of paradox and insecurity has become intolerable to them. They are in need of constant reassurance as to the existence of one and only one truth. They take scriptural texts literally, so that ambiguity might be overcome there as well. Revelation is to them literally the voice of God about which no doubt can be allowed. In these circles the feeling of community is particularly well-developed, where everyone is his brother's keeper (Genesis 4:9). Jung says,[71]

Religion is a 'revealed' way of salvation. Its ideas are products of a pre-conscious knowledge which, always and everywhere, expresses itself in symbols. Even if our intellect does not grasp them, they still work, because our unconscious acknowledges them as exponents of universal psychic facts. For this reason faith is enough—if it is there. Every extension and intensification of rational consciousness, however, leads us further away from the sources of the symbols and, by its ascendancy, prevents us from understanding them. That is the situation today.

This is not only the dichotomy drawn by Buber between philosophy and believing Judaism, but it is the same split experienced by many intelligent people of our time, for example, many scientists. In their consciousness and their daily lives, they represent an enlightened rationalism, and on Sunday they listen devoutly and piously to the maxims being intoned from the pulpit. For many pastors as well, faced with this dichotomy between consciousness and the unconscious—between understanding and feeling, between knowing and believing—there remains only the escape into neurosis. People are lacking today in the understanding that could help them believe.

Faith versus Experience

To insist on faith is of no use to those who turn their back on the church. *Faith is a mercy (charisma).* Whoever has it, has no need of having it elucidated. Yet those many who in their modern mentality have lost it, do need explanations.

Jung shied away from judging metaphysical statements from the standpoint of their truth content; this is the task of theology. He regarded them as psychological statements, worthy of regard as phenomena in their own right, whatever significance might be attributed to them. As symbolum, they are preeminently real—for millennia they served for millions of people as valid statements about things that cannot be seen with the eye or touched with the hand. Wherever we come upon metaphysical truths—whether in a symbolum (avowal of faith) or dogma—we run up against the bounds set by the extraverted practice of religion. At this point, the introverted religious attitude necessarily takes over the lead role.

One of the causes of today's religious crisis lies in the suppression by the institutions of the living spirit that once brought spirit forth. Dogmas ossify into empty formulas, and rites into meaningless behavior. The denominations are externalized schema emptied of life. In both the life of an individual and the life of religion, a renewal of vitality will not be found in further externalization, but in a radical turn inward. Perhaps one of the root causes of the problem of drug addiction—against which we are so seemingly helpless—is that it represents a failed path inward. In the Gospel of John (18:36), Jesus responded to Pilate by saying that His realm was not in this world, but that He came into the world to testify to the truth, so that everyone who was of the truth would hear his voice. This betrays an introverted attitude. The organization of the church has gone too far in presenting itself as the realm of Christ for it to remain credible—at least, for many people. No one wants to get God from this world, as pious as she might be, when the corruption is simply there for all to see. "For, when God is outside," according to Jung's commentary on Meister Eckhart,[72]

> he is necessarily projected into objects, with the result that all objects acquire a surplus value. But whenever this happens, the object exerts an overpowering influence over the subject, holding him in slavish dependence. Eckhart is evidently referring to this subjection to the object, which makes the world appear in the role of God, i.e., as an absolutely determining factor. Hence he says that for such a person "God has not yet become the world," since for him the world has taken the place of God. The subject has not succeeded in detaching and introverting the surplus value from the object, thus turning it into an inner possession. Were he to possess it in himself, he would have God (this same value) continually as an object, so that God would have become the world.

Jung does not here simply express a view that is complementary to Buber's—as extraversion is to introversion—but presents a new and more mature level of insight. It has nothing to do with the mysticism that Buber reviled. Although Buber also dealt with Meister Eckhart, he did not approach this level of understanding Eckhart's insight. It is astonishing what a feel for the "psychological" Meister Eckhart had.

When the great religions take the position of not "being of this world," that probably means that attention has been turned to the inner aspect of the subject, i.e., to the unconscious. The external object declines in significance to the extent that the withdrawal of the projections returns the libido, previously localized on the external, back onto the subject. The withdrawal of libidinal cathexis in the object[73] leads the psyche back to the inner world by the same path that it lost to cathexis at the beginning of time. This leads to a resolution of the compulsive unconscious bonds to the object and to a feeling of "redemption." This feeling comes from the inward stream of psychic energy, experienced as liberation from the world. This is not to "negate the world," a tendency which Buber believed he identified in the mystics.[74] Instead, it is the discovery of the inner world, where a yet richer world than the outer one is to be found—this, owing to the correspondence between the macrocosm and microcosm. The "withdrawal and introversion [of libido] create in the unconscious a concentration of libido," writes Jung,[75]

> which is symbolized as the "treasure," as in the parables of the "pearl of great price" and the "treasure in the field." Eckhart interprets the latter as follows:

> > Christ says, "The kingdom of heaven is like a treasure hidden in a field" (Matthew 13: 44). This field is the soul, wherein lies hidden the treasure of the divine kingdom. In the soul, therefore, are God and all creatures blessed.

> This interpretation agrees with our psychological argument: the soul is a personification of the unconscious, where lies the treasure, the libido which is immersed in introversion and is allegorized as God's kingdom. This amounts to a permanent union with God, a living in his kingdom, in that state where a preponderance of libido lies in the unconscious and determines conscious life. The libido concentrated in the unconscious was formerly invested in objects, and this made the world seem all-powerful. God was then "outside," but now he works from within, as the hidden treasure conceived as God's kingdom. If, then, Eckhart reaches the conclusion that the soul is itself God's kingdom, it is conceived as a function of relation to God... The determining force (God) operating from these depths is reflected by the soul, that is, it creates symbols and images, and is itself only an image. By means of these images the soul conveys the forces of the unconscious to consciousness; it is both receiver and transmitter, an organ for perceiving unconscious contents. What it perceives are symbols. But symbols are shaped energies, determining ideas whose affective power is just as great as their spiritual power... The organ of perception, the soul, apprehends the contents of the unconscious,

and, as the creative function, gives birth to its dynamis in the form of a symbol. The soul gives birth to images that from the rational standpoint of consciousness are assumed to be worthless. And so they are, in the sense that they cannot immediately be turned to account in the objective world. The first possibility of making use of them is artistic, if one is in any way gifted in that direction; a second is philosophical speculation; a third is quasi-religious, leading to heresy and the founding of sects; and a fourth way of employing the dynamis of these images is to squander it in every form of licentiousness... The latter two modes of application were especially apparent in the Encratic (ascetic) and Antitactic (anarchic) schools of Gnosticism.

The conscious realization of these images is, however, of indirect value from the point of view of adaptation to reality—one's relation to the surrounding world is thereby freed of admixtures of fantasy. Nevertheless, their main value lies in promoting the subject's happiness and well-being, irrespective of external circumstances... This [development of symbolic fantasies] produces a new attitude toward the world, whose very difference offers a new potential. I have termed this transition to a new attitude the transcendent function. In the regenerated attitude the libido that was formerly sunk in the unconscious emerges in the form of some positive achievement. It is equivalent to a renewal of life, which Eckhart symbolizes by God's birth.

To be compared with these remarks by Jung, which clarify the great testimony of Meister Eckhart, is Buber's concept—as stated by E. L. Fackenheim[76]—according to which,

a religion whose essence is feeling is either the mere solitary disport of the soul with itself, cut off from God; or, if not cut off from God, not a relation; or, if a relation, not immediate. But the first—subjective feeling by itself—is not religion but merely the pseudoreligion of a degenerate age. The second—God found in and identified with religious feeling—is mysticism, and mysticism is only a grandiose illusion. The third—God inferred from religious feeling—is at once pseudo-religion and bad philosophy... Absorption with God-images too is a mere corruption; and this corruption is by no means overcome by an attempt to proceed by inference from the God-image to God Himself. For the God-image is a mere part of the self, and the inferred God a mere It.

If there were such a thing as genuine religion, it could only consist in a direct dialogical encounter of the human I with a divine Thou.

As Jung explained in a letter of 1958, there is in this a kernel of truth:[77]

The image of God corresponds to its manifestation; i.e., such religious experience produces such an image... The most shocking defectuosity of the God-image ought to be explained or understood. The nearest analogy to it is our experience of the unconscious: it is a psyche whose nature can only be described by paradoxes: it is personal as well as impersonal, moral and amoral, just and unjust, ethical and unethical, of cunning intelligence and at the same time blind, immensely strong and extremely weak, etc.... The unconscious is a piece of Nature our mind cannot comprehend. It can only sketch models of a possible and partial understanding... The real nature of the objects of human experience is still shrouded in darkness. The scientist cannot concede a higher intelligence to theology than to any other branch of human cognition. We know as little of a supreme being as of matter. But there is as little doubt of the existence of a supreme being as of matter. The world beyond [consciousness] is a reality, an experiential fact. We only don't understand it.

Note, Jung expresses himself very carefully in these matters; there is no question here of transgressing boundaries. At the same time, he holds the theologians to the same standard. It is part of human nature to be constantly making statements about the divine; this is a psychological matter that can, and must, be investigated. A statement that is an expression of the psyche betrays in the best of cases something about the psyche's activity and nature, without our having the slightest idea what causes it to do what it does. Critics of Jung's psychological investigations of religious phenomena often think that Jung understands them as "merely" psychic, thus associating him with psychologism. "Faced with such a situation," Jung questions his critics in turn,[78] "we must really ask: How do we know so much about the psyche that we can say "only" psychic?"

> For this is how Western man, whose soul is evidently "of little worth," speaks and thinks. If much were in his soul he would speak of it with reverence. But since he does not do so we can only conclude that there is nothing of value in it. Not that this is necessarily so always and everywhere, but only with people who put nothing into the souls and have "all God outside." (A little more Meister Eckhart would be a very good thing sometimes!)...
>
> Even the believing Christian does not know God's hidden ways and must leave him to decide whether he will work on man from outside or from within, through the soul... It would be blasphemy to assert that God can manifest himself everywhere save only in the human soul. Indeed the very intimacy of the relationship between God and the soul precludes from the start any devaluation of the latter. It would be going perhaps too far to speak of an affinity; but at all events the soul must contain in itself the faculty of relationship to God, i.e., a correspondence, otherwise a connection could never come about. This correspondence is, in psychological terms, the archetype of the God-image.

From this comes the reproach that Jung deified the psyche. "Not I but God himself has deified it!" he cried to his critics.[79]

> It may easily happen, therefore, that a Christian who believes in all the sacred figures is still undeveloped and unchanged in his inmost soul because he has "all God outside" and does not experience Him in the soul. His deciding motives, his ruling interests and impulses, do not spring from the sphere of Christianity, but from the unconscious and undeveloped psyche, which is as pagan and archaic as ever... In his soul the Christian has not kept pace with external developments. Yes, everything is to be found outside—in image and in word, in Church and Bible—but never inside. Inside reign the archaic gods, supreme as of old; that is to say, the inner corre-

spondence with the outer God-image is undeveloped for lack of psychological culture and has therefore got stuck in heathenism.

Very early in the history of Christianity there evidently were people who could not content themselves with an external understanding of the salvation message. For them the "tidings of joy" were not merely a narrative about external occurrences, however edifying they may have been as such. The echo that the story evoked in their souls was much more important to them. They received the reports not simply as historical events, but introjected them. To the extent that they based their views on the Bible, they were not apostates. Their reactions came directly out of the collective unconscious, which accounts for the form of their inflated prose. This is a compensatory attitude that they adopted toward the external practice of religion—at attitude we denote as Gnostic, although it appears as well among other heretics and mystics. Nothing gives us the right to characterize this orientation as inferior or "apostate"—particularly since there are introverted aspects in the canonical Gospel of John, as well. We do not know just how the founder of Christianity wanted his message to be understood. Certain extracanonical quotations attributed to Jesus leave open the possibility that some things that came out of his mouth were suppressed because a simple mentality was unable to understand them.

Orthodoxy cannot be measured exclusively as the attitude that triumphed over Gnosis. Historically, the struggle against the Gnostics provided the developing orthodox church with an important means of clarifying its own standpoint. In the first two centuries, practically no one thought of making a doctrine or a system out of the scanty information that was handed down about Jesus' life and works. Only with the increasing organization of the church did this idea take form. To distinguish itself from philosophy and from Gnosis, the institutional church was obliged to formulate its own standpoint and to develop it into a system: this was the origin of orthodox theology. The process can be seen very nicely in Origen's *Contra Celsum*. The process by which Origen found his own position occurred against the background of other views, view which provide a contrast that distinguish his position. Seen in this way, Gnosis was a necessary development in order for orthodoxy to arise in the first place.

As I have already explained, there are in principle two attitudes: one I termed devotion; and the other, Gnosis. The devotional attitude regarded Gnosis as an enemy and historically was responsible for undertaking a brutal assault upon it. Today we must recognize that the Gnostic position represented, relative to orthodox theology, a more developed process of integration of the soul.

Of course, the Gnostics lacked the modern psychological perspective necessary to understand what they were doing. And while this is the source of a certain degree of eccentricity in their writings, it should not dissuade us from taking them seriously. They might even offer a new source of exploration for modern people who find their received religion too superficial and too external. Nevertheless, I have to disappoint those who believe they might find in Gnosis a ready-made religion, which they can simply take over. It is much more a matter of attaining a new attitude, which might point the way toward a new understanding. The majority of Gnostics did not see redemption in the Son of God descending from heaven, but instead charged individuals with the task of Gnosis (knowing). Some critics will characterized this as "self-redemption"—but they do so without experience of how arduous the path is, and how dependent humans are on grace to gain the necessary insights. In this respect, an examination of the role of the redeemer in Gnosis can deepen our self-understanding.

Chapter 4

On the Nature of Gnosis

We come now to the extremely difficult question of what the nature of Gnosis actually is, aside from being an introverted religious attitude.

What motivated Martin Buber, and following him Maurice Friedman,[1] to categorize Jung as a Gnostic is the position he adopted toward evil. Evidently, neither of them was aware of two articles— "A Psychological View of Conscience" (1957)[2] and "Good and Evil in Analytical Psychology" (1958)[3] —in which Jung laid out in detail his views on the issue. Buber[4] charges Jung with "relativizing evil" and "denying the individual as a moral instance." In Buber's view, the birth of the "pneumatic man" entails the elevation of judgment above the opposition between good and evil; he thinks "pneumatic man" lacks the moment of the forceful repression of instinct, and this constitutes a hysterical overlay on spirituality. It corrupts it. "The man who lives with his instincts," he quotes Jung,[5] "can also detach from them, and in just as natural a way as he lived with them." This is clearly a Carpocratian motif, as Jung himself points out in *Psychology and Religion*.[6] Carpocrates, the legendary Gnostic or Neoplatonic philosopher of the second century—and a licentious heretic, in Buber's views—stated, as Jung describes,

> that good and evil are merely human opinion and that the soul, before its departure from the body, must pass through the whole gamut of human experience to the very end if it is not to fall back into the prison of the body. It is as if the soul could ransom itself from imprisonment in the somatic world of the demiurge by complete fulfillment of all life's demands. The bodily existence in which we find ourselves is a kind of hostile brother whose conditions must first be known. It was in this sense the Carpocratians interpreted Matthew 5:25f. (also Luke 12:58f.)... It is natural that the more robust mentality of the Church Fathers could not appre-

ciate the delicacy and the merit of this subtle and, from a modern point of view, immensely practical argument. It was also dangerous, and it is still the most vital and yet the most ticklish ethical problem of a civilization that has forgotten why man's life should be sacrificial, that is, offered up to an idea greater than himself. Man can live the most amazing things if they make sense to him. But the difficulty is to create that sense. It must be a conviction, naturally; but you find that the most convincing things man can invent are cheap and ready made, and are never able to convince him against his personal desires and fears.

It strikes me as noteworthy that Buber[7] should be particularly attentive to the Carpocratian motif and that he criticizes Jung for deifying the instincts, rather than sanctifying them in faith. In Friedman's opinion,[8] "The most important issue between Jung and Buber is what happens to the drives toward evil, what the Talmud and the Hasidim call the 'evil urge.'" This is obviously an unresolved question, and one to which the Gnostics likewise sought answers.

Yet, concealed in a Westerner's sweeping condemnation of the "mystical deification of the instincts," there is deep-seated fear of the psychic stratum—manifest not least in the worship of the golden calf (Moses 2:32). The calf represents an archaic stage in the Jewish image of God, to which the people reverted in the absence of their leader Moses, when he was on the sacred mountain. The people apparently experienced a particular difficulty here because they had distanced themselves too little from their instincts.

In his "Autobiographical Fragments,"[9] Martin Buber describes a telling episode from his childhood: During summer vacation on his grandparents' estate, he was in the habit of sneaking as often as he could into the stables, to visit his beloved horse—a broad dapple-gray—and to comb out its mane.

> It was not a casual delight but a great...but also deeply stirring happening... What I experienced in touch with the animal was the Other, the immense otherness of the Other, which, however, did not remain strange... When I stroked the mighty... sometimes astonishingly wild [mane], and felt the life beneath my hand, it was

as though the element of vitality itself bordered on my skin... The horse...very gently raised his massive head... then snorted quietly, as a conspirator gives a signal meant to be recognizable only by his fellow-conspirator; and I was approved. But once...it struck me about the stroking, what fun it gave me, and suddenly I became conscious of my hand.

Suddenly, he emerged from the childish "participation mystique." He did not conclude from this experience that the numinous must also be received on a new level of consciousness, a consciousness he had happened upon spontaneously in archaic form. The symbolic meaning of the horse, whose strength we still use today as a measure of power, most likely stems from similar experiences of a strong inner kinship between horse and man, between steed and rider. Jung writes: "In the present context, therefore, the hero and his horse seem to symbolize the idea of man and the subordinate sphere of animal instinct."[10]

Legends attribute properties to the horse which psychologically speaking belong to the unconscious of man: there are clairvoyant and clairaudient horses, path-finding horses who show the way when the wanderer is lost, horses with mantic powers. In the Iliad (xix), the horse prophesies evil. They hear the words the corpse utters on its way to the grave—words which no human can hear... Horses also see ghosts. All these things are typical manifestations of the unconscious.

Buber could have learned from this image of the steed and rider that the individual is not simply consigned to the primary instinct, but has domesticated it and developed an amicable relationship with it. The close feeling of relationship to the horse and its divinity might have conveyed to him the experience of the other: that which is both alien and related.

In his memoirs,[11] Jung describes "God's world," the cosmos of his youth, as follows:

I love all warm-blooded animals who have souls like ourselves and with whom, so I thought, we have an instinctive understanding. We experience joy and sorrow, love and hate, hunger and thirst, fear and trust in common—all the essential features of existence with the exception of speech, sharpened consciousness, and science.

This illustrates what a natural relationship Jung had with nature, which appeared to him as the God-world. This is why much later in life, upon learning of the natural philosophers called the alchemists, he welcomed this knowledge enthusiastically. They obviously shared a similar world-image: God had placed his secret inside his creation, where it could be found through the study of nature. The entire macrocosm was not only to be discovered, but also to be redeemed—a task that Christianity had failed to accomplish. In his focus on the material, Buber relates to the problem of instincts, he hit by accident on a central point in which the introverted religious attitude moves ahead of the extraverted one. At issue is not "this or that" Gnostic doctrine, but the fact that Gnosis has in view a more comprehensive and complete cosmos. "The theriomorphic attributes of the gods," writes Jung,[12] "show that the gods extend not only into superhuman regions but also into the subhuman realm. The animals are their shadows, as it were, which nature herself associates with the divine image."

Buber criticized Jung because, "He oversteps with sovereign license the boundaries of psychology in its most essential point. For the most part, however, he does not note it and still less account for it."[13]   But what Buber has failed to notice is that where Jung finds rational consideration running up against a boundary, he follows the hints supplied by the unconscious in order to elaborate a concept of the unknowable. "My hypothesis is that we can do so with the aid of hints sent to us from the unconscious—in dreams, for example," he writes in his memoirs.[14]

Usually we dismiss these hints because we are convinced that the question is not susceptible to answer. In response to this understandable skepticism, I suggest the following considerations. If there is something we cannot know, we must necessarily abandon it as an intellectual problem. For example, I do not know for what reason the universe has come into being, and shall never know. Therefore I must drop this question as a scientific or intellectual problem. But if an idea about it is offered to me—in dreams or in mythic traditions—I ought to take note of it. I even ought to build up a conception on the basis of such hints even though it will forever remain a hypothesis that I know cannot be proved... Reason sets the boundaries far too narrowly for us, and would have us accept only the known—and that too with limitations—and live in a known framework, just as if we were sure how far life actually extends. As a matter of fact, day after day we live far beyond the bounds of our consciousness; without our knowledge, the life of the unconscious is also going on within us. The more critical reason dominates, the more impoverished life becomes; but the more of the unconscious, and the more of myth we are capable of making conscious, the more life we integrate. Overvalued reason has this in common with political absolutism: under its dominion, the individual is pauperized.

The unconscious helps by communicating things to us, or making figurative allusions. It has other ways, too, of informing us of things that by all logic we could not possibly know. Consider synchronistic phenomena, premonitions, and dreams that come true... When one has such experiences...one acquires a certain respect for the potentialities and arts of the unconscious. Only, one must remain critical and be aware that such communications may have a subjective meaning as well. They may be in accord with reality, and then again, they may not. I have, however, learned that the views I have been able to form on the basis of such hints from the unconscious have been most rewarding. Naturally, I am not going to write a book of revelations about them, but I will acknowledge that I have a "myth" which encourages me to look deeper into this whole realm. Myths are the earliest form of science.[15]

Myth and Gnosis

Gnosis is not a philosophy; it does not stem from a desire to rationally understand the world. It is much closer to myth, which is the formulation of an unconscious content. "Myth is the natural and indispensable intermediate stage between conscious and unconscious cognition," explains Jung.[16]

True, the unconscious knows more than the consciousness does; but it is knowledge of a special sort, knowledge in eternity, usually without reference to the here and now, not couched in the language of the intellect. Only when we let statements amplify themselves...does it come within the range of our understanding; only then does a new aspect become perceptible to us.

Myth is not only the preconscious stage of unconscious content, but also has a therapeutic effect. Precisely in regard to the unknown, it is of incalculable value to develop some conception of it. For without some such idea, we are left helpless in the face of all manner of horrors and images stemming from the collective unconscious. Whatever the modern consciousness is unable to define, it takes to be abnormal, objectionable, or pathological. Archetypal contents in dreams and fantasies can indeed take the form of the grotesque and ghastly. And in the face of profoundly experienced nightmares and obsessive fearful images, the rational consciousness is powerless. Thus is it of pressing importance to provide a context for the fantasy images that emerge in this way and that are so alien—indeed threatening—to consciousness, in order to make them more understandable.

To achieve this understanding, we must reach back to the immediate historical predecessors of the modern consciousness. Present-day consciousness is the product of two components: the spirit of the established church in the West, on the one hand; and science, on the other. The ineradicable remnants of the classical spirit and sense of nature found asylum in medieval natural philosophy. Through the increasing differentiation of rites and dogma in the church, the collective consciousness drifted more and more out of contact with its natural roots in the unconscious. Alchemy and astrology played a compensatory role in not allowing the bridges with nature to deteriorate. They favored searching by means of knowledge rather than accepting what can be found constituted through belief. In doing so, they recaptured the primary experience in which every belief originates.

Dogma is no arbitrary invention or unique miracle, as people like to portray it, and thus remove it for plausible reasons from the natural context. The central ideas of Christianity are rooted in Gnostic philosophy, which, in terms of a psychological explanation, necessarily developed in a period in which the classical religions had lost their truth content. Whenever the over-arching ideas ruling human life undergo deterioration, the unconscious process of symbol formation involved in individuation begins anew. In our contemporary world as well a growing number of people find themselves increasingly in the grip of powerful numinous archetypes, the latter pressing to the surface in the process of forming a new dominant. The phenomenon is in every case apparent in the way that those being moved by the images identify themselves with the contents of them, as opposed to understanding that the content being recognized is exercising an influence on their lives. The number of new prophets and reformers, along with the associated flood of esoteric literature, shows that they do not recognize the role being pressed upon them as the effect of a content that is yet to be understood. Throughout Western history there have always been people who have not been satisfied with the Christian dominant of conscious life. Whether in secret or by indirect means, whether to their well-being or their peril, they have sought to recapture the primal experience of their own roots and followed out the fascination presented by their disquieted unconscious.

As diverse as may have been the cultural precursors feeding historically into the formation of any given dominant of consciousness, they nevertheless are based on an archetypal foundation that remains everywhere the same. This explains the accessibility to understanding that is characteristic of all historical products of the mind. Modern people experience the emergence of Gnostic, or alchemical symbols and motifs, out of this same stratum of the collective unconscious, without the slightest indication that these contents were otherwise known to them or transmitted in any way.

Jung states:

> Although in crude form, we find in Gnosticism what was lacking in the centuries that followed: a belief in the efficacy of individual revelation and individual knowledge. This belief was rooted in the proud feeling of man's affinity with the gods, subject to no human law, and so overmastering that it might even subdue the gods by the sheer power of Gnosis... In Gnosticism we see man's unconscious psychology in full flower, almost perverse in its luxuriance; it

contained the very thing that most strongly resisted the regula fidei, that Promethean and creative spirit which will bow only to the individual soul and to no collective ruling.[17]

This is a compensatory phenomenon for all of those who do not feel themselves taken up and included in the collective, extraverted faith. The Gnostics differentiated people according to type, including the pneumatikoi (spiritual men), the psychikoi (animate men), and the hylikoi (material men), corresponding generally to the psychological functions of thinking, feeling, and sensation. "The inferior rating of the psychikoi," writes Jung,[18]

was in accord with the spirit of Gnosticism, which, unlike Christianity, insisted on the value of knowledge. The Christian principles of love and faith kept knowledge at a distance. In the Christian sphere the pneumatikoi would accordingly get the lower rating, since they were distinguished merely by the possession of Gnosis, i.e., knowledge... Owing to the predominantly practical trend of early Christianity the intellectual hardly came into his own, except when he followed his fighting instincts by indulging in polemical apologetics. The rule of faith was too strict and allowed no freedom of movement. Moreover, it was poor in positive intellectual content. It boasted of few ideas, and though these were of immense practical value they were a definite obstacle to thought. The intellectual was much worse hit by the sacrificium intellectus than the feeling type. It is therefore understandable that the vastly superior intellectual content of Gnosis, which in the light of our present mental development has not lost but has considerably gained in value, must have made the greatest possible appeal to the intellectual within the Church. For him it held out in very truth all the temptation of this world [e.g., Augustine's Manichaeism].

Gnosis is characterized by the hypostatizing of psychological apperceptions, i.e., by the integration of archetypal contents beyond the revealed "truth" of the Gospels.

Jung responds elsewhere to an interviewer:[19]

Hippolytus still considered classical Greek philosophy along with Gnostic philosophies as perfectly possible views. Christian Gnosis to him was merely the best and superior to all of them.

St. Paul had to make allowances for what his cultivated listeners— among them, Epicureans and Stoics in Athens—were able to accept. On the Areopagus, the old seat of the government and court, he maneuvered his way out of a dangerous situation by proclaiming the "unknown God" whom they, too, without knowing it, would be worshipping in their temples (Acts 17: 16-34). This was not the last of the concessions made to a culture that, while unwilling to accept Eastern revelation as a matter of faith, had produced remarkable achievements by way of the thinking function. Christian theology was ultimately an amalgam of revelation and philosophy, provoking the conflict between faith and knowledge. Theology sought to use philosophy as a way of pouring revelation into a belief system that could serve as the foundation on which to build a church. The Gnostics—who had less use for ecclesiology of any sort—opened themselves up to, and ultimately succumbed to, the danger of fragmentation into many small sects.

Thus it was necessary for Christian doctrine to be reinterpreted in order to conform to the Hellenistic world, as can be seen in the reactions of its most outstanding defender, Justin the Martyr.[20] As a young man, he had educated himself in all known schools of philosophy, of which Platonism was the only one that offered satisfaction—he was evidently an introverted thinking type. One day as he strolled along the beach engrossed in philosophical contemplation, a dignified old man joined him. In dialogue, the old man quickly forced him to the conclusion that Platonic philosophy was likewise incapable of satisfying the mind and heart of man. If one wanted to achieve inner peace, explained the old man, one had to turn away from the philosophers, and turn to the prophets.[21] Their holiness—and the miracles and divinations for which they were responsible—were the organs of the holy spirit and the intermediaries to the truth. From their writings came knowledge of the creator of the universe, of God the father, and of the Christ who was sent by the father. One could seek, through the entreaty of prayer, the grace of being able to understand their words. This conversation awakened Justin's love for the prophets and for Christ, as he tells in the first

chapter of his "Dialog with the Jew Tryphon." He never saw the vener-
able teacher again. Justin was convinced by the extraverted feeling so
impressive manifest in the steadfastness of Christians; this led to his
own conversion. From then on—as we know from Eusebius—Justin
wandered through the Hellenistic world in the coat of a philosopher,
preaching Christianity as the sole reliable and useful philosophy.

"A myth remains a myth even if certain people believe it to be the
literal revelation of an eternal truth, but it becomes moribund if the
living truth it contains ceases to be an object of belief. It is therefore
necessary to renew its life from time to time through a new interpretation."[22] The myth must be re-narrated in a new spiritual language.
Experience shows that a psychological understanding is capable of
immediately reviving the essential Christian doctrines, filling them
with the breath of life. The effect, to be precise, is that the apparently
unbridgeable chasm between knowing and believing is rendered moot:
with psychological insight, scientific knowledge and understanding fall
into correspondence with the symbolic expression of the myth.

In the scene mentioned above on the Areopagus, Paul told of how
God overlooked times of ignorance (agnoia) but has now declared
himself (Acts 17: 30). In I Corinthians he is yet more explicit:

Where is the wise? where is the scribe? where is the disputer of this
world? hath God not made foolish the wisdom of this world? For
after that in the wisdom of God the world by wisdom knew not
God, it pleased God by the foolishness of preachers to save them
that believe. For the Jews require a sign, and the Greeks seek after
wisdom: But we preach Christ crucified, unto the Jews a stumbling
block, and unto the Greeks foolishness; But unto them which are
called, both Jews and Greeks, Christ the power of God, and the
wisdom of God (1: 20-24).

This appeal the Gnostics understood as meaning that neither philosophy nor prophecy alone led to truth and knowledge, but rather their
specific psychic reaction to the figure and message of Christ as it clashed
with the pagan world. Jung designated this a "phenomenon of assimilation" [Rezeptionserscheinung].[23] The countless Gnostic amplifications
may seem, to the modern understanding, more to obscure than clarify

the message. Yet recognizable from start to finish even in these is the transformation of sensuous extraversion into introverted symbolism. The phenomenon of assimilation represents, first of all, the reaction of the unconscious. Having been plunged into turmoil by the message, the unconscious responds with archetypal images, thus showing just how deeply the message has penetrated into the psyche and how the unconscious interprets the appearance of Christ. The fundamental problem of Christianity was, indeed, the moral and spiritual agnosia of the natural human being.

Today Christian peoples are faced with a similar problem: their Christianity has fallen into a slumber. Jung explains[24] that over the course of the centuries they have neglected to further construct their myth.

They do not realize that a myth is dead if it no longer lives and grows. Our myth has become mute, and gives no answers. The fault lies not in it as it is set down in the Scriptures, but solely in us who have not developed it further, who, rather, have suppressed any such attempts. The original version of the myth offers ample points of departure and possibilities of development... A further development of the myth might well begin with the outpouring of the Holy Spirit upon the apostles, by which they were made into sons of God, and not only they, but all others who through them and after them received the filiatio—sonship of God—and thus partook of the certainty that they were more than autochthonous animalia sprung from the earth, that as the twice-born they had their roots in divinity itself. Their visible, physical life was on this earth; but the invisible inner man had come from and would return to the primordial image of wholeness, to the eternal Father, as the Christian myth of salvation puts it.

"If the spiritual adventure of our time," as Jung says in his concluding lecture on Psychology and Religion,[25]

is the exposure of human consciousness to the undefined and indefinable, there would seem to be good reasons for thinking that even the Boundless is pervaded by psychic laws, which no man invented,

but of which he has "Gnosis" in the symbolism of Christian dogma. Only heedless fools will wish to destroy this; the lover of the
soul, never.

The age brought forth by Christianity and Gnosis was one in which
man, the world, and the godhead no longer formed an untroubled
unity—the Greek critique of the world having already had its effect.
Now new questions were being raised concerning such issues as the
origin of evil, the imperfection of creation, the meaning of suffering,
etc. Running parallel to this was the need for redemption, or for a
redeemer. The tendency of the extraverted attitude was to expect salvation in the form of a redeemer, while the introverted attitude looked for
it in knowledge, or as we would say today, *in becoming conscious*. This
attitude continues to be met with dismissal. It is seen as self-
redemption, although it should be apparent that this is the path that
has been followed successfully in the East for several millennia.

The Gnostic Christ

It is particularly interesting to pursue the question of the Gnostic
reception of Christ, because in this the two attitudes join hands. For
most Gnostics, Christ remains the redeemer, although he does so in a
form thoroughly worked over by the unconscious. The "world of the
son"[26] is characterized by the onset of an independent understanding; it
is an the overcoming of the extraverted fidelity to the law of the "world
of the father."[27] Justin the Martyr—who was discussed briefly above—
wrote in his *Apology*, that we do not remain "the children of necessity
and of ignorance, but may become the children of choice and
knowledge." In this same spirit, Clement of Alexandria declared, "how
necessary is it for him who desires to be partaker of the power of God,
to treat of intellectual subjects by philosophizing!"[28] He explains further: "Knowledge, accordingly, is characterized by faith; and faith, by a
kind of divine mutual and reciprocal correspondence, becomes characterized by knowledge."[29] He adds that through Gnosis, "faith is
perfected, inasmuch as it is solely by it that the believer becomes perfect."[30] And finally, "And knowledge [Gnosis] is the strong and sure
demonstration of what is received by faith."[31] In these statements, it

becomes clear how tightly interwoven and mutually influential are theology, philosophy, and Gnosis—in spite of whatever enmity in principle may have divided them. Jung makes the point:[32]

> As can plainly be seen from Gnosticism and other spiritual movements of the kind, people are naively inclined to take all the manifestations of the unconscious at their face value and to believe that in them the essence of the world itself, the ultimate truth, has been unveiled.
>
> This assumption does not seem to me quite as unwarranted as it may look at first sight, because the spontaneous utterances of the unconscious do after all reveal a psyche which is not identical with consciousness and which is, at times, greatly at variance with it. These utterances occur as a natural psychic activity that can neither be learnt nor controlled by the will. The manifestation of the unconscious is therefore a revelation of the unknown in man... In these archetypal forms, something, presumably, is expressing itself that must in some way be connected with the mysterious operation of the natural psyche—in other words, a cosmic factor of the first order.

The inflation characteristic of the Gnostics, which is responsible for their sometimes bombastic language, stems from the self-identification of the enlightened subject with his interior light (Gnosis)—the subject has mistaken the ego for the self, and imagines himself to have risen above his own darkness (agnoia). He forgets that light only makes sense where there is darkness to be illumined, and that his enlightenment can be of service only if it helps him to recognize his own darkness.

> Recognizing the danger of Gnostic irrealism, the Church, more practical in these matters, has always insisted on the concretism of the historical events despite the fact that the original New Testament texts predict the ultimate deification of man in a manner strangely reminiscent of the words of the serpent in the Garden of Eden: "Ye shall be as gods." (Genesis 3:5).[33]

Had the Gnostic not identified with the self in this way he would have been obliged to recognize the extent of the darkness within him. Modern people much more easily gain this insight into our personal darkness, and it is the cause of many associated complaints. However, despite all the unfortunate consequences of the Gnostics' inflation, they did attain to both religio-psychological and religious insights from which we can still learn a thing or two. They peered deeply into the background conditions of Christianity, and thus also into its future development.

On the one hand, Christianity compensated for the spiritual disorientation of the Roman world; but on the other hand, it had to defend itself against what Jung described as "the excessive pretensions of some of its adherents, including those of the Gnostics."

> Increasingly it [Christianity] had to rationalize its doctrines in order to stem the flood of irrationality. This led, over the centuries, to that strange marriage of the originally irrational Christian message with human reason, which is so characteristic of the Western mentality. But to the degree that reason gradually gained the upper hand, the intellect asserted itself and demanded autonomy.[34]

"This Gnostic Christ, of whom we hear in the Gospel according to St. John, symbolizes man's original unity and exalts it as the saving goal of his development."[35] This intuition exalted and redeemed the individual by connecting him with his center, which is at once the midpoint of the universe. This intuition presupposes a robust ego-consciousness that does not succumb to the temptation to identify with the self. The danger in this, however, is that the ego all too often identifies with the inner Christ, encouraged by a false understanding of the imitatio Christi. This is why the church failed to make much of the dictum "Christ is in you" (Romans 8:10).

> For the less mindful [consciousness] is of the unconscious, the greater becomes the danger of its identification with the latter, and the greater, therefore, the danger of inflation, which, as we have experienced to our cost, can seize upon whole nations like a psychic epidemic.[36]

From various hints dropped by Hippolytus, it is clear beyond a doubt that many of the Gnostics were nothing other than psychologists. Thus he reports them as saying that "the soul is very hard to find and to comprehend" (Elenchos, V, 7, 8) and that knowledge of the whole man is just as difficult.[37]

The majority of the Gnostics may sound like theologians (Valentinus and Basilides are examples), but to a considerable extent—in contrast to orthodox theologians—they opened themselves up to the influence of natural inner experience.[38] This is the grounding of a psychological viewpoint.

Differentiating Light and Dark

Gnosticism cannot escape criticism for its oft one-sided spirituality. From the perspective of modern depth psychology, we need not however take its "pessimistic flight from the world" literally. We can view it as a development from a state of unconsciousness, characterized as evil, to the enlightenment or knowledge (Gnosis), associated with the light. Even so, however, the Gnostics verge on a dualism; this took its most radical form in Manichaeism.

In the untitled text of the Bruce Codex, the Lord of Glory separated matter into two lands, one on the right and one on the left. The one on the right is the land of life and light, and on the left is the land of death and darkness. The protogenitor spread a veil over the lighted region, "In order to separate that which is from that which is not. That which is not is the evil, which appeared in matter."[39] Today we designate "that which is not" as the unconscious, a concept just as "negative" as that of the Gnostics—with consciousness we are unable to define "the unconscious" more precisely. There has been a tendency to understand this "negative" of the unconscious as chaos and the embodiment of evil—as did Freud with his concept of "id." This is incorrect insofar as instincts, or inborn behaviors,[40] are also present in both humans and animals, and they dwell within this undifferentiated unconscious realm as life-sustaining structures. The Gnostics quite generally neglected these more chthonic parts of the psyche in favor of the intellect. This one-sidedness of ancient Gnosticism probably should be understood in terms of the spiritual situation of the time, in which the libidinal parts of the psyche played a preponderant role in people's lives. Their one-sidedness in the division of the world into good and evil stems from the fact that they had to compensate for a one-sided mentality of their age.

Marie-Louise von Franz, in her essay "Jung's Discovery of the Self," addressed the so-called boundary violation by Jungian psychology—the reproach of "psychologism" in its attitude to religion. As she explains: [41]

> From time to time the metaphysical concepts and statements of theologians of all culturally more highly developed religions seem to lose touch with their experiential basis, and then they can no longer evoke the primal experience that is so charged with meaning. The words no longer have any living content; they have degenerated into sterile ideas. It is like people clinging to possessions that once meant wealth; the more ineffectual and incomprehensible and lifeless they become, the more obsessed with them people become. Through inner psychological experience, on the other hand, the words can once again be connected with the understanding of the ego and again become actual in the sense of active.

Gnosis is an unconscious reaction to the collapse of the old system of religion, just as was Christianity. In the late Roman Empire, Gnosis was the philosophy that arose to displace the Roman religion in decline. On the one hand, it was magical thought; on the other, it included the irrational element. Gnosis and Christianity united both these aspects in a new, vital form.

Similar spontaneous compensatory reactions are also observed in modern individuals confronted with collapse of an "old system." People entering analysis suddenly experience "big," i.e., religious dreams. "So if this is a case of boundary violation," von Franz continues,

> then it is one committed by the unconscious of the patients, not by the analysts. But the analyst usually cannot send the patient on to a theologian, because as a rule patients resist this. They want to understand their dreams in the framework of the inner experience they have had up to this point. If there is a priest or minister with

sufficient understanding, and if the patient is willing to seek him out, then of course one can refer the patient to him. And Jung in fact did this, mostly with Catholic patients. For the most part, however, theologians today are still too inexperienced to be able to help in any way. For instance, once a peasant woman came to me who from her earliest childhood had had vivid visions, primarily visions of light. She was completely normal. "I went to the minister with this," she told me, "but, you know, they don't understand anything about it. The minister even gave me a frightened look, as though I were crazy." And conversely, it also has happened not infrequently that priests and ministers have been very impressed with the religious visions of people who have consulted them, without realizing that they were dealing with a case of schizophrenia.

Since the unconscious of patients spontaneously produces religious symbols and since it is precisely in them that a potential for bringing about a cure lies, the therapist cannot leave them aside. As a result, he often finds himself, willy-nilly, suddenly deeply involved in discussing ultimate religious questions, which formerly were the province of priests and ministers.

Chapter 5

Law versus Personal Responsibility

The modern debate over differentiating various historical strains of Gnosis is often defined by the diverse forms in which Gnostic texts utilized Biblical scriptures.[1] But the intellectual atmosphere in the early centuries of Christianity was so saturated by classical mythology and philosophy, in addition to Judaic and Christian ideas, that it appears impossible to trace precisely the "first" sources underlying various texts.

Historians have a constant tendency, when speaking of tradition, to think exclusively in terms of consciously or textually received tradition. Unconscious tradition—that which in a certain sense is absorbed unrecognized but nonetheless influences collective culture—is, however, conceivably much more important. Even today in an analytical practice we remain insufficiently aware of how analysands are capable of breathing new life into archaic cultural possessions within their dreams and fantasies.

Jean-Pierre Mahé (of the Sorbonne) is a scholar with a deep knowledge of the Nag Hammadi texts. I have found particularly useful his critical engagement[2] with an article by K. Koschorke, entitled "Die Polemik der Gnostiker gegen das kirchliche Christentum" ("The Gnostics' polemic against church Christianity").[3] Koschorke conceived of Gnosis in terms of *the development of a higher consciousness*.[4] My understanding of Gnosis coincides with that of Koschorke. According to the Gnostics, the meaning of the events reported in the Bible should be understood in a spiritual and symbolic sense, rather than the literal or historical sense adopted by the established church. This view bestows a permanent validity on the events recorded, as if they were constantly recurring anew. Not even the church fathers were entirely able to avoid this kind of understanding in their interpretations of the record. Thus in the writings of Augustine, the Father continually begets the Son. And in Meister Eckhart, God is ever again reborn in the human heart.

It may be true that the opposed views of *devotio* and *gnosis* are mutually exclusive on a logical plane. But like all oppositions, they share a secret identity at bottom: both are formative of the whole of which each is a part.

The emergence of Gnosis was a providential development for the Christian church. Opposition from the Gnosis motivated the church to formulate a rational basis for its articles of faith. Christian theology took form from within the tension of this interaction, as well as in the interactive tension with classical philosophy. It was through interaction with these other, so-called heterodox, viewpoints that orthodoxy first defined itself. When the anti-Gnostic church fathers point so triumphantly to revelation as a source of guidance for all believers, not only did they match the arrogance of the Gnostics, but they also betray the limitations of their own standpoint.[5]

The Nag Hammadi texts establish that, with the possible exception of Hippolytus, the critics of Gnosis failed altogether to appreciate the specificity of the views advanced under the rubric of Gnosis. They were much more involved in trying to comprehend a system underlying all the various Gnostic tendencies. However, scarcely a single Nag Hammadi text coincides with the supposed Gnostic doctrinal systems the church fathers constructed in their critiques of Gnosis. This may suggest that the "Gnostic revelation" was never systematic in the first place—orthodox attempts at systemization of the Gnosis were artificial constructs made by its opponents. (The single doctrinal text from the Nag Hammadi corpus that might be described in systematic terms is "The Tripartite Tractate."[6])

In the second century, the church fathers were busy ordering the canon. The Gnostics, however, were not theologians in this systematic sense. They were individuals who had been seized by the Christian message, and hence, they gave expression to the reactions of the unconscious. For them, it was more important to confront the internal paradoxes of Christianity than to elaborate an orthodoxy. And this challenge, in turn, must have powerfully motivated the church fathers to create an authoritative theology.

It is no accident that the Gnostics were opposed in particular to "the law,"[7] to the Jewish religion based on laws, and to the adoption by the established church of a legal basis for the new faith. In fact, the relationship between the Old and New testaments[8] posed a serious difficulty for the church; it was able to formulate its own position only as the result of serious internal conflict. This fact illustrates that the orthodox view was not the only one possible. Christ says (Matthew 5:17f):

> Think not that I have come to abolish the law and the prophets; I have come not to abolish them but to fulfill them. For truly, I say to you, till heaven and earth pass away, not an iota, not a dot, will pass from the law until all is accomplished. Whoever then relaxes one of the least of these commandments and teaches men so, shall be called least in the kingdom of heaven; but he who does them and teaches them shall be called great in the kingdom of heaven. For I tell you, unless your righteousness exceeds that of the scribes and Pharisees, you will never enter the kingdom of heaven.[9]

In the last sentence, we find a suggestion of what distinguishes the new *evangelium Christi* from the religion of the Old Testament age: The gospel of love calls the law into question. Thus Paul declares explicitly (Romans 13:10): "Love does no wrong to a neighbor: therefore love is the fulfilling of the law."

Jesus is recorded to have said in a so-called apocryphal text: "And Yeshua beheld a man working on the Sabbath, and He said to him, man, if you know what you are doing, you are blessed, for you are not breaking the law in the spirit; but if you don't know, you are accursed and a transgressor of the law."[10] Says such as this could only survive outside the developing orthodox canon.

This is a dangerous truth for morally weak individuals, who are better suited to following the law. Nevertheless, even in the canonical gospels there are passages that nullify or relativize legality. One example is David eating "the bread of the Presence" on the Sabbath (Luke 6:1-5). This text concludes: "the Son of man is lord of the Sabbath." Another is the parable of the dishonest steward (Luke 16:1-9), in which the Lord praises the steward for having acted shrewdly, saying: "make friends for yourselves by means of unrighteous mammon, so that when it fails they may receive you into the eternal habitation."

Law and Transgression

Transgressing the law is legitimate only at the behest of an internal moral judgment. In their anthropology, the Gnostics discovered the self—the great or true individual—who can dispense with legality.[11] As the Abbot Joachim of Fiore demonstrated many centuries later, the law belongs to the age of the father.[12] It signifies fear and bondage. The Gnostics overcame this status of bondage to law, becoming sons of the one invisible father. They took the message of Matthew 23:8-9 seriously: "But you are not to be called rabbi, for you have one teacher and are all brethren. And call no man your father on earth, for you have one Father, who is in heaven." In the Gnostic text, "The Interpretation of Knowledge,"[13] we find:

> Do not call out to a father upon the earth. Your Father, who is in heaven, is one. You are the light of the world [Matthew 5:14]... For what use is it if you gain the world and you forfeit your soul? [Matthew 16:26]. For when we were in the dark we used to call many "father," since we were ignorant of the true Father.[14]

The "Gospel of Philip" lays out the logic of the case as follows: "The father makes a son, and the son has not the power to make a son. For he who has been begotten has not the power to beget, but the son gets brothers for himself, not sons."[15] The one father is the begetter of all the sons, which is why, among themselves, the Gnostics regarded each other as brothers. This is a process that continually repeats itself, and thus remains forever current: "If the sons of Adam are many, although they die, how much more the sons of the perfect man, they who do not die but are always begotten."[16]

As detailed in chapter four of the "Untitled Text" in the Bruce Codex (47-48), the Lord of Glory separated matter into two parts, or lands. The one on the right is the land of life and light, the one on the left that of death and darkness. These designate the respective spheres of those who serve the Lord and those who rise up against him. The ones on the right receive the commandments, which they must observe in order to be saved. This bifurcation corresponds to the Valentinian system, in which the psychikoi are on the right; so long as they obey the law, they are promised salvation. The pneumatikoi, in contrast, are secure in salvation without condition.[17]

The Gnostics thought of themselves members of a new aeon characterized by the rise of the spiritual man. In the new aeon there is no hierarchy, as there is in the established church, and no directeur de conscience. As sons of the *teleios anthropos*, the self, they must assume moral responsibility for their own lives. No wonder, then, that the critics of Gnosis could see only libertinism when confronted with the nullification of the law. And, indeed, this danger is not to be denied. But Mahé demonstrates persuasively that the Gnostics were devoutly committed to an ascetic lifestyle—confirming the old psychological adage that prohibitions and commandments are more likely to inspire transgression than is freedom.[18] Thus, the "Second Treatise of the Great Seth" proudly declares, "the...nobility of the Fatherhood is not guarded, since he guards only him who is from him, without word and constraint."[19] The redemption sought by the Gnostics began in emancipation from the tyranny of the paternal authority of the law.[20]

It seems to me telling that precisely in this point it was impossible for Martin Buber, a scholar of the book, to understand Jung, calling him a Gnostic—indeed even a Carpocratian. Jung does in fact cite the doctrine of Carpocrates.[21] Nevertheless, it is essential to keep in mind the context in which he does so. He introduces the topic by saying:

> Unfortunately there can be no doubt that man is, on the whole, less good than he imagines himself or wants to be. Everyone carries a shadow, and the less it is embodied in the individual's conscious life, the blacker and denser it is. If an inferiority is conscious, one always has a chance to correct it. Furthermore, it is constantly in contact with other interests, so that it is continually subjected to modifications. But if it is repressed and isolated from consciousness, it never gets corrected, and is liable to burst forth suddenly in a moment of unawareness. At all events, it forms an unconscious snag, blocking the most well-meant attempts.[22]

The only response the established church could find to the problem of the shadow was repression—the source not only of ecclesiastical neuroses among the clerics, but also of a legacy of unconsciousness among lay churchgoers of a degree that we simply can today no longer afford.[23] If in our own times Gnosis has once again become contemporary, it is not least due to its striving after consciousness. In contrast to the surreptitious dualism of the established church, Gnosis emphasizes unity in the knowledge of the one: the "Valentinian Exposition" appeals to those "who [have known him who] is, the Father, that [is, the Root] of the All, the [Ineffable One who] dwells in the Monad."[24]

The church of the Gnostics is therefore an *ecclesia spiritualis* (a church of the spirit),[25] cast in the image of the church of the pleroma.[26] This is not, as Mahé would have it,[27] simply for the sake of purity, but in response to the shadow tendencies responsible for disfiguring the power structure of an institutional ecclesia. The early Christian church was ridden with conflict over the correct understandings, which came to be increasingly displaced onto the hierarchy. As demonstrated by spiritual alchemy, the *ecclesia spiritualis* is free of this problem when it consists no longer of rulers and subjects, but exclusively of brothers.

The orthodox church fathers, such as Irenaeus[28] and Clement of Alexandria,[29] share Martin Buber's reservations about the dangers of creeping libertinism, unleashed whenever the law is to be overcome. But if one reads Irenaeus' report carefully, it is impossible to mistake his own uncertainty regarding the claims of libertinism among the Gnostics.[30] Likewise, the logic of the Gnostic doctrine was anything but libertine, given that the believer, along with his inner antagonist, is bound to confront the (eternal) judge, who would otherwise hand down an indictment.[31] The general tendency of the Gnostics was to free themselves from this world, refusing its temptations, in order to avoid being reborn and confined once again in a body. This kind of misunderstanding of a person's dealings with the shadow side of life can only occur to someone who has never had any practical experience with it. Those who free themselves of the law fall victim immediately to the tyranny of the shadow. If they do not want simply to trade the one tyranny for the other, there remains only the arduous path of coming to terms with the shadow brother.

I insist on this point, because it is the root of many misunderstandings in the established church today, and because the church cannot evade the reproach of having raised a flock of unconscious sheep, rather than of mature individuals who take responsibility for themselves. The former are easy prey for spiritual infections, whether of a religious or a political nature.

Gnosis and the Spiritual Man

The system of Valentinus will be taken as an example to facilitate the following discussion. It illustrates a trichotomy typical to many Gnostic systems. Three elements exist in this Gnostic view: the material (*hyle*), which comes from the passion of the fallen Sophia Achamoth, the lower Sophia; the psychic (*psychikos*), which stemming from her turn to higher matters; and the spiritual (*pneumatikos*), or the element corresponding to her own spiritual essence.[32] This three-fold division reflects in the typology of humans, who also fall into three groups.

When the demiurge brought man into being, he made the material (earthly = physical) man (cf. I Corinthians 15:47) by taking the liquid aspect of matter and blowing the animate human being into it. This is man made "in the image" of God (Genesis 1:26), who is similar to God. Psychic man is created "after [the] likeness" of God (Genesis 1:26) out of the spirit of life. Finally, he is clothed in a garment of fur (Genesis 3:21), by which is meant the sensuous flesh.

The spiritual man, the pneumatikoi, was however created by Achamoth, behind the back of the demiurge, out of her own spiritual substance; these are the Gnostics. The pneumatikoi may have their soul from the demiurge, their invisible body from the earth, and their flesh from matter, but they come spiritually from their mother Achamoth.[33] The end of the material world comes when everything related to spirit within matter has been formed, perfected and liberated by Gnosis— when the pneumatikoi have achieved complete Gnosis about God and have been initiated into the mysteries of Achamoth.[34] For the pneumatikoi, the true Gnostic,

> It is impossible that they themselves should ever come under the power of corruption, whatever the sort of actions they indulged. For even as gold, when submersed in filth,[35] loses not on that account its beauty, but retains its own native qualities, the filth having no power to injure the gold, so they affirm that they cannot

in any measure suffer hurt, or lose their spiritual substance, whatever the material actions in which they may be involved.[36]

The psychikoi—the "psychic man," the second group in this trichotomy of human types—are however sustained by works and simple faith. These are the ordinary people of the church. The third and last group, the hyletic or choical (material) men, are beyond the reach of salvation, just as there is no salvation possible for matter itself.
This Valentinian typology, as described above by Irenaeus, is key to understanding our problem. The most primitive level of humanity is that of material man (choics or hyletics), who never gets beyond what is concrete, or what is accessible to sensuous experience. For material man the real is comprised simply of what is palpable, what can be apprehended by means of the senses. The hyletic is sensuous man, for whom the world is a source of sensuous pleasure, and who is capable of fully enjoying the beauties and hedonic aspects of the world. It is through his senses that he is mediated to the environment. He finds orientation according to the immediate realities that confront him, in terms of the small pleasures of life. In the negative case, he remains mired in unconsciousness and tribulation. All people bear something of this aspect in themselves.

The psychikoi are graced with an additional element, stemming from the conversion, from Achamoth's turn to higher things. This is a spiritual aspect, which, because God is spirit (John 4:24), makes them similar to God. By turning to spirit, they are able to lift themselves out of the unconsciousness of merely natural man. In so doing, they can achieve redemption through knowledge (gnosis). To this end they require good works, the law, faith, and Christ the redeemer.

The pneumatikoi occupy the highest level. This is spiritual man, who yet bears traces of the previous levels, but is made of the same spiritual substance as the mother Sophia. Because of this, he has complete gnosis, even before his birth, and thus the certainty of redemption. Of course, this sounds arrogant in the extreme! It strikes me as similar to the certainty of redemption expressed by Christians in the established church, singing "I know that my Redeemer lives" (Job 19:25).

It is perhaps possible to identify the inborn sensitivities of some people to invisible spiritual realities, which are not explicable by reference to life experience. Nonetheless, we are in no position to judge with any certainty as to which category our fellow human beings might ultimately belong. Even one of the criminals crucified with Christ, in the final moment of his life, achieved the gnosis necessary to acknowledge Christ (Luke 23:40-43). We must therefore take great care in consigning someone to one or the other of these categories: the seed planted in him might only in the future bear fruit.

Likewise, no individual can be confident of belonging in a certain category, but must make an effort to work up from the lower to the higher ones—and when once he rises to the status of the pneumatikoi, it is not his merit that has taken him there, according to the texts, but his destiny. Nor can he then begin to "sin," trusting that nothing can annul his redemption as one of the pneumatikoi. Only having once arrived at the goal can he see in retrospect whether his gold has escaped defilement by the filth of the world. Later on, the alchemists sought for the philosophical gold (*aurum nostrum*) in people, for that indestructible divine kernel—there for all the world to see, and yet disdained by fools (*spernitur a stultis*).

It should not be held against the Gnostics that they felt superior to the *agnosia* (ignorance) of the members of the established church. They had indeed found, in introversion, a fundamentally new path to redemption, one that left them largely independent of external means of grace. In the proud knowledge that both sin and redemption were matters internal to their being, they trusted in their own spiritual powers. Thus, from today's perspective, they were the first depth psychologists: they plumbed the depths of divinity (1 Corinthians 2:10). The Gnostics' aim was therefore to disparage the established church as something that had been overcome. It is a psychological law that any developmental stage that has been newly overcome continues for a time to be experienced as a threat, due to the possibility of regression. In the Gnostic text "The Testimony of Truth" we read:

> For no one who is under the Law will be able to look up to the truth, for they will not be able to serve two masters. For the defilement of the Law is manifest; but undefilement belongs to the light [that is, to gnosis]. The Law commands (one) to take a husband (or) to take a wife, and to beget, to multiply like the sand of

the sea [Genesis 1:22]. But passion, which is a delight to them, constrains the souls of those who are begotten in this place, those who defile and those who are defiled, in order that the Law might be fulfilled through them. And they show that they are assisting the world; and they [turn] away from the light, who are unable [to pass by] the archon of [darkness] until they pay the last [penny] [Matthew 5:26].[37]

Like the comment of Carpocrates, this passage relies on Matthew 5:26, but the point now is to cast blame on the members of the established church for having allowed passion to bind their souls to the archon of the world, thus rendering them incapable of freeing themselves from the darkness.

My inclination, based on this passage, is to conclude that the church fathers and the Gnostics—armed with fundamentally different presuppositions—were incapable of understanding each other; they were engaged in a process of reciprocal projection. Thus, not every misunderstanding necessarily sprang from disreputable motives. An exceptional figure among the "enemies" of the Gnostics in the early third century was Hippolytus of Rome.[38] Hippolytus may have secretly been a Gnostic—as Jung points out—and an admirer of those he supposedly opposed. Perhaps for this reason his reports concerning their doctrines are quite extensive and accurate.

With these reservations in mind, let us have a look at the testimony of Irenaeus.[39] He says of the Gnostics:

They maintain, therefore, that in every way it is always necessary for them to practice the mystery of conjunction. And that they may persuade the thoughtless to believe this, they are in the habit of using these very words, "Whosoever [sc. Gnostics] being in this world does not so love a woman as to obtain possession of her, is not of the truth, nor shall attain to the truth. But whosoever [sc. Psychics] being of this world has intercourse with woman, shall not attain to the truth, because he has so acted under the power of concupiscence."

On this account, they tell us that it is necessary for us whom they call psychic men, and describe as being of the world, to practice continence and good works, that by this means we may attain at length to the center habitation, but that to them who are called "the spiritual and perfect" such a course of conduct is not at all necessary. For it is not conduct of any kind which leads into the Pleroma, but the seed sent forth thence in a feeble, immature state, and here brought to perfection.[40]

To adduce a modern comparison here, the psychikoi conduct themselves in regard to the pneumatikoi as Freud to Jung. Freud, who had a biological understanding of sexuality, never accounted adequately for his own fascination with sexuality, such that he could never stop talking about it. Jung, in the last great work of his life—his magnum opus the *Mysterium Coniunctionis*—elaborated on the spiritual content of sexuality, as found in particular in philosophical alchemy. Jung addresses this point in his memoirs:[41]

Freud, I concluded, must himself be so profoundly affected by the power of Eros that he actually wished to elevate it into a dogma—aere perennius—like a religious numen. It is no secret that "Zarathustra" is the proclaimer of a gospel, and here was Freud also trying to outdo the church and to canonize a theory. To be sure, he did not do this too loudly; instead, he suspected me of wanting to be a prophet. He made his tragic claim and demolished it at the same time. That is how people usually behave with numinosities, and rightly so, for in one respect they are true, in another untrue. If Freud had given somewhat more consideration to the psychological truth that sexuality is numinous—both a god and a devil—he would not have remained bound within the confines of a biological concept. And Nietzsche might not have been carried over the brink of the world by his intellectual excesses if he had only held more firmly to the foundations of human existence.

Wherever the psyche is set violently oscillating by a numinous experience, there is a danger that the thread by which one hangs may be torn. Should that happen, one man tumbles into an absolute affirmation, another into an equally absolute negation. Nirdvandva (freedom from opposites) is the Orient's remedy for this. I have not forgotten that. The pendulum of the mind oscillates between sense and nonsense, not between right and wrong. The numinosum is dangerous because it lures men to extremes, so that a modest truth is regarded as the truth and a minor mistake is equated with fatal error.

This passage helps clarify the nature of the axiomatic differences that existed between the psychikoi (the members of the established church who are subject to the law), and the pneumatikoi (the chosen ones). The former regard revelation as closed, using it to construct a body of doctrine that is as consistent as possible in logical terms, and that ultimately works as a defense against primary experience. From this effort stems the typical attitude of *devotio*. The latter, the pneumatikoi, are in the grip of experience. They have an immediate contact with numinal revelation, which leads them to give ever-changing expression to the images and myths springing from their souls in the response to revelation. Thus they run the risk of becoming filled to excess with their reaction to the numinous, and being "carried over the brink of the world."

The psychikoi content themselves with the modest truth of a religious creed, so as not to lose contact with this world. The pneumatikoi strive instead to free themselves from the imperfection and doubtfulness of this world, pursuing redemption through contact with the plenitude of being. The former are captives of the material-physical world, from which they hope to be saved by a redeemer, based on their good behavior. The latter experience themselves as strangers in a dark material world; they seek to free themselves from whatever binds them to it, and this freedom is what redemption means to them. Both claim to be in possession of the one true faith, neither noticing what a one-sided attitude they have. Gilles Quispel, in his general treatment *Gnosis as Weltreligion*,[42] simplifies somewhat in suggesting that Gnosis was "neither in its origin nor in its essence...Christian"[43]—even though the Gnostic movement in the West sought, as on the other hand Quispel states,

merely to illumine received doctrine from its own point of view, indeed...sought no more than to offer an interpretation, if the correct and timely one, of Christianity.[44]

The Gnostic attitude was complementary to our own modern attitudes, and an unbiased study of their views could teach us a great deal that compensates our own one-sidedness.[45] The approach of the modern Christian church and of our entire culture remains today one-sided; its focus is on the external, neglecting the reactions of the soul. We see only the surface of things, failing to penetrate their depths.

This same one-sided attitude also characterizes present-day research into Gnosis—scholars stop short of plumbing the depths and using modern psychology to assist their understanding. While people are indeed fascinated by their study of the old texts, they collectively remain bound unconsciously to the traditional mentality. The ongoing orthodox condemnation of Gnosis also stems from this same unconscious predisposition, in which "the law" has not yet been overcome. The overcoming of the law does not result in libertinism, as many fear, but leads instead, via individuation, to the primacy of the soul. Where the law had been, the independent judgment of the soul now reigns. It is therefore no surprise that the Nag Hammadi texts document a demanding ascetic attitude.[46]

Sexuality and Coniunctio

The Gnostics, in preference to the customary baptism by water, practiced baptism by the spirit (Matthew 3:11; Mark 1:8; Acts 1:5), the "baptism of the truth."[47] According to The Testimony of Truth, a text found at Nag Hammadi:

> Some enter the faith [by receiving a] baptism on the ground that they have [it] as a hope of salvation, which they call "the [seal]." They do not [know] that the [fathers of] the world are manifest to that [place]... For [the Son] of [Man] did not baptize any of his disciples. But [...if those who] are baptized were headed for life, the world would become empty. And the fathers of baptism were defiled.
>
> But the baptism of truth is something else; it is by renunciation of [the] world that it is found. [But those who] say [only] with the tongue [that they] are renouncing it [are lying], and they are coming to [the place] of fear.[48]

Baptism by water, as initiation into an attitude adopted toward the world, constitutes for the psychikoi their tie to the archons, to the fathers of this world. For the pneumatikoi, it is a renunciation of this world. From this perspective, their presumed rejection of sexuality can be understood. Quispel often cites this rejection of sexuality, because the essence of sexuality is a surrender to the world of the archons. "The Testimony of Truth" reports John the Baptist's understanding of the reversal of the current of the Jordan River as signifying the end of the dominance of physical propagation:

> The Jordan River is the power of the body, that is, the senses of pleasures. The water of the Jordan is the desire for sexual intercourse. John is the archon of the womb.[49]

We do not know whether the Gnostics understood this passage literally. In symbolic terms it signifies a state "beyond the pleasure principle" and thus an introversion of libido (psychic energy). We are bound by our senses to this world, and entangled in it.[50] The unconscious and thus compulsive emotional ties we have to objects leave us in a state of non-redemption. Salvation is to be sought by way of severing these ties, through the introversion of libido and through knowledge (gnosis), i.e., the withdrawal of projections.

This does not necessarily entail a rejection of biological sexuality. People in antiquity were bound to their environment by a "participation mystique" to a much greater extent than are we. Because of this, they were very much at the mercy of their passions. Socrates tried to free people of this scourge with his philosophy of *apatheia* (passionlessness). The only way for this to be achieved at that time was through reason. The Gnostics, with their encratic attitude, took another path: they withdrew libido from the world, diverting it to the unconscious. The result was to invigorate the unconscious enormously, giving rise to the mythological images we encounter in the Nag Hammadi texts, and constituting an alternative, numinous goal to be sought in preference to worldly objects. This process by which projections are withdrawn from the environment, along with the associated intensification of the inner life, is experienced as redemption. Anyone who knows the pain involved in the renunciation of loved objects or ideas will not be inclined to speak lightly of "self-redemption."

The grace, or the external circumstance occasioning this process, consists in the fact that only the suffering due to a conflict (crucifixion) can set in motion the inner dynamic that is the necessary condition of psychic development. Those who choose to avoid suffering and indulge the "pleasure principle" receive negative impulses (including nightmares) from the unconscious. This is the deeper reason for the asceticism of the Gnostics. The path to self-becoming is unique and must be found by the individual. The soul, and not paternal authority, is the guide. It consists in the vital interaction between the ego and the self, or with God. The Gnostics thus had no need of an external church as a means to salvation, or of baptism by water, as opposed to the spiritual baptism represented in the Nag Hammadi texts.[51] Sufficient for them was an ecclesia spiritualis, a relation of solidarity, with eternity as its goal. And yet, if the condition of the whole is this relation (eros), then at issue here is a dialectical process between the human individual and God.

Irenaeus asserts above[52] that the Gnostics were incapable of entering into truth if, during their time in this world, they had not "so love[d] a woman as to obtain possession of her." At the same time he asserts that they rejected baptism by water because the Jordan signified lust and sexuality.[53] There is, however, no contradiction between the two statements. In citing this Gnostic view, Irenaeus indicates the relationship with a woman that transcends the purely biological, and in which the eternal comes to expression. Just prior to the above passage, Irenaeus writes:

> but...they themselves have grace as their own special possession, which has descended from above by means of an unspeakable and indescribable conjunction [syzygy]; and on this account more will be given them. (Luke 19:26) They maintain, therefore, that in every way it is always necessary for them to practice the mystery of conjunction [see above].[54]

The Gnostics apparently accorded the feminine an equal role with the masculine,[55] because everything comes into being out of syzygy.

Redemption now consists in the reunification of that which has been separated. The world comes into being out of the separation of the syzygies, as, for example, in the fall of Sophia Achamoth. Creation and life in this world are therefore deficit conditions that should be overcome. Unification with a woman constitutes the mysterium coniunctionis in the true sense and it has a redemptive effect.[56] The psychikoi, who see only the external, were able to recognize only the biological aspect in this union. And the doctrine of Carpocrates, it seems to me, stems from just these considerations. According to this internal logic, the Gnostic mentality properly understood, strives not toward *libertinism*, as the psychikoi thought, but toward *redemption*.

In the above discussion, I have employed Martin Buber's misunderstanding of the works of C. G. Jung to illustrate a central issue: the Gnostics were pneumatikoi; they rejected members of the institutional church as psychikoi. An understanding of this distinction and viewpoint opens the way for a deeper understanding of the Gnostics and their attitude. It is a way that leads not merely to an external perspective on what we term Gnostic, but to an understanding of Gnosis "from the inside, out."

C. G. Jung was a pioneer who noted the numerous similarities that exist between the experiences people have today in the course of individuation, and the strivings of the ancient Gnostics for redemption.[57] The empirical findings of modern depth psychology could thus provide a valuable tool to students researching the phenomenon of Gnosis. For this reason it is worthwhile studying the works of C. G. Jung and Marie-Louise von Franz to gain an understanding of Gnosis. At least for some scholars, their works could open up a new perspective. Above all, however, they make a thousand-year old spiritual attitude current once again.

Was it perhaps not a truly meaningful coincidence—a synchronicity, as Peter Sloterdijk[58] suggests—that the Nag Hammadi library was found in 1945, just after the Second World War at the moment of the West's greatest spiritual crisis?

Chapter 6

Jung and Gnosis

The texts found near Nag Hammadi in late 1945 were unfortunately not available to C. G. Jung. The first codex, presented to him on November 15, 1953, was named after him in recognition of his contribution to the understanding of Gnosis, and he followed with great interest the translation and editing of the editio princeps. The results appeared in a study series put out by the Jung Institute at lengthy intervals for a considerable period after his death (1956, 1963, 1968, 1973-1975).

Despite the worldwide significance of these Gnostic texts, and intensive research undertaken in Cairo by Jean Doresse from 1947 to 1953 and James M. Robinson from 1966 to 1981,[1] the story of how they were discovered remains spotty. Prominent scholars have reacted with skepticism to the reconstruction of the events thirty years later, based on interviews with surviving witnesses. It is known that twelve codices and eight pages of a thirteenth codex were found ten kilometers (as the crow flies) northeast of the bridge over the Nile at Nag Hammadi, 129 kilometers downstream from Luxor, the ancient city of Chenoboskion. The site lies nine kilometers west of the ruins of the Basilica of St. Pachomius, prompting much speculation about possible connections between this Coptic library and the monastic communities. The codices were found inside clay jars, and following the discovery were divided into eight equal parts, causing certain materials to be lost, some of which were later recovered. Codex III was the first to come into the possession of the Coptic Museum in Cairo, under the directorship of Togo Mina (1906-1949). Mina showed the codex to the orientalist Henry Corbin, who suspected that it was a Gnostic text because appearing on the cover sheet was the title "The Apocryphon of John." This suspicion was confirmed the following summer (1947) by Antoine Guillaumont, based on a comparison with the Papyrus Berolinensis 8502 (BG 2). Jean Doresse took photographs of the text to Paris at the end of 1947, where on January 10, 1948, the discovery was announced by a Cairo publisher. Doresse and his teacher, Henri-Charles Puech, informed the Académie des Inscriptions et Belles-Lettres in Paris of the find on February 29, 1948. Hasty preparations were undertaken to publish the materials, but all efforts thus far were lost in the coup d'état of July 23, 1952, that toppled King Faruk.

Part of Codex I, later called the Jung Codex, was sold to a grain merchant in Nag Hammadi, where Phocion J. Tano (d. 1972) bought part of that. Another part found its way to dealers in Cairo and ultimately to Albert Eid (1885-1950), a Belgian antique dealer, proprietor of the Old Shop. Eid had the Gnostic status of the text verified by the expert B. Couroyer, and he then offered forty-one sheets to the Fine Arts Museum in Boston. The museum declined (November 1946). The University of Louvain was also approached and likewise turned down the offering, although plans for publication had been made (March 1948). In the meantime (between October 1947 and November 1948) the rest of Codex I turned up, so that Eid was able to put the complete text, which he had smuggled out of Egypt, up for sale in America. In August 1948, Gilles Quispel made an offer to the Bollingen Foundation to buy the codex for $12,000. The bid was rejected. Toward the end of 1949, Eid returned to Cairo, having left the codex in a safe in Brussels. He died in Cairo at the end of November 1950.

Quispel had informed Professor C. A. Meier, director at the time of the C. G. Jung Institute in Zurich, about the codex. Meier obtained an agreement from Eid's widow to buy it for 35,000 Swiss francs. He gathered the necessary funds from a number of donors, and on May 10, 1952, he was able to take possession of the codex in Brussels. On November 4, 1952, Meier invited Henri-Charles Puech, along with Quispel, Michel Malinine, and W. C. Van Unnik, to publish the codex.

It has already been noted that Quispel brought the codex to Zurich for presentation to C. G. Jung in a ceremony on November 15, 1953, where it was officially named after Jung. Following Jung's death an agreement was reached between the family and the Egyptian authorities, stipulating that following publication, the Codex would be returned to Egypt. In exchange, Egypt made available to the publishers excellent photographs of the missing pages.

James Robinson[2] found it disconcerting that the codex lay for an extended period in a bank safe on Zurich's Bahnhofstrasse, where it was accessible to only a few scholars—a situation that caused delay in publication. In his usual thorough manner, he has reviewed the exchange of letters about the case, determining C. G. Jung himself was never responsible for the codex having been kept from interested researchers. At the end of September 1975, the codex finally was received into the collection at the Coptic Museum in Cairo, and facsimile editions of the texts are to be found in larger libraries throughout the world.

The address delivered by Jung in 1953 at the ceremony in the Zunfthaus zum Rüden, at which he was presented with the codex that had been named after him, has been published in the Collected Works.[3]

Jung had undertaken an intensive study of the Gnostics, using as his sources the polemics that written by church fathers. These texts, aside from the Pistis Sophia, the Bruce Codex, and a few Oxyrhynchos fragments, contained the only known original Gnostic writings at the time. Jung made such a thorough study of them, however, that he was able to round out an adequate picture of Gnosis.

The modern revival of general interest in Gnosis can be traced in no small measure to Jung; he is responsible for opening a new angle of access to these materials. Even nowadays, Christian theologians can be nonplussed by the topic of Gnosis. For example Werner Foerster,[4] in his introduction to the modern textual edition put out by Artemis Verlag, treats Gnosis like a fossil from the remote past. It will no doubt be many years yet before the new understanding initiated by Jung finds general acceptance. It is thus premature to undertake a final investigation of Jung's influence on research into Gnosis. Only a few pioneers, Gilles Quispel among them, have so far distinguished themselves in this regard. Yet recognizing Gnosis as a phenomenon is of more than merely historical or theological significance. Many people could find in it assistance in overcoming their personal spiritual crises, because of the compensatory relation it offers to orthodox Christianity. The Gnostics, rather than following the institutional church in projecting the archetype of Anthropos— the god-man or great-man—onto the figure of the historical Christ, introjected or internalized the image. In this process, they raised the value of the human psyche to a higher level. Modern depth psychology, in its compensatory relation to extraverted Western materialism, has arrived at a similar conclusion. In contrast to the Eastern intellectual traditions (Buddhism, Zen, Taoism, etc.), which remain fundamentally alien to Western persons, Gnosis has its roots in our own Western culture. It is the introverted, mystical undercurrent of occidental Christianity.

In what follows, I must first introduce readers to the pertinent biographical details about Jung himself—and here, I will draw upon sources that are not generally accessible. In the second part, I will try to bring out a few central Gnostic motifs that have also been significant for alchemy and Jungian psychology. My desire in pursuing these matters is to show the contemporary relevance of Gnosis. As a non-specialist Gnostic studies, I have refrained from taking positions in ongoing controversies over the historical origins of Gnosis or other specialized matters. Historians of religion will likely object to the "unhistorical manner" in which comparisons are drawn—both by Jung and myself—between like motifs belonging to different times or cultures. Yet, other recognized scholars have also adopted the same approach. Claudio Moreschini offers one example, when he states: "Un fenomeno culturale non si delimita–con confini rigorosi, tanto meno con limiti cronologici." ("A cultural phenomenon does not confine itself with rigorous boundaries, much less with chronological limits.")[5] Another example is G. Quispel, who points out[6] that in Gnostic tradition, "the systems change, but the fundamental baseline remains the same."

The Jungian method of "amplification," that is, bringing a symbol or idea to conscious understanding by comparing it to similar ideas with the same meaning, is the only means by which their vital meaning can be maintained. The method is based on the recognition that the collective unconscious, in the present, just as in the past, is constantly reproducing similar ideas independent of tradition. Jung compared this psychic faculty for reproducing the similar to a matrix, designating the latter an "archetype." The fact that this ability is general to humanity is what makes it possible for us to understand documents from the remote past, such as those pertaining to Gnosis. If we know today that the Gnostics produced their writings from out of the collective unconscious, then our modern experience with depth psychology offers us a key to understanding them. The method of amplification might initially alienate historians, who are used to materials distinguished precisely according to time and place. It takes a psychological understanding to appreciate the value of amplificatory methods, even while such an understanding is not as yet widely prevalent. The value of what might seem a tiresome comparison with similar ideas will become apparent to readers, if only they are able to muster a provisional acceptance of them.

The numinosum by which the Gnostics were seized is not the same as the one current in the Christian church. By attempting to trace Jung's own attachment to this Gnostic numinosum, using his writings and the Gnostic texts to relativize it for ourselves, we will achieve genuine access to Gnosis. Gnosis has no doubt been alive in one form or another throughout the course of Western history, but more often as an undercurrent.[7] The goal of this work is to bring it back to life for readers, to give them a sense of why it came to hold such significance for Jung and his psychology.

Several authors have already attempted to describe Jung's relationship to Gnosis. Stephan Hoeller's *The Gnostic Jung and the Seven Sermons to the Dead* is available in several editions. Robert A. Segal's *The Gnostic Jung* lists the literature devoted to Jung and Gnosis, and includes excerpts from the texts relevant to our topic, taken mostly from Jung's Collected Works. Christine Mailland wrote an interpretation of *Les Sept Sermons aux Morts* that is well worth reading. But I am intentionally refraining from offering an evaluation of what has been written on the matter by other authors thus far. In conscious distinction to these works, and writing as a practicing analyst, I here attempt to make Gnosis accessible to readers from a psychological point of view. In doing so, I must assume some minimal familiarity on the part of the reader with Jungian psychology.

Gnostic Studies

Gnosis played a significant role in the life of C. G. Jung (1875-1961).[8] In 1913 he broke definitively with Sigmund Freud (1856-1939), with whom he had enjoyed a fruitful scientific friendship for more than six years. A thick volume of letters[9] offers eloquent testimony of this relationship. The years between this break and the end of World War I coincide with Jung's "confrontation with the unconscious."[10] In the period of crisis attending his separation from the world of established science, his unconscious came vibrantly to life, and he was obliged to undergo his own personal journey through the underworld. He record- ed his phantasies in abbreviated gothic script in the so-called Red Book.*

In 1916 he felt impelled to give form to his unconscious experienc- es and published in a private edition his *Septem Sermones ad Mortuos* (Seven Sermons to the Dead),[11] with the subtitle, "Written by Basilides in Alexandria, the City where the East toucheth the West." The ser- mons begin, "The dead came back from Jerusalem, where they found not what they sought. They prayed me let them in and besought my word, and thus I began teaching."[12] The world of orthodox Christian spirituality no longer offered adequate sustenance to the spirit, and Jung (alias Basilides) was called upon to seek for it out of his own depths. This text is written in a Gnostic style and makes use of Gnostic ways of thinking. Later he characterized the published work—which was never available in book stores—as a "youthful sin" and only reluc- tantly, for the sake of honesty, did he give his approval for the sermons to be printed in his *Memories, Dreams, Reflections*.[13] (Through a mean- ingful coincidence, a so-called synchronicity, I ran across this booklet in 1979 in the catalog from a second-hand bookstore in Vienna; I pur- chased it for just a few schillings—the bookseller had thought it really was a translation of an ancient Gnostic text!)

Jung said, speaking about this period in his life:[14]

Though the [mythopoeic] imagination is present everywhere, it is both tabooed and dreaded, so that it even appears to be a risky ex- periment or a questionable adventure to entrust oneself to the uncertain path that leads into the depths of the unconscious. It is considered the path of error, of equivocation and misunderstand- ing... The second part of Faust...is a link in the Aurea Catena which has existed from the beginnings of philosophical alchemy and Gnosticism down to Nietzsche's Zarathustra. Unpopular, am- biguous, and dangerous, it is a voyage of discovery to the other pole of the world.

---

* For an evaluation of this period that includes new details supplied by publication of Jung's *The Red Book: Liber Novus*, see the Foreword by Lance Owens.

Not only was Jung in his "initiation illness" required to undergo the primal experience, but he had to attempt to provide it with a historical foundation in his scientific work. For, in recognizing the emotional power and numinosity of these internal images, he sensed quite clearly they did not merely represent his personal experience, but were the collective possession of humanity—of which, however, the science of his time contained no adequate conceptualization. These deep psychological strata, common to humanity as a whole, Jung termed the "collective unconscious"[15] or the "objective psyche." People still have difficulty accepting the reality of a layer of unconsciousness that is independent of time and culture, because they are all too accustomed to thinking historically. Moreover, only a few people in the modern age, including those who are uneducated, have access to dreams and fantasies in which images and ideas from the most distant times spontaneously appear. The discovery of an objective psyche is Jung's contribution to depth psychology; in this he ventured beyond Freud and all other contemporary psychologists. The discovery has given us the key to understanding many of humanity's spiritual achievements, not the least of which are Gnosis and alchemy.

This phase of Jung's inner development came to a provisional conclusion in 1918 with the discovery of the function of the mandala as an expression of psychological wholeness. Is it any wonder then, that Jung, in the ensuing years (1918-1926), occupied himself very intensively with the Gnostics, since they too were acquainted with the primal world of the unconscious? For his evidence, he had to depend primarily on the opponents of Gnosis—the church fathers—among whom he valued Hippolytus in particular, as noted above. Because of the marked empathy apparent in Hippolytus' study of Gnostic doctrines, Jung regarded him as a secret Gnostic who concealed his allegiance under the guise of opposition.

Direct historical comparisons between our modern understandings of the unconscious and Gnostic documents are destined to fail, however, since the Gnostics had not yet developed a concept of the psychological; we cannot know the psychological experiences that lay behind their statements. "The tradition that might have connected Gnosis with the present seemed to have been severed," according to Jung,[16] and for a long time it proved impossible to find any bridge that led from Gnosticism—or Neo-Platonism—to the contemporary world. But when I began to understand alchemy I realized that it represented the historical link with Gnosticism, and that a continuity therefore existed between past and present. Grounded in the natural philosophy of the Middle Ages, alchemy formed the bridge on the one hand to the past, to Gnosticism, and on the other into the future, to the modern psychology of the unconscious.

Indeed, Gnostic motifs were already unwittingly present in theories put forward by the pioneers of depth psychology: Freud introduced classic Gnostic motifs of sexuality and the malignant paternal authority. Freud's myth betrays his Gnostic Yahweh and demiurge as disappointed by his creation of a world filled with illusion and suffering. His development toward materialism is anticipated in alchemy and its concern with the secret of matter. In Hermetic philosophy the feminine principle plays a major role, equal to the masculine, in opposition to the paternal domination evident in the Protestant and the Jewish world. The "vessel" not only plays a central role in Hermeticism and Gnosis (Poimandres) as the mythical site of the transformation of substances, but is prominent as well throughout alchemy. It corresponds to "individuation" (self-becoming) in modern psychology, as a process of inner transformation.

Prior to Jung's rediscovery, alchemy languished as a forgotten and disparaged discipline, understood very inadequately—if at all—by historians of science. Alchemical books were to be found on the market for a relative pittance. Jung was led to alchemy not by conscious curiosity, but through the guidance of his unconscious. He found the same motif appearing continually in his dreams, of an additional wing or structure, standing next to his house, of which he had no knowledge. Each time he wondered how it could be that he did not know it, although it had always been there. Finally, in one dream, he made his way into this other wing, where he discovered a wonderful library of mostly sixteenth- and seventeenth-century books. On every wall were large folios bound in pig leather, filled with bizarre etchings or illustrations of marvelous symbols, such as he had never seen. In the dream the books, indeed the library as a whole, held for him an indescribable fascination. "The unknown wing of the house," Jung' explains in commentary on his dream, "was a part of my personality, an aspect of myself; it represented something that belonged to me but of which I was not yet conscious. It, and especially the library, referred to alchemy, of which I was ignorant, but which I was soon to study. Some fifteen years later I had assembled a library very like the one in the dream."[17]

Alchemical Studies

Embarking on his study of alchemy, Jung browsed through the Zentralbibliothek in Zurich and sent his students to the much older library at the University of Basel (founded in 1460, as opposed to 1833 in Zurich). He quickly realized, however, that the collections were very meager, and the old books could not be checked out long enough for intensive study. Therefore, he asked a Munich bookseller to inform him of whatever alchemy books happened to come into his hands. He soon made his initial acquisition, purchasing the second edition of *Artis Auriferae, quam Chemiam vocant*, in two volumes. This was a collection of Latin treatises, quite a few of them in translations from the Arabic. "I left this book lie almost untouched for nearly two years," relates Jung,[18]

> Occasionally I would look at the pictures, and each time I would think, "Good Lord, what nonsense! This stuff is impossible to understand." But it persistently intrigued me, and I made up my mind to go into it more thoroughly. The next winter I began, and soon found it provocative and exciting. To be sure, the texts still seemed to me blatant nonsense, but here and there would be passages that seemed significant to me, and occasionally I even found a few sentences which I thought I could understand. Finally, I realized that the alchemists were talking in symbols—those old acquaintances of mine. "Why, this is fantastic," I thought. "I simply must learn to decipher all this." By now I was completely fascinated, and buried myself in the texts as often as I had the time. One night, while I was studying them, I suddenly recalled the dream that I was caught in the seventeenth century.[19] At last I grasped its meaning. "So that's it! I am condemned to study alchemy from the very beginning."

It was a long while before I found my way about in the labyrinth of alchemical thought processes, for no Ariadne had put a thread into my hand. Reading the sixteenth-century text, "Rosarium Philosophorum," I noticed that certain strange expressions and turns of phrase were frequently repeated. For example, "solve et coagula," "unum vas," "lapis," "prima materia," "Mercurius," etc. I saw that these expressions were used again and again in a particular sense, but I could not make out what that sense was. I therefore decided to start a lexicon of key phrases with cross references. In the course of time I assembled several thousand such key phrases and words, and had volumes filled with excerpts. I worked along philological lines, as if I were trying to solve the riddle of an unknown language. In this way the alchemical mode of expression gradually yielded up its meaning. It was a task that kept me absorbed for more than a decade.

Jung's fascination with alchemy had a long history. When he was eleven, on his long walk to school one day, he was overcome by a feeling of having just emerged from a dense fog, possessed suddenly with the consciousness that "now I am myself!"[20] It was a kind of awakening for him, like the one represented in the so-called Mutus Liber (mute book), first published in La Rochelle in 1677. In this story, two angels on the ladder to heaven blow their trumpets to awaken an alchemist sleeping on the ground.

On his way to the gymnasium as a student, Jung experienced his first elaborate fantasy.[21] He welcomed the way it shortened the walk along the Rhine. In his fantasy, the Rhine was suddenly a large lake, covering the whole of Alsace and dotted with sailboats. On a rock rising out of the lake was "a well-fortified castle with a tall keep, a watchtower." Among the simple paneled rooms was "an uncommonly attractive library where you could find everything worth knowing." The nervus rerum was the secret of the keep, and only Jung knew about it:

For, inside the tower, extending from the battlements to the vaulted cellar, was a copper column or heavy wire cable, which ramified at the top into the finest branches...like a taproot with all its tiny rootlets turned upside down and reaching into the air. From the

air they drew a certain inconceivable something which was conducted down the copper column into the cellar. Here I had an
equally inconceivable apparatus, a kind of laboratory in which I
made gold out of the mysterious substance... This was really an arcanum, of whose nature I neither had nor wished to form any
conception. Nor did my imagination concern itself with the nature
of the transformation process. Tactfully...it skirted around what
actually went on in this laboratory. It was a kind of spiritual essence that the roots drew out of the air, which became visible down
in the cellar below in the form of gold coins.

Without any knowledge of the tradition, the adolescent Jung thus
dreamed the thousand-year-old dream of the alchemists. Today we
would call this a spontaneous experience of active imagination. The
alchemists must have had a similar experience; they must have found
themselves overwhelmed by what they were imagining, without knowing exactly what it was supposed to mean, though clearly in the grip of
the secret. This experience made it possible for Jung later to understand
alchemy from within.

Marie-Louise Franz, Jung's later student and collaborator on these
questions, likewise had spontaneous alchemical fantasies as a child, as
she told me. She grew up in the country, and as a ten year old often
played in a little hut in the garden attached to the henhouse. One time
she read that amber was fossilized resin that had been washed in sea-
water. This prompted fantasies about making an amber yellow pearl.
She realized she would have to accelerate the process, which otherwise
took place over thousands of years. She took salt from the kitchen and
iodine from her father's pharmacy, and mixed them together to make
sea water (called *aqua pontica* by the alchemists). Then she gathered
resin from all the trees in the neighborhood. Since it was impure, she
had first to purify it (*purificatio*), which she did by melting and sifting it
to remove the impurities (*scoria*). Melting this substance in a pot she
had taken secretly, she was overcome with compassion for the resin,
which was being tormented in the heat. She spoke to it: "Look, you
might be suffering terribly now, but you will be a beautiful yellow
amber pearl, so it is worth it to endure the heat." The whole experiment
came unexpectedly to a sudden end when the pot caught fire and she

singed her eyebrows, causing her parents to find out what she was doing and put a stop to it.[22]

Found here, as well as in certain other branches of science, are two different kinds of researches: those in which the subject matter is approached from the outside, and those in which experience comes from within. These "childish" fantasies tend toward the second path. And this is the sense in which Hippolytus understood Gnosis. He, like Jung and von Franz, had fallen into the eternal stream of Gnostic (or alchemical) fantasies and been enchanted. Anyone who has had such an experience understands that neither Gnosis nor alchemy represent merely historical undercurrents of Christian culture, but make up part of the permanent, vital stock of the human soul that can break through to the surface at any time. Today we are in the midst of a virtual renaissance of Gnosis, demonstrating how it has been kept alive over the centuries.[23]

We left Jung making his long and boring way to school, absorbed in his alchemical fantasy. Jung continued with this highly pleasurable occupation for a few months, until it lost its appeal and he began viewing it as ridiculous and stupid. Now, instead of dreaming, he began to build castles and village squares. Not until he was 38 years old, when he surrendered to his unconscious impulses during the crisis he experienced after the break with Freud, did this childhood memory come back to him. Along with it there came a certain emotion. "Aha," he said to himself. "This is life! The little boy is still there, filled with the creative vitality the grown man lacks." The only remaining alternative was to return to that earlier place and resume the childhood game, hoping for the best. This moment, as he said, was a turning point in his life: he began collecting a vast number of stones from the lakeshore and set to building an entire village.

In the course of a year, this project released a stream of fantasies, which he wrote down in the Red Book—the source as well for the Gnostic *Septem Sermones ad Mortuos*. The whole development culminated in the mandala as the ultimate expression of the whole, or, as Jung termed it, the self. While he was still working with another mandala image, "the golden, well-fortified castle,"[24] the sinologist Richard Wilhelm sent him a thousand-year-old Chinese Taoist alchemical treatise entitled The Secret of the Golden Flower.[25] The text provided unanticipated confirmation of his ideas about the mandala and circling around a center. It offered him a way out of his loneliness, because here was something of a related nature that he could hold on to and use for a comparative commentary.

Gnosis in Jung's Alchemical Notebooks

The text about the golden castle as the germinal core of the immortal body constituted a transition for Jung, and led to the study of alchemy. For Jung, Gnosis and alchemy were historical confirmations of his own experiences. More than other sciences, psychology is subject to the personal circumstances of the observer. Today we are awash in psychologies of the most varied sorts, making it impossible for the layperson to navigate them all. Everyone takes his own truth to be universal. This is the reason it was so important to Jung to have unprejudiced historical material corresponding to his own experiences with the collective unconscious. Using evidence provided by independent historical documentation, he was able to claim to have stumbled upon an impersonal layer of the psyche that is common to humanity. Jung explained:[26]

> The possibility of comparison with alchemy, and the uninterrupted intellectual chain back to Gnosticism gave substance to my psychology [of the unconscious]. When I pored over these old texts everything fell into place: the fantasy-images, the empirical material I had gathered in my practice, and the conclusions I had drawn from it. I now began to understand these psychic contents meant when seen in historical perspective... The primordial images and the nature of the archetype took a central place in my researches, and it became clear to me that without history there can be no psychology, and certainly no psychology of the unconscious.

Jung had an excellent memory and was not accustomed to having to keep notes about what he was reading. It was thus with reluctance that he began in 1935 collecting notations from his alchemical readings in a small oilcloth notebook. This became the first of several subsequent "alchemical notebooks." These unpublished notebooks provide a detailed guide to Jung's studies over the next decade. To start, he made quick notes about the most important aspects of the six volumes comprising the *Theatrum Chemicum* (1602-1661). Later, after having gained an overview of alchemy, he would return to these volumes in greater detail.

The notebooks document that in 1935 Jung also returned to Gnostic texts for another thorough study, starting with the *Refutatio* of Irenaeus.[27] Having arrived at an overview of alchemy, he was clearly searching for connections to Gnosis. The edition of Irenaeus then studied must have been a German edition of the work (probably the one put out by the Bibliothek der Kirchenväter; Munich 1912), because a short while later (1936) he made use of a Greek-Latin bilingual edition, published by W. Wigan Harvey (Cambridge 1857): *Sancti Episcopi Lugdunensis Libros Quinque Adversus Haereses*. Later still, he studied the Greek alchemists in an edition by Marcelin Berthelot: *Collection des Anciens Alchimistes Grecs* (Paris 1887/88), in the very inadequate translation by Ch. Em. Ruelle.[28] (More than a hundred years later, only two volumes of a planned twelve-volume critical edition of the Greek alchemists have appeared in the Collection des Universités de France.[29])

Jung had the help of the classical philologist Marie-Louise von Franz for his interpretation of the Zosimos texts, which he felt substantiated the historical link between Gnosticism and Alchemy. Marie-Louise von Franz's work resulted in the production of a coherent Greek version of Zosimos and a faithful translation based on a proper understanding of the text itself. In 1937, Jung also turned to the *Corpus Hermeticum*,[30] where he discovered parallels to Plato's Timaeus, which he had studied again a short time before.[31] In the same year, he examined the Arab alchemists in Marcelin Berthelot's edition of *La Chimie du Moyen Age* (Volume III, Paris 1893), taking extensive notes about them as well.

Jung took his next notebook along on the trip to India in 1938. It contains excerpts from the first volume of the *Theatrum Chemicum*, to which he turned in a certain sense as an antidote to Indian spirituality. "India affected me like a dream," he reports, "for I was and remained in search of myself, of the truth peculiar to myself. The journey formed an intermezzo in the intensive study of alchemical philosophy in which I was engaged at the time."[32]

The introverted culture of India had possessed knowledge of the psyche—and the collective unconscious—for thousands of years. Descriptions of it are found in its religious philosophy. Jung had evidently previously studied the theosophical literature during his encounter with the unconscious. *Symbols of Transformation* (CW 5) offers sufficient evidence that by 1912 he was already quite familiar with Indian religious history.

Jung was, however, in search of his own roots, and of his own historical predecessors in the Western psychology of the unconscious. Borrowing from Indian culture, as the theosophists were then doing, would not work for him. In Gnosis and alchemy he found the Western roots of his own tradition, and this was prompting his inner defenses against Indian influences. While in India, only when he encountered striking parallels to Western traditions—such as the one between the Naga godhead (the snakelike water goddesses) and the *serpens Mercurii*—did he open himself up to a foreign cultural spirit.[33]

It is no surprise, then, that following the trip to India, he turned back to the Gnostics, specifically to a study of the works of Hans Leisegang.[34] Studying Gnosis along with his concurrent reading of the alchemical literature—in particular the works of the Frankfurt physician and Paracelsist, Gerhard Dorn—were complementary activities. In both, the symbolism derives from the same level of the soul. The difference is that the philosophical alchemists give much more extensive expression to their ideas, making them at the same time a valuable guide to understanding Gnostic intuitions.

Beginning in 1933, Jung took part in the Eranos conferences in Ascona, which had been instituted with his support. Following a series of addresses—"A Study in the Process of Individuation" (1934), "The Archetypes of the Collective Unconscious" (1934), "The Idea of Redemption in Alchemy" (1936), and a lecture about the visions of Zosimos (1937)—in 1939 he began the preliminary work for "Transformation Symbolism in the Mass." He presented this work in two lectures at Ascona in 1941. The two themes are closely connected internally, as shown by Jung's opening remarks on how the mass remained a living mystery, with beginnings reaching back to the early Christian period.[35] While the visions of Zosimos depict an individual experience of sacrifice and transformation, the mass is a collective form.

Jung indeed compares these two forms explicitly in a chapter on their parallels with the mystery of transformation.[36] All the while Gnosis remained an intermittent object of interest; his next study was of the *Gnostische Mysterien* by Leonhard Fendt (Munich 1922).

Following along with his intensive study of alchemical works, Jung returned his attention to Gnosis. This study is documented in his private notebooks, the *Extracta philosophica*, beginning in 1939. There we find notes from his renewed reading of Hippolytus in the English translation by J. H. Macmahon (Edinburg, 1911)—a source I have not been able to find cited in the Collected Works. References to Hippolytus in the Works are always to the edition provided by Paul Wendland, *Die griechischen christlichen Schriftsteller der ersten drei Jahrhunderte* (Leipzig, 1916). Both these works are found in C. G. Jung's library.[37] He took extensive detailed notes on the latter work.[38] These notes suggest a renewed and deepened concern with the pre-Socratics and the Gnosis. This focus continued in his reading of *Ancoratus* by Epiphanius (Volume 38, *Bibliothek der Kirchenväter*)—a volume not now found in his library, nor cited in the bibliography to the Collected Works.

In between—as indicated by the notebooks—there comes a further series of alchemical studies, leading ultimately to Wilhelm Bousset's *Hauptprobleme der Gnosis* (Göttingen 1907). Jung examined this work on Gnosis very closely[39], and it left a lasting impression. In his later works, he quotes Bousset copiously, although there remains a noticeable contrast between the few actual ideas taken over from Bousset, as opposed to the many excerpts. Jung's primary interest here is in the Anthropos doctrine: the concept of the invisible father, of the original human being (Urmensch) as light, and of the darkness of matter. Bousset is recognized for having attempted to go beyond merely locating the ideas of Gnosis in the cultural and historical landscape to which they belonged. His approach was very congenial to Jung's synoptic way of thinking, according to which, rather than simply posing questions about the tradition, he sought after archetypical images wherever he could find them. This practice may not be congenial to historians, yet it fills in gaps in the evidence—gaps which otherwise leave us completely in the dark on many issues arising from this intellectual tradition.

Jung was a thorough empiricist. He had personal experience of the spontaneous appearance of archetypal Gnostic or alchemical ideas. He had witnessed this event in himself and in other modern people. Therefore, he knew that such ideas are capable of emerging spontaneously at any time, and without having been conveyed historically by tradition. This understanding, however, did not stop Jung from emphasizing the historical Gnostic provenance of certain alchemical ideas. In *Hauptprobleme der Gnosis*, Bousset had clearly organized archetypal ideas in terms of the various intellectual tendencies they represented. This accorded nicely with Jung's own intention. My impression is that Bousset went about his work with a genuine analytical flair; for that reason, he became a rich intellectual and historical source for Jung.

In the late 1940s—again, based on his notebooks—Jung undertook a very thorough study of Richard Reitzenstein's *Poimandres* (1904).[40] He did this even while he continued to pursue other issues—reading, for example, Carl Bezold's *Syrische Schatzhöhle* (1883) and Plutarch's *De Iside et Osiride* in the edition by Gustav Parthey (Berlin, 1850). Working through the second volume of the alchemical anthology *Theatrum Chemicum*, he came across the "hieroglyphic monad" of John Dee (1527-1608), the source of the remarkable hieroglyph for the seven planets. From there, he went on to the *Chymische Hochzeit* by Christian Rosencreutz, where the same signs appears in a letter. By the time of the publication of the *Chymische Hochzeit* by Johann Valentin Andreae in 1616, alchemy was already in decline. This fantasy was a final original product of the tendency, and also a sign that alchemy—philosophical alchemy to be precise—was coming to an end. Individual alchemists would continue to appear, but the profundity of the movement had given way to uninteresting theosophical speculation.

Jung later took up the *Acta Archelai* of Hegemonius, in the edition by Charles Henry Beeson (Leipzig, 1906).[41] Scattered through the pages of alchemical textual notations, Jung includes quotations on Gnosis—a testimony of his continuing interest. Stuck to these pages are handwritten notes by Marie-Louise von Franz, whom Jung dispatched to the Zentralbibliothek for research into certain specialized questions. She was Jung's "bloodhound": he would put her onto a scent and she would follow it. The topics he assigned to her were always outside currently established research areas, where no one anticipated finding anything of value. Von Franz worked through the whole of the *Musaeum Hermeticum* (Frankfurt, 1678) for him. In addition, these notes are testimony to the close collaboration that took place between the two, as indeed is noted by Jung in the foreword to *Mysterium Coniunctionis*.

Marie-Louise von Franz was born on January 4, 1915, in Munich, where her mother was on a visit to her sister when she went into labor and gave birth. After the first World War, fearing a communist takeover in Austria, the family left Vienna for St. Galler Rheintal in Switzerland, and in this rural setting Marie-Louise grew up. She went to gymnasium and university in Zurich, deciding on account of an archetypal dream to study classical philology instead of mathematics. Her love for the latter took visible form only years later when, at 55 years of age, she published the book *Zahl und Zeit*. While at the university, she became acquainted with C. G. Jung, who was lecturing at the time at the Eidgenössische Technische Hochschule as part of his teaching duties.[42] She was still a young student when Jung drew her into his work on alchemy, entrusting her in particular with working through the *Aurora consurgens*.

During his study of the *Artis Auriferae* of 1593 Jung had come across part two of the *Aurora consurgens*. Jung thought it odd that part one would be missing, in particular that the explanation given by the printer Conrad Waldkirch had already appeared in the first edition of 1572 by Petrus Perna. It says there that part one of *Aurora consurgens* had been left out because it was full of allegories and parables from Holy Scripture, in order to represent alchemy in the manner of the obscurantists (antiqua more tenebrionum). It further noted that even the most sacred miracle of the incarnation and death of the Lord Christ had been profaned into a Lapis Mysterium. This is not the result of any ill will—so believed the editor, Perna—because the author seems to have been a pious man. Perna thus regarded such a work to be inappropriate for the representation of the art.[43]

This missing first part of the *Aurora consurgens* which had piqued Jung's interest, initially became available to him later in the form of a photocopy from the rare volume of Johannes Rhenanus, *Harmoniae imperscrutabilis chymico philosophicae Decades duae* (II, pp. 175ff).[44]

Jung took up this remarkable text with great excitement—quickly recognizing in it a unique testament to the coexistence of Christian belief and alchemical knowledge. The author finds in alchemy the wisdom of God (Sapientia Dei). As the queen of the south wind (or the south), this wisdom comes from the east like the rising sun (aurora consurgens). Jung's excerpts from this treatise testify to his intense preoccupation with it.[45] He was impressed—as Perna remarked correctly—by the way the author brought holy scripture, in particular the Song of Songs, into alchemy, undertaking the wildest reinterpretations in all good conscience, without the slightest awareness of what he was doing.[46] No wonder Jung—with complete justification, as it turned out—considered this text worthy of thorough analysis, a task he entrusted to his young student, Marie-Louise von Franz.

Only in the course of analyzing the treatise did it emerge as unique in yet other respects. In contrast to the chaotic state of other alchemical sources, this treatise was extant in six (or in the more recent edition, seven) fifteenth- and sixteenth-century texts. From these it was possible to compile a critical edition of the text, which is unique among alchemical works. The other novel feature concerns authorship. Alchemical treatises published under the name of a famous philosopher (Aristotle, Plato, Raymund Lull) are not to be understood as forgeries; the pseudepigraphic use of a famous name is meant merely to lend more weight to the text. Jung initially doubted the authorship of St. Thomas Aquinas. Obviously, *Aurora consurgens* had been written by someone— probably a cleric—who knew his vulgate by heart. Nonetheless, Jung found it difficult to imagine that the famous theologian not only had an interest in illicit alchemy, but also prized it highly. If authorship of the *Aurora consurgens* by St. Thomas were to be confirmed, the status of medieval alchemy and its relationship with Christianity would be cast in an entirely new light. In her final chapter, von Franz proved conclusively—in my opinion—that Aquinas really was the author of *Aurora Consurgens*. Alchemy in the middle ages thus did have the status of science, and it was taken seriously by leading figures. Since the enlightenment, the symbolic understanding necessary to its reading has been lost, and only thus did it fall into disrepute.

This does not explain, however, how it was that the famous author of the scholarly *Summa theologiae* and *Summa contra gentiles* could have composed such an ecstatic alchemical text. Indeed, *Aurora consurgens* is still put into the category of the "Falsa" by scholars, and is considered ill-befitting the image of the strict logician and systematizer. From friends and intimates of St. Thomas it is stated that he suddenly broke off his Summa at the paragraph on penance, because what he had written seemed to him like straw. He is said to have fallen into a state of agitated silence, and became profoundly alienated from his surroundings. He is supposed to have revealed, under a pledge of secrecy, the inner images he was having to brother Reginald von Piperno, his best friend, who had pressed him to explain the reasons for the extraordinary state into which he had descended. On the journey to the Council of Lyon (1274), Aquinas collapsed, and was taken to the Cistercian cloister of St. Maria de Fossa-Nuova, where he lived out his final months. Biographers report how, in a remarkable state on his deathbed, he interpreted the Song of Songs for the monks. As death approaches, visions similar to the *Aurora consurgens* recur frequently.

The Coniunctio symbolism of the Song of Songs and alchemy are expressions of the ultimate unification of opposites, as they often appear in the motif of the death wedding in dreams experienced by the dying. It is known that St. Thomas often dictated in a state of ecstasy (in raptu mentis). The assumption that the *Aurora consurgens* represents the words of the dying St. Thomas thus becomes a certainty.[47]

I have gone into such detail concerning the *Aurora consurgens* in part to shed light on the collaboration between Jung and von Franz, showing how they independently worked together, but also because the figure of St. Thomas reveals both the high regard for alchemy in the middle ages and its compensatory relation to Christianity. People have long underestimated alchemy's religious character,[48] with Jung being one of the first to draw attention to the "Introduction to the Religious and Psychological Problems of Alchemy."[49] In his work on the "spirit Mercurius"[50] Jung designates Christ as the archetype of the (collective Western) consciousness and the alchemist Mercurius as the archetype of the unconscious. Alchemy constituted a compensatory undercurrent of Christian culture.

We left Jung in his studies of alchemy as he enlisted the aid of his talented young student M.-L. von Franz, who collaborated with him on research and also helped him freshen up his knowledge of Latin and Greek, which had fallen in to disuse. In the publications on alchemy, it was she who translated the Latin and Greek quotations for the modern reader. Beginning in the mid-1930s, Jung lectured on his studies of alchemy at the Eranos conferences. These lectures included: "Traumsymbole des Individuationsprozesses" (1935), which was integrated into Psychology and Alchemy[51] (1944); "Einige Bemerkungen zu den Visionen des Zosimos" (1937), included in a revised and expanded version (1954) in the Collected Works[52]; and "The Spirit Mercurius" (1942), in Collected Works 13, § 239, in the expanded version of 1948. On October 8, 1949, at the Zurich Psychological Club he delivered a lecture entitled "Faust and Alchemy,"[53] in which he lay great emphasis on Goethe's opus magnum, *Faust*—this was the work that had made a great impression on him in his youth.[54] He compared *Faust* to *Chymische Hochzeit* by Christian Rosencreutz (mentioned above), establishing the primarily alchemical motifs of the works.

Around 1950 Jung's creative powers had reached a high point. He read a great many books, the fruits of which are apparent in the texts he then authored. In "A Psychological Approach to the Dogma of the Trinity" (1948),[55] he emphasized the pre-Christian parallels of the idea of the trinity; and in "Transformation Symbolism in the Mass" (1940/1954),[56] he referred to parallels with the mystery of transformation in the Aztec teoqualo (the eating of god) and in Zosimos' vision of the priest who had to eat himself. He also had gathered considerable material for his book *Aion*,[57] which includes a collection of essays on the symbolism of the self in Christianity, in alchemy, and in Gnosis. He also drew on an increasing number of collaborators for information regarding various individual themes.

Jung's oeuvre culminated in the opus magnum, *Mysterium Coniunctionis*.[58] Therein he dealt not only with the entire alchemical literature but with a good portion of the Western intellectual tradition as well. He attempted to represent the whole of alchemy as a kind of psychology; alchemical psychology became a foundation for depth psychology. "With Mysterium Coniunctionis," Jung said,[59] "my psychology was at last given its place in reality and established upon its historical foundations. Thus my task was finished, my work done, and now it can stand. The moment I touched bottom, I reached the bounds of scientific understanding, the transcendental, the nature of the archetype per se, concerning which no further scientific statements can be made." Jung concludes his notebooks of *Extracta* on September 10, 1953.

The Significance of Gnosis for Jung

Following an illness in 1944 which brought Jung to the edge of death, an extremely productive period of work got underway in earnest.[60] During this period he wrote the majority of his major works. His notebook excerpts in this period are widely varied and short: he had now achieved an overview, and was able to work from the fullness. "The insight I had had, or the vision of the end of all things," he writes,

> gave me the courage to undertake new formulations. I no longer attempted to put across my own opinion, but surrendered myself to the current of my thoughts. Thus one problem after the other revealed itself to me and took shape... I have also realized that one must accept the thought that go on within oneself of their own accord as part of one's reality. The categories of true and false are, of course, always present; but because they are not binding they take second place. The presence of thoughts is more important than our subjective judgment of them. But neither must these judgments be suppressed, for they also are existent thoughts which are part of our wholeness.

With this, he had come full circle: following his encounter with the unconscious, Jung was drawn to look for historical precedents for what he had undergone. The Gnostics, although he had spent many years studying them, remained too vaguely articulated in extant literature to form bridge to his own experience. It was only after he came upon alchemy, having been led there by his dreams, that he found the "missing link" between the "thinkers of the unconscious" and his experience. The "Mater Alchimia" was ultimately a daughter: "It owes its real beginnings," Jung writes in *Aion*,[61]

> to the Gnostic systems, which Hippolytus rightly regarded as philosophic, and which, with the help of Greek philosophy and the mythologies of the Near and Middle East, together with Christian dogmatics and Jewish cabalism, made extremely interesting at-

tempts, from the modern point of view, to synthetize a unitary vision of the world in which the physical and mystical aspects played equal parts. Had this attempt succeeded, we would not be witnessing today the curious spectacle of two parallel world-views neither of which knows, or wishes to know, anything about the other.

The attempt to encompass both of these realities within the same view—which was also the project of Greek alchemy[62]—had failed. As result, the medieval scholastics were already having to deal with the dichotomy between faith and knowledge, to which they gave a preliminary response in the formula *credo ut intelligam*. This same split became increasingly pressing in the eighteenth century. "Faith lacked experience and science missed out on the soul," wrote Jung.[63]

> Now for the Gnostics—and this is their real secret—the psyche existed as a source of knowledge just as much as it did for the alchemists. Aside from the psychology of the unconscious, contemporary science and philosophy know only of what is outside, while faith knows only of the inside, and then only in the Christian form imparted to it by the passage of the centuries, beginning with St. Paul and the gospel of St. John. Faith, quite as much as science with its traditional objectivity, is absolute, which is why faith and knowledge can no more agree than Christians can with one another.[64]
>
> Our Christian doctrine is a highly differentiated symbol that expresses the transcendent psychic—the God-image and its properties, to speak with Dorn. The Creed is a "symbolum." This comprises practically everything of importance that can be ascertained about the manifestations of the psyche in the field of inner experience, but it does not include Nature, at least not in any recognizable form. Consequently, at every period of Christianity there have been subsidiary currents or undercurrents that have sought to investigate the empirical aspects of Nature not only from the outside but also from the inside.[65]
>
> We are rooted in Christian soil. The foundation does not go very deep, certainly, and...has proved alarmingly thin in places, so

that the original paganism, in altered guise, was able to regain possession of a large part of Europe.[66]

This modern development is in line with the pagan currents that were clearly present in alchemy and have remained alive beneath the Christian surface ever since the days of antiquity. Alchemy reached its greatest efflorescence in the sixteenth and seventeenth centuries, then to all appearances it began to die out. In reality it found its continuation in natural science, which led in the nineteenth century to materialism and in the twentieth century to so-called "realism," whose end is not yet in sight. Despite well-meaning assurances to the contrary, Christianity is a helpless bystander.[67]

Empirical reality and faith have thus drifted ever farther apart. The inner experience formulated as dogma becomes an empty formula, while nature has lost its gods.

If we wish to understand what alchemical doctrine means, we must go back to the historical as well as the individual phenomenology of the symbols, and if we wish to gain a closer understanding of dogma, we must perforce consider first the myths of the Near and Middle East that underlie Christianity, and then the whole of mythology as the expression of a universal disposition in man. This disposition I have called the collective unconscious, the existence of which can be inferred only from individual phenomenology.[68]

Physicians who were versed in alchemy had long recognized that their arcanum healed, or was supposed to heal, not only the diseases of the body but also those of the mind. Similarly, modern psychotherapy knows that, though there are many interim solutions, there is, at the bottom of every neurosis, a moral problem of opposites that cannot be solved rationally, and can be answered only by a supraordinate third, by a symbol which expresses both sides. This was the "veritas" (Dorn) or "theoria" (Paracelsus) for which the old physicians and alchemists strove, and they could do so only by incorporating the Christian revelation into their world of ideas. They continued the work of the Gnostics (who were, most of them, not so much heretics as theologians) and the

Church Fathers in a new era, instinctively recognizing that new wine should not be put in old bottles, and that, like a snake changing its skin, the old myth needs to be clothed anew in every renewed age if it is not to lose its therapeutic effect.[69]

Had there not been an affinity...between the figure of the Redeemer and certain contents of the unconscious, the human mind would never have been able to perceive the light shining in Christ and seize upon it so passionately. The connecting link here is the archetype of the God-man, which on the one hand became historical reality in Christ, and on the other, being eternally present, reigns over the soul in the form of a supraordinate totality, the self. The God-man, like the priest in the vision of Zosimos, is a "kyrios ton pneumaton," not only "Lord of the spirits," but "Lord over the (evil) spirits," which is one of the essential meanings of the Christian Kyrios.[70]

This long excerpt from Jung's *Aion*[71] allows us to see how contemporary the concerns of the Gnostics and early alchemists really are—though the knowledge gained from modern depth psychology offers a necessary supplement. Depth psychology observes that comparable material appears in the dreams, fantasies, or the psychotic ideas of modern individuals who are completely unaware of this historical material.

The explanation of Gnostic ideas "in terms of themselves," i.e., in terms of their historical foundations, is futile, for in that way they are reduced only to their less developed forestages but not understood in their actual significance.[72]

Gnostic ideas are not "mere symptoms of a certain historical development, but creative new configurations which were of the utmost significance for the further development of Western consciousness."[73] The extent to which Gnostic images reflect genuine inner experience, or the degree to which they are the outcome of philosophical elaboration, is extremely difficult to say. "That they may be spontaneous experiences we know from our experience with patients," including the observation that "the pictures they occasionally draw are very often spontaneous recreations of images which have a religious significance."[74]

More than once Jung has been castigated for being a "Gnostic." This is not only because he appraised the Gnostics so highly and quoted them often, but because his psychology of individuation is regarded by these critics as a form of "self-redemption." The individuation process does in fact share a good bit in common with Gnostic systems. This should be understood, however, as the merit due the Gnostics for having raised the question of the sources of evil, a problem that arises whenever psychological therapy becomes at all deep. Jung explains:[75]

Valentinus as well as Basilides are in my view great theologians, who tried to cope with the problems raised by the inevitable influx of the collective unconscious, a fact clearly portrayed by the "gnostic" gospel of St. John and by St. Paul, not to mention the Book of Revelation, and even by Christ himself (unjust steward and Codex Bezae to Luke 6:4). In the style of their time they hypostatized their ideas as metaphysical entities. Psychology does not hypostatize, but considers such ideas as psychological statements about, or models of, essential unconscious factors inaccessible to immediate experience... In our days there are plenty of people who are unable to believe a statement they cannot understand, and they appreciate the help psychology can give them by showing them that human behaviour is deeply influenced by numinous archetypes. That gives them some understanding of why and how the religious factor plays an important role. It also gives them ways and means of recognizing the operation of religious ideas in their own psyche.

I loved the Gnostics in spite of everything, because they recognized the necessity of some further raisonnement, entirely absent in the Christian cosmos. They were at least human and therefore understandable.[76]

Gnosis is characterized by the hypostatizing of psychological apperceptions, i.e., by the integration of archetypal contents beyond the revealed "truth" of the Gospels. Hippolytus still considered classical Greek philosophy along with Gnostic philosophies as perfectly possible views. Christian Gnosis to him was merely the best and superior to all of them.[77]

The Gnostics were of such great interest to Jung because they had a view of the unconscious. According to a letter by Valentinus[78] excerpted by Epiphanius: "[In] the beginning, the Self-Progenitor [*Autogenes*] encompassed all things within himself, though they were within him in ignorance [*agnosia*]." Literally, the term agnosia means "non-knowledge".[79] Likewise, the term *anoeton* in Hippolytus[80] is best translated as "unconsciousness."[81]

> He whom some call ageless Aeon, ever new, both male and female, who encompasses all and is yet unencompassed—the Ennoia within him (desired to break the eternal bonds). Her some have called Ennoia, others, Grace, but properly—since she has furnished treasures of the Majesty to those who are of the Majesty...

Ennoia is probably to be understood here as a latent possibility of consciousness. The Pauline concept of agnoia (ignorantia), as an initial state of unconsciousness, is not very distant from agnosia (Acts 17:30; Ephesians 4:18; 1 Peter 1:14, 2:15). The Gnostics even regarded the human state of agnosia as the "original sin," although "Gnosis" (consciousness) was not apportioned equally among all individuals (cf. Asclepius, chapter 7).

For Hippolytus the wretched condition of unconsciousness is the lot not only of the first humans, but also of the Gnostic God. The transformation of the image of God was not only a change from the God of the Old Testament to the New Testament God affirmed among Christians. In the Gnostic systems, it was additionally characterized as a transformation toward increasing consciousness.[82]

Consciousness presupposes a distinction—and thus a relationship—between subject and object. Where there is not yet an "other," there is no possibility of consciousness. Only when the "Son" of this First Father appears to himself as a person, does he become conscious of himself. Just as the deity is essentially unconscious, so, according to Meister Eckhart, is the individual, who lives in God:

> ...for when a man's existence is of God's eternal species, there is no other life in him: his life is himself.

But we say that it [happiness] consists neither in knowledge nor in love, but in that there is something in the soul, from which both knowledge and love flow... To know this is to know what happiness depends on.

For [my] unconditioned being is above god and all distinctions. It was here [in unconditioned being] that I was myself, wanted myself, and knew myself to be this person [here before you], and therefore I am my own first cause, both of my eternal being and of my temporal being" (Sermon 32: "Beati pauperes spiritu;" Matthew 5:3).[83]

Jung frequently praises the insight of Meister Eckhart, noting:

The world-embracing spirit of Meister Eckhart knew without discursive knowledge, the primordial mystical experience of India as well as of the Gnostics, and was itself the finest flower on the tree of the "Free Spirit" that flourished at the beginning of the fourteenth century... Such utterances on the nature of the Deity express transformations of the God-image which run parallel with changes in human consciousness, though one would be at a loss to say which is the cause of the other. The God-image is not something invented, it is an experience that comes upon man spontaneously... The unconscious God-image can therefore alter the state of consciousness, just as the latter can modify the God-image once it has become conscious... Psychologically, however, the idea of God's agnosia, or of the anennoetos theos, is of the utmost importance, because it identifies the Deity with the numinosity of the unconscious.[84]

These symbols represent in a certain sense the character of a whole, and they presumably signify "wholeness."

As a rule they are "uniting" symbols, representing the conjunction of a single or double pair of opposites, the result being either a dyad or a quaternion. They arise from the collision between the conscious and the unconscious and from the confusion which this causes (known in alchemy as "chaos" or "nigredo"). Empirically, this confusion takes the form of restlessness and disorientation...

For the present, it is not possible for psychology to establish more than that the symbols of wholeness mean the wholeness of the individual. On the other hand, it has to admit, most emphatically, that this symbolism uses images or schemata which have always, in all the religions, expressed the universal "Ground," the Deity itself.[85]

In his memoirs,[86] in the chapter entitled "Late Thoughts," Jung writes of how the Christian nations had neglected over the course of the centuries to continue developing their myth, with the effect that their Christianity has fallen into a state of slumber. Jung understands myth as the irrational formulation of psychic functions and contents.[87] It consists of a series of images in the soul that, while often originating in external reality, represent an inner world. A myth that is no longer in the process of self-renewal is dead. The Christian myth has fallen mute, and no longer has any answers to offer, although in its original formulation it would have contained the necessary potential for development.

In an unorthodox manner, the Gnostics and the alchemists cultivated the myth further, seeking answers that were not available from the orthodoxy of their time. The original church fathers likewise were at work on the myth in a creative sense, continuing to develop it until, along with the institutionalization of the church, it fell into the ossified state of dogmatism and formalism. The further development of the myth was supposed to take place with the outpouring of the Holy Spirit over the congregation, turning the individual members into the sons and children of God. Thus would they partake of the certainty that they were,

> more than autochthonous animalia sprung from the earth, that as the twice-born they had their roots in divinity itself. Their visible, physical life was on this earth; but the invisible inner man had come from, and would return to, the primordial image of wholeness: to the eternal Father, as the Christian myth of salvation puts it.[88]

Chapter 7

The Septem Sermones ad Mortuos

Not least of the motivations for Martin Buber's criticism of Jung for being a Gnostic was a mythopoetic text written by Jung in 1916 and published in the form of a series of instructions left by the Gnostic Basilides.* That Jung allowed the document to appear at all, in a private edition offered as a gift to friends—which he later (and perhaps ingeniously) stated regretting as a "youthful transgression"—seems to me evidence of a fascination of the time, and as such is understandable. He no doubt *did not* regret having written the fantasy, but only having naively made it available to a few individuals who were not in a position to understand it. Thus, it was only "for the sake of honesty" that he permitted it to be printed in his memoir, *Memories, Dreams, Reflections*, recorded by Aniela Jaffé.[1]

In the prior chapter on "Jung and Gnosis" I already described developments leading to the confrontation with his unconscious fantasies, which he had already experienced in the form of alchemical images as a child walking to school. The fantasies of middle age initially appeared as arresting dreams.[2] According to Jung:[3]

> I dreamed I was sitting in a very beautiful Italian loggia, something like the Palazzio Vecchio in Florence. It was most luxurious, with columns, floor, and balustrade of marble. I was sitting in a golden chair, a Renaissance chair, in front of a table of green stone like emerald. It was of an extraordinary beauty. I was sitting looking out into space, for the loggia was on top of a tower belonging to a castle. I knew that my children were there too. Suddenly a white bird came flying down and gracefully alighted on the table. It was like a small gull, or a dove. I made a sign to the children to keep quiet, and the dove suddenly became a little girl with golden hair,

---

* For an updated evaluation of this period, see the Foreword by Lance Owens.

and ran away with the children. As I sat pondering over this, the little girl came back and put her arms around my neck very tenderly. Then all at once she was gone, and the dove was there and spoke slowly with a human voice. It said, "I am allowed to transform into a human form only in the first hours of the night, while the male dove is busy with the twelve dead." Then it flew away into the blue sky and I awoke.

Jung found himself at a loss to interpret the dream at the time. He was certain only was that it demonstrated extraordinary activity on the part of his unconscious. The emerald table prompted him to think of the story of the "Tabula Smaragdina" from the alchemical legends of Hermes Trismegistus, who is supposed to have left behind a tablet engraved in Greek with the essential tenets of alchemy. Jung associated the twelve dead with the twelve apostles.

The dream took place prior to a moment of extraordinary clarity in which Jung looked back over his life to that point. He asked himself, what had he accomplished? He had explicated the myths of earlier peoples and written a book about heroes, about the mythology in terms of which human beings had always lived (*Transformations and Symbols of the Libido*, 1912).[4] This raised the question of the guiding mythology today—of Christianity, for example. "Do you live in it?" he asked himself.[5] "To be honest, the answer was no. For me, it is not what I live by." But then came the question, "What is your myth—the myth in which you do live?" At this, Jung reports his dialog with himself becoming uncomfortable. He had arrived at a dead end and quit thinking.

Jung found himself at the midpoint of his life and noted that he had fallen away from the Christian mythology. Here began his search for his own mythology, intended also to serve more generally as orientation in the modern world.[6] Already in this first dream there had appeared the motif of the dead, attended by the dove in the first hours of the night. Jung reports having had a recurring fantasy at this same time in which something dead was yet alive.[7] Night is the realm of mysterious transformation in the Egyptian Amduat, the "book of the hidden space." Its theme is the nightly journey through the underworld of the sun-god in his barque.[8] It narrates the myth of the "night-sea journey"[9] of the sun-god, and of the prevailing collective consciousness of daily renewal. The concept of the night-sea journey comes from the ethnologist Leo Frobenius, who was able to demonstrate the existence of this myth throughout the world. The sun-god travels in the womb from west to east, where he rises reborn after withstanding a variety of dangers. The myth's universal existence proves that it expresses a psychic reality independent of history and culture: this is the renewal of consciousness that takes place through regression. It is the intrapsychic resurrection that is the psychic equivalent and basis of all resurrection beliefs. Consciousness, which separates itself from its source in the morning of life, sinks back into its ultimate origins, the unconscious, in order to reemerge enriched with new contents to once again confront the world. This experience is common in midlife, when the first phase of conforming to the demands of the world has come to an end and a second phase of adaptation to that which lies behind life begins. Typical of the experience is this moment of sudden clarity in regard to life thus far, of gaining an objective overview, as in the moment of death.

The dream setting as such evokes a southern historical atmosphere. It is a Renaissance castle with sumptuous décor. The historical period of the Italian renaissance marked a new stage in European history, a transformation of the medieval spirit into a modern one. It was not so much a rebirth of antiquity as the assimilation of the classical sense of the world with the Christian worldview of the Middle Ages. The previously unified world image had collapsed, and a new era was struggling to be born amid great labor pains. Playing a considerable role in this process were the alchemists, who had maintained continuity with antiquity as an intellectual undercurrent of Christianity.

The exquisitely beautiful emerald table is a reference to alchemy, which just twenty years later would become an important element in Jung's life. The "Smaragdine tablet"[10] is supposed to have been produced by Hermes, the ultimate alchemical authority, who is said to have summarized the wisdom of alchemy in brief mnemonics on the tablet and hidden it. And in fact it would be given to Jung himself to discover this wisdom, although he could have had no such idea of any such eventuality at the time. The emerald is the stone of Hermes, the god of revelation[11] in alchemy. Jung was indeed on the threshold of a great revelation, bearing on the renewal of the Western spirit.

In the course of the dream, the white bird is identified as a dove. In the Christian tradition, this is the third member of the trinity. The prevailing spirit of the Renaissance was not so much Christian as genuinely classical. The dove is the bird of Artemis and Aphrodite, or the great Near Eastern goddess of love as such. The founding of the oracle of Dodona goes back to a dove. Dione is the feminine counterpart of Zeus, comparable to the Roman Diana, and is called the goddess of the bright sky. In Dodona she is worshipped as the wife of Zeus and the goddess who is the source of the oracle. The great hunter Orion, with his close association with the chaste huntress Artemis, was in pursuit of a host of divine young maidens (or according to other narratives a single maiden, named Pleione), who were transformed into wild doves (peleiades) and cast into the heavens. The mother of the Pleiades is called Pleione or Aithra, the "bright." Her daughters made up the virgin cohort of Artemis. It was a companion of Artemis, the nymph Maia, who bore Zeus's son, Hermes, the bringer of dreams.[12]

From these amplifications from Greek mythology it appears that the white dove has to do with a heavenly virgin love goddess, who establishes intimate relations that perplexed Jung; and she even frolics around with his children in the castle. Jung himself sits in a lofty position high up above the crowd, on a golden throne in the tower like a king. This is taken to suggest that he, as the metamorphosing king, has come into a first fleeting contact with the inspiring bird anima. In a later dream the motif of the dead appeared once again:

I was in a region like the Alyscamps near Arles. There they have a lane of sarcophagi which go back to Merovingian times. In the dream I was coming from the city, and saw before me a similar lane with a long row of tombs. They were pedestals with stone slabs on which the dead lay. They reminded me of old church burial vaults, where knights in armor lie outstretched. Thus the dead lay in my dream, in their antique clothes, with hands clasped, the difference being that they were not hewn out of stone, but in a curious fashion mummified. I stood still in front of the first grave and looked at the dead man, who was a person of the eighteen-thirties. I looked at his clothes with interest, whereupon he suddenly moved and came to life. He unclasped his hands; but that was only because I was looking at him. I had an extremely unpleasant feeling, but walked on and came to another body. He belonged to the eighteenth century. There exactly the same thing happened: when I looked at him, he came to life and moved his hands. So I went down the whole row, until I came to the twelfth century—that is, to a crusader in chain mail who lay there with clasped hands. His figure seemed carved out of wood. For a long time I looked at him and thought he was really dead. But suddenly I saw that a finger of his left hand was beginning to stir gently. [13]

The dream is evidence not only of an unusually active unconscious, but in terms of its meaning refers back to a much earlier dream: [14]

I was in a house I did not know, which had two stories. It was "my house." I found myself in the upper story, where there was a kind of salon furnished with fine old pieces in rococo style. On the walls hung a number of precious old paintings. I wondered that this should be my house, and thought, "Not bad": But then it occurred to me that I did not know what the lower floor looked like. Descending the stairs, I reached the ground floor. There everything was much older, and I realized that this part of the house must date from about the fifteenth or sixteenth century. The furnishings were medieval; the floors were of red brick. Everywhere it was rather dark. I went from one room to another, thinking, "Now I really must explore the whole house." I came upon a heavy door, and opened it. Beyond it, I discovered a stone stairway that led down into the cellar. Descending again, I found myself in a beautifully vaulted room which looked exceedingly ancient. Examining the walls, I discovered layers of brick among the ordinary stone blocks, and chips of brick in the mortar. As soon as I saw this I knew that the walls dated from Roman times. My interest by now was intense. I looked more closely at the floor. It was of stone slabs, and in one of these I discovered a ring. When I pulled it, the stone slab lifted, and again I saw a stairway of narrow stone steps leading down into the depths. These, too, I descended, and entered a low cave cut into the rock. Thick dust lay on the floor, and in the dust were scattered bones and broken pottery, like remains of a primitive culture. I discovered two human skulls, obviously very old and half disintegrated. Then I awoke.

In Jung's own analysis of the dream, the house represented a kind of image of the psyche—that is, the state of his consciousness at that time (1909), including elements which to that point remained unconscious. Consciousness was characterized by the salon, which had a lived-in atmosphere despite the old-fashioned style. The first floor was already referring to the unconscious. The deeper he ventured, the more unfamiliar and dark it all became. In the cellar he discovered the remains of a primitive culture, that is, the world of primitive man within himself, to which consciousness has only scant access and is nearly incapable of illuminating. The primitive soul of man merges with the life of the animal soul. The layers of the unconscious represent past times and stages of consciousness that have been overcome. They go all the way back to the foundations of cultural history. The house in the dream can be regarded as a structural diagram of the human soul, a thoroughly impersonal kind of prerequisite: This is the collective a priori of the individual psyche, a certain sensing of earlier ways of operating, which Jung later recognized as instinctual forms, terming them archetypes (primal forms).

The dream of the sarcophagi uses another image to signify composition of our psyche out of many historical layers and former patterns of behavior, just as the development of the embryo (ontogenesis) has been perceived as going through old structural phases (phylogenesis) in the history of human development. For the majority of people these holdovers are dead. Yet if one attends to them, they come back to life. Just prior to this dream, he had had another that suggested this fact to him:[15]

I was in an Italian city, and it was around noon, between twelve and one o'clock. A fierce sun was beating down upon the narrow streets. The city was built on hills and reminded me of a particular part of Basel, the Kohlenberg. The little streets which lead down into the valley, the Birsigtal, that runs through the city, are partly flights of steps. In the dream, one such stairway descended to Barfüsserplatz. The city was Basel, and yet it was also an Italian city, something like Bergamo. It was summertime; the blazing sun stood at the zenith, and everything was bathed in an intense light. A crowd came streaming toward me, and I knew that the shops were closing and people were on their way home to dinner. In the midst of this stream of people walked a knight in full armor. He mounted the steps toward me. He wore a helmet of the kind that is called a basinet, with eye slits, and chain armor. Over this was a white tunic into which was woven, front and back, a large red cross.

One can easily imagine how I felt: suddenly to see in a modern city, during the noonday rush hour, a crusader coming toward me. What struck me as particularly odd was that none of the many persons walking about seemed to notice him. No one turned his head or gazed after him. It was as though he were completely invisible to everyone but me. I asked myself what this apparition meant, and then it was as if someone answered me—but there was no one there to speak: "Yes, this is a regular apparition. The knight always passes by here between twelve and one o'clock, and has been doing so for a very long time [for centuries, I gathered] and everyone knows about it."

The dream made a deep impression on Jung, but he did not understand it at the time. He was depressed and troubled, and completely at a loss as to what to do. He thought a great deal about the puzzling figure of the crusader, without being able to fully comprehend its significance. He knew already in the dream that the crusader belonged to the twelfth century. This was the onset of European alchemy and the quest for the Holy Grail.[16] The grail stories had played a large role in his thoughts from his youth onward, and he suspected that a secret lay yet concealed there. Thus it appeared quite natural to him that the dream would evoke the quest, because that was the deepest meaning of his world.

We owe Jung an extraordinary debt for having shared with us these dreams that led him to the specific understanding of the historical psyche for which he is known. They came to him not as finished revelations from heaven, but in symbolic form. They prompted him to mediation, and ultimately to come upon the vein out of which the Gnostics and alchemists had emerged in earlier times. Because the psyche itself is historical in nature, these dreams cease appearing as alien forms, and become accessible to us from within. These insights came to him as a natural revelation, and so he was able to confirm them a thousand times over in his later works.

Evidently, the crusader had been around for centuries as a "specter," because he is unredeemed. Just as certain problems remain unresolved from childhood and must be worked out in one's adult years, so do conflicts in the psychic history of mankind resist becoming conscious. The seeds of positive developments that have been blocked lie concealed in every conflict. And conflicts, insofar as they are not acknowledged, persist in the form of an inhibition to healthy growth. For the Christian world, the crusades represent just such a problem, which is not understood and which is manifest today in the form of the threat to Western Europe by Islamic fundamentalism. The quest for the Holy Grail was the unfinished attempt to combine oriental Christianity and the predatory practices of medieval knights into a chivalric culture. Likewise does Gnosticism resist resolution, because at the beginning of the Christian era, Gnosis was simply suppressed as an heretical understanding of Christianity, rather than having been consciously integrated.

The average European has no awareness of the existence of these problems in his or her psyche. A psychological problem that is not perceived as such often finds expression in the outer world, leaving Europeans to simply wonder at why the political history of the continent has followed such a remarkable course. An unacknowledged psychological problem leaves its trace on historical developments. It is thus of inestimable importance when particular individuals are led, as if by fate, to historical problems, thereby bringing them to general consciousness and contributing to a resolution. Research into Gnosis is currently undergoing a renaissance; something present in it remains yet unresolved. By confronting this resolution, the European spirit can gain new impulses.

Buber and Jung embody two different, paradigmatic positions on the numinous: one is passive-submissive, and the other is active-acknowledging. One shies away from eating of the tree of knowledge, because to do so is to commit original sin and be driven out of paradise;

the other must eat of the tree precisely because the meaning of life consists in becoming conscious.

In this sense, the Gnostics reversed the usual paradise narrative: Among the Ophites (Irenaeus, Adversus haereses, 30.7), Yaldabaoth is the creator of man. But his mother is described as lending assistance to the first human pair, using the snake to tempt them to transgress Yaldabaoth's commandment. "But when they were eating, they recognized the supreme power..." (Genesis 3:7, "Then the eyes of both were opened, and they knew that they were naked; and they sewed fig leaves together and made themselves aprons.") In the Gnostic text, The Hypostasis of the Archons (NHC II 4), the figure giving instruction is the female spirit in the snake:

> "What did he say to you? Was it, 'From every tree in the garden shall you eat; yet—from the tree of recognizing good and evil do not eat'?"
>
> The carnal woman said, "Not only did he say 'Do not eat,' but even 'Do not touch it; for the day you eat from it, with death you are going to die.'"
>
> And the snake, the instructor, said, "With death you shall not die; for it was out of jealousy that he said this to you. Rather your eyes shall open and you shall come to be like gods, recognizing evil and good." And the female instructing principle was taken away from the snake, and she left it behind, merely a thing of the earth.
>
> And the carnal woman took from the tree and ate; and she gave to her husband as well as herself; and these beings that possessed only a soul, ate. And their imperfection became apparent in their lack of knowledge; and they recognized that they were naked of the spiritual element, and took fig leaves and bound them upon their loins (89, 31-90,10; 13-19).[17]

Returning now to Jung's biography: In a previous chapter I described how around 1913 he felt compelled to play with stones at the lake, and enter his imagination. A flood of fantasies was eventually evoked; they continued for several years and were constellated in his Red Book. In these fantasies, eventually there appeared a male figure, whom Jung called Philemon. He was a pagan, conjuring up an Egyptian-Hellenist mood with a Gnostic coloration. In the imaginative conversations that followed, Philemon became Jung's psychagogue, the source of enlightening ideas.

Gradually there emerged an urge to give form to what Philemon had to say. Thus it was, in 1916, that the Septem Sermones appeared, written in their peculiar language. I want to let Jung speak for himself:[18]

> It began with a restlessness, but I did not know what it meant or what "they" wanted of me. There was an ominous atmosphere all around me. I had the strange feeling that the air was filled with ghostly entities. Then it was as if my house began to be haunted. My eldest daughter saw a white figure passing through the room. My second daughter, independently of her elder sister, related that twice in the night her blanket had been snatched away; and that same night my nine-year-old son had an anxiety dream. In the morning he asked his mother for crayons, and he, who ordinarily never drew, now made a picture of his dream. He called it "The Picture of the Fisherman." Through the middle of the picture ran a river, and a fisherman with a rod was standing on the shore. He had caught a fish. On the fisherman's head was a chimney from which flames were leaping and smoke rising. From the other side of the river the devil came flying through the air. He was cursing because his fish had been stolen. But above the fisherman hovered an angel who said, "You cannot do anything to him; he only catches the bad fish!" My son drew this picture on a Saturday.
>
> Around five o'clock in the afternoon on Sunday the front doorbell began ringing frantically. It was a bright summer day; the two maids were in the kitchen, from which the open square outside the front door could be seen. Everyone immediately looked to see who was there, but there was no one in sight. I was sitting near the doorbell, and not only heard it but saw it moving. We all simply stared at one another. The atmosphere was thick, believe me. Then I knew that something had to happen. The whole house was filled as if there were a crowd present, crammed full of spirits. They were packed deep right up to the door, and the air was so thick it was scarcely possible to breathe. As for myself, I was all a-quiver with the question: "For God's sake, what in the world is this?"

Then they cried out in chorus, "We have come back from Jerusalem where we found not what we sought." That is the beginning of the Septem Sermones.

Then it began to flow out of me, and in the course of three evenings the thing was written. As soon as I took up the pen, the whole ghostly assemblage evaporated. The room quieted and the atmosphere cleared. The haunting was over.

The experience has to be taken for what it was, or as it seems to have been. No doubt it was connected with the state of emotion I was in at the time, and which was favorable to parapsychological phenomena. It was an unconscious constellation whose peculiar atmosphere I recognized as the numen of an archetype. "It walks abroad, it's in the air!" [Faust, Part Two] The intellect, of course, would like to arrogate to itself some scientific, physical knowledge of the affair, or, preferably, to write the whole thing off as a violation of the rules. But what a dreary world it would be if the rules were not violated sometimes!

Shortly before this experience I had written down a fantasy of my soul having flown away from me. This was a significant event: the soul, the anima, establishes the relationship to the unconscious. In a certain sense this is also a relationship to the collectivity of the dead; for the unconscious corresponds to the mythic land of the dead, the land of the ancestors. If, therefore, one has a fantasy of the soul vanishing, this means that it has withdrawn into the unconscious or into the land of the dead. There it produces a mysterious animation and gives visible form to the ancestral traces, the collective contents. Like a medium, it gives the dead a chance to manifest themselves. Therefore, soon after the disappearance of my soul the "dead" appeared to me, and the result was the Septem Sermones. This is an example of what is called "loss of soul"—a phenomenon encountered quite frequently among primitives.

From that time on, the dead have become ever more distinct for me as the voices of the Unanswered, Unresolved, and Unredeemed; for since the questions and demands which my destiny required me to answer did not come to me from outside, they must have come from the inner world. These conversations with the dead formed a kind of prelude to what I had to communicate to the world about the unconscious: a kind of pattern of order and interpretation of its general contents.

Jung writes in his memoirs that he "worked...through a mountain of mythological material, then through the Gnostic writers" for his book *Transformations and Symbols of the Libido* (1911/12).[19] I was able to identify three books as possible sources for the Gnostic material he might have read in this period, all of which were in his library: Wolfgang Schultz, *Dokumente der Gnosis* (Jena 1910), Charles William King, *The Gnostics and their Remains, Ancient and Medieval* (London 1864), and G. S. R. Mead, *Fragments of a Faith Forgotten* (London 1906). Of his Gnostic subsequent studies in the following years, he states:[20]

Between 1918 and 1926 I had seriously studied the Gnostic writers, for they too had been confronted with the primal world of the unconscious and had dealt with its contents, with images that were obviously contaminated with the world of instinct. Just how they understood these images remains difficult to say, in view of the paucity of the accounts—which, moreover, mostly stem from their opponents, the Church Fathers. It seems to me highly unlikely that they had a psychological conception of them.

In the books Jung read during his early studies, the discussion of Gnosis took place in the context of ancient religious history; therein, Jung took note of the name of the Gnostic teacher Basilides and the significance of the city of Alexandria. We find ourselves today in a more comfortable situation, in which we are able to corroborate and complete Jung's suggestions on the basis of modern knowledge.

Jung begins his Gnostic treatise with a preface:[21]

Septem Sermones ad Mortuos
The Seven Sermons to the Dead
Written by Basilides in Alexandria, the City
Where the East toucheth the West

Little is known about Basilides. He is supposed to have been active in Alexandria during the reigns of Emperor Hadrian (117-138) and Antoninus Pius (138-161). Outstanding among his followers was his son Isidoros, who spread his teaching. His sect is supposed to have existed as late as the fourth century in Lower Egypt. According to the report by Hippolytus,[22] he claimed to have received from the apostle Matthew the secret sayings of Jesus himself. But this is a very common trope in Gnostic texts, and need not be taken literally from today's point of view, but rather as a "revelation in the spirit of the Lord."

We possess two very different reports concerning his doctrine: first from Irenaeus[23] and Epiphanius,[24] but also one from Hippolytus,[25] as well as a few scattered mentions in other sources.[26] How the contradictions appearing in these sources might be reconciled remains a puzzle even to scholars. Nevertheless, the problems raised for discussion in the texts are interesting for our purposes, and they prove Basilides to have been one of the great theologians. A Basilides fragment quoted by Clement of Alexandria sheds light on our question:

> For if one by nature knows God, as Basilides thinks, who calls intelligence of a superior order at once faith and kingship, and a creation worthy of the essence of the Creator; and explains that near Him exists not power, but essence and nature and substance; and says that faith is not the rational assent of the soul exercising free-will, but an undefined beauty, belonging immediately to the creature; the precepts both of the Old and of the New Testament are, then, superfluous, if one is saved by nature, as Valentinus would have it, and is a believer and an elect man by nature, as Basilides thinks.[27]

The Gnostics also speak of "faith," but in a quite different sense from people of the Church. I mentioned above that Jung, in an interview toward the end of his life with John Freeman, was asked whether he believed in God. He replied, "I know. I don't need to believe. I know." This remark elicited a flood of letters from the public, some of which were forwarded to him, in response to which he elaborated his standpoint:

Mind you, I didn't say "there is a God." I said: "I don't need to believe in God, I know. Which does not mean: I do know a certain God (Zeus, Yahweh, Allah, the Trinitarian God, etc.) but rather: I do know that I am obviously confronted with a factor unknown in itself, which I call "God" in consensu omnium… I remember Him, I evoke Him, whenever I use his name, overcome by anger or by fear, whenever I involuntarily say: "Oh God." That happens when I meet somebody or something stronger than myself. It is an apt name given to all overpowering emotions in my own psychic system, subduing my conscious will and usurping control over myself. This is the name by which I designate all things which cross my willful path violently and recklessly, all things which upset my subjective views, plans, and intentions and change the course of my life for better or worse. In accordance with tradition I call the power of fate in this positive as well as negative aspect, and inasmuch as its origin is beyond my control, "God," a "personal God," since my fate means very much to myself, particularly when it approaches me in the form of conscience as a vox Dei with which I can even converse and argue…

Yet I should consider it an intellectual immorality to indulge in the belief that my view of a God is the universal, metaphysical Being of the confessions or "philosophies." I commit the impertinence neither of a hypostasis nor of an arrogant qualification such as: "God can only be good." Only my experience can be good or evil, but I know that the superior will is based upon a foundation which transcends human imagination. Since I know of my collision with a superior will in my own psychic system, I know of God, and if I should venture the illegitimate hypostasis of my image, I would say of a God beyond Good and Evil, just as much dwelling in myself as everywhere else.[28]

It seems to me very important for the reader to understand what Jung means when he speaks of "God." Since most scholars of Gnosis are theologians or theologically oriented historians, this is also where the threat of misunderstanding is greatest. For the same reason, in order to come to know the "Gnostic Jung," it is not enough to simply print out the texts in which Jung speaks about Gnosis. *Jung's conception of Gnosis permeates the entirety of his systematic psychology, from which it is not possible to extract a single part in ignorance of the rest.*

Theologians have frequently criticized Jung for statements he has made about God,[29] without seeing that these statements follow from an utterly contrary initial image. They either hypostasize their own personal experience in a way that is not justified, or they give expression to their faith—which, as noted above, is in psychological terms a projection. Faith is a matter of grace and cannot be created as an object of the will. Wherever faith has been lost, it must be replaced by experience and understanding. To do this is to reclaim the projection, without falling prey to agnosticism.

The "superior faith" mentioned by Basilides appears to consist of an inner illumination, which is distinct from the sort of belief usually encountered among members of the church. This superior faith he also characterizes as the "rational consent of a free soul." Individuals acceding to this agreement are taken "to be closer to the creator," which involves a shift from the limited form of the conscious ego to that of the non-egoistic self, a state that can be compared to the satori experience of Zen Buddhism.

Whoever is identical with his or her ego standpoint is thus wholly incapable of understanding the transformed standpoint of a Basilides. The standpoint of the ego entails a limitation in one's view of the world, and this cannot be overcome by the understanding, no matter how clever it might be. The breakthrough to the self signifies a broadening of horizons, comparable to the "eternal beauty of an immediate creation," says Basilides. Satori is likewise the achievement of a point of view, rather than some kind of mystical vision of God. It means to have cast a gaze into the original nature of human being or the knowledge of the original human beings. It is the belief in the power of redemption in the individual.

This shift from the standpoint of the ego to the self is one of the central points of Gnosis. It speaks often of a subordinate demiurge that says of himself: "I am the Lord, and there is none else; besides Me there is no god" (Isaiah 45:5). For the Ophites mentioned above, this is Yaldabaoth,[30] and similar statements from the demiurge are to be found in the Apocryphon of John,[31] in the Ptolemaic system described by Irenaeus,[32] in Hippolytus's report on the Valentinians,[33] and in

Epiphanius.[34] These passages were confirmed by the texts found at Nag Hammadi, in the Apocalypse of Adam,[35] and the Hypostasis of the Archons.[36]

It may be that all of these passages represent hostile formulations aimed against the Old Testament God JHWH, but yet more importantly, they take aim against the ego's claim of exclusivity, a standpoint that is likewise in need of being overcome because it is inadequate. From a psychological point, the demiurge—the master in charge of building the world—is consciousness. *The world exists only insofar as a consciousness is present.* Because consciousness has its developmental basis in a matrix (Mutterboden), it has the nature of being derived, of being something secondary, "the son of the mother," the sum of the contents of the unconscious that have been made conscious. Its subject is the ego, which is always smaller than the whole. This, however, is the driving force behind the becoming conscious of these contents. If the sense of the dynamic brought forth by the ego is lost, the ego takes itself to be the sole creator and ultimate commander. This is the "evening knowledge" of Augustine, the *scientia hominis*, which loses itself in ten thousand worldly things. All creation ends in this, before returning to its beginnings in the "morning knowledge,"[37] the *scientia creatoris*.

The Gnostics, and Basilides in particular, had an intuitive recognition of something similar to this, and so allotted a subordinate role to the demiurge. From this perspective, it is self-evident that the world is incomplete, and this is the source of the longing for an origin. This is not a regressive longing for the lost innocence of paradise, but one aiming at the world of the manifold (pleroma) out of which the Gnostics came. This desire for the whole stems from a transformed perspective, as Basilides puts it, a "scientia creatoris," which strives for knowledge of the unknowable father. Such a perspective renders superfluous "the commandments of the Old and New Testaments," to the dismay of Clement of Alexandria. The church fathers were no more able than Buber to hear a statement like this without getting a chill up the spine. From the standpoint of the ego, in which both remain caught, the end result of such an understanding is nothing short of libertinism. Only a psychological understanding is capable of mediating between these two irreconcilable positions. Martin Buber, because he rejected analytical psychology as "psychologism," denied himself access to such a perspective.

I do not know how thoroughly Jung was acquainted with the ideas and the system of Basilides. Not wanting to wrongly ascribe his "revelation" to knowledge of this source,[38] I prefer to regard the similarity between Basilides' ideas and his own as a case of synchronicity.

Later Jung also became interested in the teachings of Isidoros, the son of Basilides,[39] who remarked:

> Were I to persuade anyone that the real soul is not a unit, but that the passions of the erring are occasioned by the compulsion of the accreted natures, no common excuse then would the worthless of mankind have for saying, 'I was compelled, I was carried away, I did it without wishing to do so, I acted unwillingly'; whereas it was the man himself who led his desire towards evil and refused to battle with the constraints of the accretions. Our duty is to show ourselves rulers over the inferior creation within us, gaining mastery by means of the rational principle.

But in a letter, Valentinus also wrote explicitly about the "accretions":

> For the many spirits dwelling in the heart do not allow it to become pure: rather each of them performs its own acts, polluting it in various ways with improper desires.[40]

Jung quoted these passages in *Aion*,[41] in order to show that through the adopting of an alternative perspective, other parts of the soul could be rendered visible. These he termed "shadows," which at the lowest level do not distinguish themselves from animal instincts. Only this new standpoint makes it necessary to recognize the existence of an unconscious psyche that functions autonomously and has the capacity to call into question the standpoint of the ego, and frustrate its aims, no matter what form is taken by the latter. The typical standpoint of the established church, as expressed by Clement of Alexandria—that we must "by acquiring superiority in the rational part, show ourselves masters of the inferior creation in us"—corresponds to the complete identification of the psyche with the ego; and this remains the prevailing opinion today. This view not only cannot do justice to the realities of the psyche, but in theological terms, winds up entangled in endless contradictions. The position on sin taken by Basilides and his son Isidoros, in particular in regard to sins committed unconsciously, represents a remarkably modern standpoint. Inextricably connected to one's understanding of what sin is, is the question of evil—another of Basilides' primary concerns. It is a measure of the extent of the intellectual kinship Jung felt toward Basilides that he would allow his instructions to the dead be spoken through the latter's mouth.

Alexandria,[42] founded by Alexander the Great at the turn of the years 322-321 BCE at the west end of the Nile River delta, was once a world-class city, comparable to Rome. The city's wealth derived from its secure harbor, which was protected by a dam extending from the mainland to the island of Pharos, the site of the famous lighthouse. Alexandria enjoyed a flourishing trade with Arabia, East Africa, and India during the reign of the Emperor Augustus, thanks to a canal connecting the Nile to the Red Sea. Lake Mareotis, in the southern part of the city, produced so much papyrus that Alexandria was able to supply the entire Mediterranean world with paper. Under the Ptolemaic dynasty the capital city was changed from Memphis to Alexandria. When Egypt became a Roman province, the imperial governor took over from the king. In 495 CE it became part of the eastern empire, and in 642 it fell to the Arabs. Although an ethnically very diverse city, Greeks, Jews, and Egyptians were segregated. The old opposition between Greeks and Jews flared up in the first century CE, and anti-Semitism went hand in hand with the Alexandrians aversion for Rome.

Alexandria was a center of Hellenic science, literature, and art. It had a large library with a catalog. Here, in the Ptolemaic period, the Septuagint was produced, the Greek translation of the Old Testament for the Hellenized Jews. Famous names associated with Alexandria include the Jewish philosopher Philo, the Christians Clement and Origen, and the Neo-Platonist Plotinus. The snake Agathos had its site there as the local daemon. Worshiped in Alexandria alongside the Olympian gods were Dionysus with his mysteries; Asclepius; Isis, who had long been Hellenized and brought into association with Tyche; gods of the Orient and Asia Minor as well as Hellenized Egyptian gods such as Osiris-Apis, who became Sarapis; and, not least, the deified Alexander. Greek and oriental gods passed over into each other; the mysteries of Dionysus and Isis, as well as the secret teachings of Hermes Trismegistus, joined one another in a colorful mix. The Christians appeared in this mix in the second century, and many of these were Gnostics. A Christian catechetic school appeared around 200, in addition to a considerable congregation, which Clement took to represent the pinnacle of education and culture. A Christian monastery was established not far from Alexandria in the Natron desert. And then, in 642, the Arabian conquest changed everything.

Septem Sermones ad Mortuos

With that introduction, we will now turn to the text of Jung's *Seven Sermons to the Dead*, evaluating the Sermons in the context of both Gnostic tradition and Jung's subsequent writings. The English translation reproduced here is the one originally prepared by H. G. Baynes in the early 1920s, with the approval of C. G. Jung. (It will be noted that Baynes used an archaic "biblical" form of English in his translation.) Only portions of each of the Sermons can be presented here; the reader is advised to additionally read the complete version of the Baynes translation of the *Septem Sermones ad Mortuos,* which is found in the appendix to *Memories, Dreams, Reflections.*[43] (Stephan Hoeller has produced a fine translation of Sermons in modern English that might also be helpful[44]—and we now find a further expanded version of the Sermons in Jung's Red Book.[45])

Excerpts from the Sermons are presented in italics, followed by my commentary. In the Sermons, "the Dead" ask questions, and a speaker answers with a *sermo*, or discourse upon the question. The identity of this speaker is ambiguous; it might be claimed that Jung is speaking, or that a visionary figure named Basilides is doing the talking. Perhaps another imaginative source could be identified (we recently have discovered that in the version of these texts recorded in Jung's Red Book, Philemon speaks the Sermons to the Dead). In my commentary, I will identify the voice speaking as Jung or "Jung's Basilides," or at other times simply as "the speaker." However the voice delivering the *Septem Sermones ad Mortuos* is named, historically Jung was the scribe: he recorded the Sermons, and in 1916 he printed this version of them for private distribution.

Sermo I

> *The dead came back from Jerusalem, where they found not what they sought. They prayed me let them in and besought my word, and thus I began my teaching.*

Jerusalem remained the center of Christianity until well into the modern period; medieval maps even chart it as the center of the world, and the most ferocious battles between Muslims and Christians were waged over possession of this spiritual center.[46] The appearance in Jung's dream of a crusader in the middle of a modern state refers to an as yet unresolved problem. Crusaders took home with them the holy lance, according to the legend of Longinus and the siege of Antioch in 1098. It forms the bridge to the grail legends, in which the fisher-king is wounded by the poisoned lance of a pagan enemy. In the "Lancelot Grail" the son of Joseph of Arimathea is wounded in the thigh by a black angel, and is later healed by the same lance.[47] The grail is taken to be the cup used by Christ at the last supper, which came later into the possession of Joseph of Arimathea and which nourishes its owner in miraculous ways. It is supposed to have been used to contain the blood of Christ. The circumstance of the grail having found its way to the West symbolizes the way in which the elements were gathered there that made possible the mystical continuation of the life of Christ.[48] This led further to the cup symbolism in alchemy, which has one of its sources in this mystical, nous-filled cup in the Corpus Hermeticum (IV 4).

All of these characteristics—merely suggested here—show that the spiritual essence of Christianity has not yet been fully absorbed in the West. It is a cultural veneer over a Germanic and Celtic polydaemonism, which manifests in every European abaissement du niveau mental. The extraverted aspect of the historical Christ has been taken in, but his spiritual message has not. The latter begins with the outpouring of the Holy Spirit on Pentecost (Acts 2:1-4). Jung states,[49]

> A further development of myth might well begin with the outpouring of the Holy Spirit upon the apostles, by which they were made into sons of God, and not only they, but all others

who through them and after them received the filiation—sonship of God—and thus partook of the certainty that they were more than autochthonous animalia sprung from the earth, that as the twice-born they had their roots in the divinity itself. Their visible, physical life was on this earth; but the invisible inner man had come from and would return to the primordial image of wholeness, to the eternal Father, as the Christian myth of salvation puts it.

When the dead return from Jerusalem, this means that some aspect of Christ's message has not yet been understood in the collective unconscious of Christians and is in need of being taught.

The opening words of Jung's sermons and the "infant spirits" associated with them, recall Goethe's *Faust*, which begins:

> Uncertain shapes, visitors from the past
> At whom I darkly gazed so long ago,
> My heart's mad fleeting visions—now at last
> Shall I embrace you, must I let you go?
> Again you haunt me: come then, hold me fast!
> Out of the mist and mirk you rise, who so
> Besiege me, and with magic breath restore,
> Stirring my soul, lost youth to me once more...
> And I am seized by long unwonted yearning,
> For that still, solemn spirit-realm...

The difference is that what reappears in Goethe are the neglected aspects of his youth. These appear in order to rejuvenate Faust, who has become paralyzed in his science. At issue likewise for Jung, as already noted above, is a royal renewal—he is, as it were, making up for the entire Western spiritual heritage. In *Faust*, the "uncertain shapes" are still personal spirits who metamorphose into the collective figures of classical mythology only in the second part of the tragedy. Faust's transformation fails in regard to the personal, because he succumbs to his shadow. This leads to Gretchen's terrible tragedy, and Faust only then breaks through to the deeper layers of the psyche.

The driving motif of the first phase in *Faust* was eros. In Christianity, this is an unmastered problem. Faust makes the change over to power, because he has lost his relationship to the world and has been disappointed in love. A certain resolution of the problem is achieved only through an encounter with the "eternal feminine," in the archetypal form of Helen, in Part Two. After Faust has drunk the magic potion, the text continues:

> With that elixir coursing through him,
> Soon any woman will be Helen to him.

The problem that remains unresolved to the end of *Faust* was that he could never retrieve his projection of the anima. In any case, *Faust*—Goethe's opus magnus—shows how problems in our culture can come to affect select individuals and become conscious.

Harken: I begin with nothingness. Nothingness is the same as fullness. In infinity full is no better than empty. Nothingness is both empty and full. As well might ye say anything else of nothingness, as for instance, white is it, or black, or again, it is not, or it is. A thing that is infinite and eternal hath no qualities, since it hath all qualities.

These instructions appear philosophically and logically correct. Are they nothing more than that? Such a "revelation" from the unconscious, as sometimes happens with dreams, might easily be underestimated. The source of the "revelation" refers here to one of the central problems of theology, whereby one says joyfully of the characteristics of God, that God is the "summum bonum." If he is truly everything, then it is impossible to ascribe any characteristics to him, unless the opposite of each is posed in every instance as a paradox.

The Neo-Platonists, from whom the Gnostics borrowed some good ideas, put particular emphasis on the transcendence of the deity. The latter so surpasses human understanding that it is impossible to assign to it either positive or negative characteristics, aside from "being" and the "One" (*Hen*) and the "All" (*Pan*). This conception comes quite close to that of a *deus otiosus* who, having created the world, completely withdraws from it. In Neo-Platonism, however, the sensible world is produced out of the supersensible by way of many hypostatizations. The One and matter are only the end points of a line on which the light of the One gradually fades, ultimately turning into the darkness of matter. Plotinus designates matter to be the opposite of being, as well as its product, and for our Basilides later on this nonbeing becomes the devil, the effective void. Nor does Plotinus evade the problem that the deity can only be described in paradoxes. On this issue, Jung writes:[50]

> Although the God-concept is a spiritual principle par excellence, the collective metaphysical need nevertheless insists that it is at the same time a conception of the First Cause, from which proceed all those instinctual forces that are opposed to the spiritual principle. God would thus be not only the essence of spiritual light, appearing as the latest flower on the tree of evolution, not only the spiritual goal of salvation in which all creation culminates, not only the end and aim, but also the darkest, nethermost cause of Nature's blackest deeps. This is a tremendous paradox which obviously reflects a profound psychological truth. For it asserts the essential contradictoriness of one and the same being, a being whose innermost nature is a tension of opposites. Science calls the "being" energy, for energy is like a living balance between opposites. For this reason the God-concept, in itself impossibly paradoxical, may be so satisfying to human needs that no logic however justified can stand against it. Indeed the subtlest cogitation could scarcely have found a more suitable formula for this fundamental fact of inner experience.

The Gnostics recognized this fundamental problem of transcendence, speaking of the "unknowable first father"—whereby the object is to know him. This formulation once again appears to pose an impossibility, which can only be overcome when the unknowable father has a son who brings news of him to those he has created, thus redeeming them from their *agnosia*. The sense here is very psychological: if the unconscious was only unconscious, we could say nothing about it, and we would not even know of it. The unknowable corresponds to those aspects of the unconscious that cannot be brought to consciousness and of archaic being,[51] an equivalence of subject and object. Only when a part of the whole distinguishes itself as such (or "emanates", in Gnostic terminology) can anything become conscious. All of the complicated and confusing Gnostic systems refer ultimately to a process of becoming conscious. Becoming conscious encompasses the meaning and the redemption of creation.

It might seem strange to equate God with "nothingness." However, this is precisely what mystics do when words fail them, or when we speak of the "unconscious": it is the ineffable. As Angelus Silesius says in The Cherubinic Wanderer:[52]

> God is an utter Nothingness,
> Beyond the touch of Time and Place:
> The more thou graspest after Him,
> The more he fleeth thy embrace.

This emptiness is also the aim of Zen Buddhism—that which is unknowable and lies beyond consciousness. Consciousness is distinction; "nothingness" is the absence of distinction, where logical categories cease to apply.

When our Basilides begins his instructions with "nothingness," he is referring to the unknowable ultimate ground of all being, all creation, and all consciousness. He is saying that we have our origin in a great mystery, which is unfathomable because it precedes all consciousness. Jung explains:[53]

> A second psychic system coexisting with consciousness—no matter what qualities we suspect it of possessing—is of absolutely revolutionary significance in that it could radically alter our view of the world. Even if no more than the perceptions taking place in such a second psychic system were carried over into ego-consciousness, we should have the possibility of enormously extending the bounds of our mental horizon.
>
> Once we give serious consideration to the hypothesis of the unconscious, it follows that our view of the world can be but a provisional one; for if we effect so radical an alteration in the sub-

ject of perception and cognition as this dual focus implies, the result must be a world view very different from any known before. This holds true only if the hypothesis of the unconscious holds true, which in turn can be verified only if unconscious contents can be changed into conscious ones—if, that is to say, the disturbances emanating from the unconscious, the effects of spontaneous manifestations, of dreams, fantasies, and complexes, can successfully be integrated into consciousness by the interpretative method.

This nothingness or fullness we name the PLEROMA. *Therein both thinking and being cease, since the eternal and infinite possess no qualities. In it no being is, for he then would be distinct from the pleroma, and would possess qualities which would distinguish him as something distinct from the pleroma.*

The reader must be informed here that a well-known Gnostic term is being used in a specific sense. What Basilides calls pleroma Jung designates at the end of his life as *unus mundus* (the One World).[54] He found this expression in the work of the physician and alchemist Gerardus Dorneus (sixteenth century) as the term for the "potential world of the first day of creation, when nothing was *in actu*..., but was yet only One." This potential world is the *mundus archetypus* of the scholastics, an all-encompassing continuum of being with its own intrinsic order,[55] which is the consciousness-transcending background of the entire world. In this vein Jung continues,[56]

Since psyche and matter are contained in one and the same world and moreover are in continuous contact with one another and ultimately rest on irrepresentable, transcendental factors, it is not only possible but fairly probable, even, that psyche and matter are two different aspects of one and the same thing. The synchronicity phenomena point, it seems to me, in this direction, for they show that the nonspsychic can behave like the psychic, and vice versa, without there being any causal connection between them. Our present knowledge does not allow us to do much more than compare the relation of the psychic to the material world with two cones, whose apices, meeting in a point without extension—a real zero-point—touch and do not touch.

In the pleroma there is nothing of a personal nature, which only emerges with ego-consciousness or with contents similar to consciousness. The pleroma cannot be spoken of in terms either of "subconsciousness" or "supraconsciousness," because each of these would presuppose a subject, while in the pleroma there is not yet any differentiation between subject and object. In mythology, this condition is symbolized by the cosmic man (Purusha, Ymir, Gayomart, etc.).[57]

In Valentinian Gnosis the pleroma contains the aeons and thus corresponds to the collective unconscious. For the Gnostic the pleroma is true being, the origin of the individual and that into which the pneumatikoi enter in redemption.

In the pleroma there is nothing and everything. It is quite fruitless to think about the pleroma, for this would mean self-dissolution.

This pleroma can be compared to the eastern Dharmakaya. This is original, formless wisdom, true experience, entirely free of error. It is the uncreated, the unformed, and the unchanged.[58] In Eastern traditions, which have been involved in the "scientific" study of the soul for much longer than we have, it is termed "universal consciousness." We are able to agree with this only to the extent that we assume a non-subjective consciousness, an "absolute" consciousness. Such would be the presumption of a mystic who had submitted fully to the will of God, having relinquished his own entirely. This kind of "emptiness" is thus conceivable only as an ideal goal, or indeed, as in the Book of the Dead, as a stage in the process of dying calling for the soul to empty itself of contents and give up its tie to the world of the senses. This is just what is meant by the dissolution of the self. In pathological cases it is psychosis, in which personal consciousness is more or less dissolved.

CREATURA is not in the pleroma, but in itself. The pleroma is both beginning and end of created beings. It pervadeth them, as the light of the sun everywhere pervadeth the air. Although the pleroma pervadeth altogether, yet hath created being no share thereof, just as a wholly transparent body becometh neither light nor dark through the light which pervadeth it.

In a letter of July 10, 1946, Jung writes to Fritz Künkel:[59]

Your view that the collective unconscious surrounds us on all sides is in complete agreement with the way I explain it to my pupils. It is more like an atmosphere in which we live that something that is found in us. It is simply the unknown quantity in the world. Also it does not by any means behave merely psychologically; in the cases of so-called synchronicity it proves to be a universal substrate present in the environment rather than a psychological premise. Wherever we come into contact with an archetype we enter into relationship with transconscious, metaphysic factors which underlie the spiritualistic hypothesis as well as that of magical actions.

That which is created necessarily comes from a creator and is something different from the latter. The creator, now understanding Basilides' pleroma in personal terms, is the beginning and end of its creature. If, instead of creator, we posit the principium individuationis as the driving force behind the consciousness of the created being, then the goal of the process becomes its unification with the origin. This is a cyclical process, symbolized by the uroboros, the snake that swallows its own tail, and which fructifies and consumes itself. Described in this way, a whole is present in every phase of the process, for having emanated a part out of itself does not diminish the creator. The creature is something outside the creator, something new and existing in its own right, which is yet pervaded by the creator.

The separation of "a consciousness as creature" does not work to diminish the unconscious matrix, because that matrix has no magnitude. The creation of consciousness is not a one-time event, but a lifelong process. Consciousness can never assume within itself the "whole" of the unconscious without suffering dissolution, which is indeed what happens whenever the ego is identified with the self. This is termed inflation: "a puffed-up ego and a deflated self," as Jung puts it.[60] This is the sort of being Nietzsche describes in terms of the superman in Zarathustra, but which also appears in less extreme form in everyday life, when the self no longer works to compensate ego-consciousness.

Returning from these introductory remarks to Basilides, as conveyed by Hippolytus, we note certain similarities, which may have provided the impetus to Jung's revelation. This is how Hippolytus describes Basilides' system:[61]

Since, therefore, "nothing" existed—(I mean) not matter, nor substance, nor what is insubstantial, nor is absolute, nor composite, nor conceivable, nor inconceivable, (nor what is sensible,) nor devoid of senses, nor man, nor angel, nor a god, nor, in short, any of those objects that have names, or are apprehended by sense, or that are cognised by intellect, but (are) thus (cognised), even with greater minuteness, still, when all things are absolutely removed— (since, I say, "nothing" existed,) God, "non-existent"... inconceivably, insensibly, indeterminately, involuntarily, impassively, (and) unactuated by desire, willed to create a world.

Now I employ, he [Basilides] says, the expression "willed" for the purpose of signifying (that he did so) involuntarily, and inconceivably, and insensibly. And by the expression "world" I do not mean that which was subsequently formed according to breadth and division, and which stood apart; nay, (far from this,) for (I mean) the germ of a world. The germ, however, of the world had all things in itself. Just as the grain of mustard comprises all things simultaneously, holding them (collected) together within the very smallest (compass), viz. roots, stem, branches, leaves, and innumerable gains which are produced from the plant, seeds again of other plants, and frequently of others (still), that are produced (from them).

In this way, "non-existent" God made the world out of nonentities, casting and depositing some one Seed that contained in itself a conglomeration of the germs of the world... All things, therefore whatsoever it is possible to declare, and whatever, being not as yet discovered, one must omit, were likely to receive adaptation to the world which was about to be generated from the Seed.

And this (Seed), at the requisite seasons, increases in bulk in a peculiar manner, according to accession, as through the instrumentality of a Deity so great, and of this description. (But this Deity) the creature can neither express nor grasp by perception... When, therefore, the cosmical Seed becomes the basis (for a subsequent development), those (heretics) assert, (to quote Basilides' own words:) "Whatsoever I affirm," he says, "to have been made after these, ask no question as to whence. For (the Seed) had all seeds treasured and reposing in itself, just as non-existent entities, and which were designed to be produced by a non-existent Deity."

Let us see, therefore, what they say is first, or what second, or what third, (in the development of) what is generated from the cosmical Seed. There existed, he says, in the Seed itself, a Sonship, threefold, in every respect of the same Substance with the non-existent God, (and) begotten from nonentities.

I leave it to the reader to decide the extent to which Jung's fantasies correspond to this "negative" Gnostic theology. People sometimes invoke the term "negative theology" casually as a slogan, using it to do away with the underlying difficulty of the ineffable. Yet it remains the case, in comparison with Jung's own statements on the matter, that this early commentary is no mere jumble of words.

We find another Gnostic parallel in the Apocryphon of John, well preserved in three Nag Hammadi codices, as well as the Codex Berolinensis 8502 (BG)—the multitude of versions still surviving may offer testimony to the esteem in which it was held among the Gnostics. Jesus revealed himself to the prophet John both as a child and as an old man (*puer—senex*), and instructed him concerning the monads:

And [I asked] to know
  He said to me
[The Monad,] since it is a unity
and nothing rules over it,
  [is] the God and the Father of the All

the holy One
the invisible One, who is above the All,
who exists as his incorruption
existing in the pure light
into which no light of the eye can gaze.
He is the Spirit.
It is not right to think of him as a god
or something similar
for he is more than a god.
He is a rule, over which nothing rules,
for there is nothing before him.
Nor does he need them.
He does not need life, for he is eternal.
He does not need anything,
for he cannot be perfected,
as if he were lacking and thus needing to be perfected;
rather he is always completely perfect.
He is light.
He is illimitable
since there is no one prior to him to set limits to him,
the unsearchable One
since there exists no one prior to him to examine him,
the immeasurable One since no one else measured him,
as if being prior to him,
the invisible One since no one saw him,
the eternal One since he exists always,
the ineffable One since no one comprehended him
so as to speak about him,
the unnameable One
since there is no one prior to him to give a name to him.
He is the immeasurable light,
the pure one who is holy and immaculate,
the ineffable One,
who is perfect and incorruptible.
He is neither perfection
nor blessedness
nor divinity,

but he is something far superior to them.
He is neither unlimited nor limited,
but he is something superior to these.
For, he is not corporeal; he is not incorporeal.
He is not large; he is not small.
He is not quantifiable,
For he is not a creature.
Nor can anyone know him.
He is not at all someone who exists,
but he is something superior to them,
not as being superior, but as being himself.
He did not to partake in an aeon.
Time does not exist for him.
For he who partakes in an aeon,
others prepared (it) for him.
And time was not apportioned to him,
since he does not receive from another who apportions.
And he is without want;
there is no one at all before him.
He desires himself alone
in the perfection of the light.[62]

What is described here is the *deus absconditus oder absolutis*. Many Christian theologians (Karl Barth among others) have claimed that God is completely independent of man, existing in a state of self-sufficiency far above or beyond the human sphere. Insofar as God is an unknowable first principle, this may be correct. In that case, it becomes necessary, in accord with the Gnostics, to concede that he exists beyond the reach of our cognitive powers and that it is possible to speak about him exclusively in negative terms: not-not, or as in Sanskrit, "neti-neti." Thus would it be "quite fruitless to think about" it. Nevertheless, the Gnostics are constantly emphasizing how the primary human task is "to know the father," which amounts to achieving knowledge of his origins and thus his "true" nature. This is only possible, however, if this unknowable God wants and gives himself to be known to human beings. This myth is central to Gnosis.

An example of this is found in the revelation of Allogenes, found at Nag Hammadi.[63] The *photes* (divine lights) instruct him as follows about the One, the Unknowable:

Now he is something insofar as he exists in that he either exists and will become, or acts or knows, although he lives without Mind or Life or Existence or Non-Existence, incomprehensibly. And he is something along with his proper being.

He is not left over in some way, as if he yields something that is assayed or purified [or that] receives or gives. And he is not diminished in any way, [whether] by his own desire or whether he gives or receives through another.

Neither does [he] have any desire of himself nor from another; it does not affect him. Rather neither does he give anything by himself lest he become diminished in another respect; nor for this reason does he need Mind, or Life, or indeed anything at all.

He is superior to the Universals in his privation and unknowability, that is, the non-being existence, since he is endowed with silence and stillness lest he be diminished by those who are not diminished.

He is neither divinity nor blessedness nor perfection. Rather it (this triad) is an unknowable entity of him, not that which is proper to him; rather he is another one superior to the blessedness and the divinity and perfection. For he is not perfect but he is another thing that is superior. He is neither boundless, nor is he bounded by another. Rather he is something [superior].

He is not corporeal. He is not incorporeal. He is not great. [He is not] small. He is not a number. He is not a [creature]. Nor is he something that exists, that one can know. But he is something else of himself that is superior, which one cannot know.

He is primary revelation and knowledge of himself, as it is he alone who knows himself. Since he is not one of those that exist but is another thing, he is superior to (all) superlatives even in comparison to (both) what is (properly) his and not his. He neither participates in age nor does he participate in time. He does not receive anything from anything else. He is not diminishable, nor does he diminish anything, nor is he undiminishable. But he is self-comprehending, as something so unknowable that he exceeds those who excel in unknowability.[64]

This tedious enumeration of negative theology ("neither...neither") is suddenly interrupted by an extremely important statement: He is the ultimate source of revelation, because he alone knows himself. This means that all self-knowledge on the part of the human individual is rooted in the self-knowledge of this unknowable being. Negative theology describes this "being" in a state of rest, a self that has not yet manifested itself and is present only in the form of the potential of being known.

Psychologically, we can say nothing about the absolute unconscious; we live in it in a condition of archaic identity,[65] and have no trace of it, although it is living. Not yet is there a knowing subject present that could perceive a knowable object. The subject continues to live fully contained and embedded in its primal ground as in an amniotic sheath or egg integument. The two still form an unquestionable unity. This condition becomes recognizable only when one steps outside of it. When the membrane of the egg is broken and a knowing subject emerges, the problem arises in the form of an opposition between the current condition of unrest and the earlier condition of rest. Thus can it happen that the subject longs to return to this earlier paradise. To muse excessively over this is not allowed, out of fear that the newly emerged subject will be taken back and dissolved in the primal fullness.

This is the problem we encounter in cases where a severe mother complex—and its associated retrospective longing—is not directed back toward the personal mother, but toward this state of unquestionable being. The church—by demanding "belief," blind acceptance and renunciation, and by desiring that everything be understood—fosters unconsciousness and encourages this regressive tendency. Not surprisingly, it offers itself as the mother, as *mater ecclesia*, in whose lap believers can once again become children. This opens the door to the power play between the sheep and the shepherds, between followers and leaders. The unconscious individual lacks the sort of competence needed to live in our civilization (we are no longer hunter-gatherers), and is thus perpetually in search of a leader. Power-hungry figures are eager to oblige, because they find satisfaction in leading others (astray).

Yet, the will on the part of this unknown and unknowable being to reveal itself means that it is in search of a knowing subject—what Gnostics called the pneumatikoi, or spiritual individuals in general. The "rest" that is being sought in this case is not regressive—the desire to creep back into the maternal womb—but progressive: the repose to be found in God, in original purity, in confronting and achieving knowledge of this deus absconditus with which the spiritual individual was formerly identical.

The creature is secondary, subordinate, yet, as the knowing subject, it is elevated. Its heritage continues to cling to it, like the egg shell clings to the chick, and can never be shed. The unconscious, no matter how complete the individual consciousness that is achieved, can never be dissolved entirely. For it remains as the creature's matrix, the constant source of the nourishment it needs. The knowing subject must emerge out of his original unconsciousness (for Gnostics, the *agnosia*) and overcome it; thus will the unconscious be constantly suffused by the subject, like the light that "everywhere pervadeth the air."

We are, however, the pleroma itself, for we are a part of the eternal and infinite. But we have no share thereof, as we are from the pleroma infinitely removed; not spiritually or temporally, but essentially, since we are distinguished from the pleroma in our essence as creatura, which is confined within time and space.

"This question, regarding the nature of the unconscious, brings with it the extraordinary intellectual difficulties with which the psychology of the unconscious confronts us," confesses Jung.[66]

Such difficulties must inevitably arise whenever the mind launches forth boldly into the unknown and invisible... Before we scrutinize our dilemma more closely, I would like to clarify one aspect of the concept of the unconscious. The unconscious is not simply the unknown, it is rather the unknown psychic; and this we define on the one hand as all those things in us which, if they came to consciousness, would presumably differ in no respect from the known psychic contents, with the addition, on the other hand, of the psychoid system, of which nothing is known directly. So defined, the unconscious depicts an extremely fluid state of affairs: everything of which I know, but of which I am not at the moment thinking; everything of which I was once conscious but now have forgotten; everything perceived by my senses, but not noted by my conscious mind; everything which, involuntarily and without paying attention to it, I feel, think, remember, want, and do; all the future things that are taking shape in me and will sometime come to consciousness: all this is the content of the unconscious. These contents are all more or less capable, so to speak, of consciousness, or were once conscious and may become conscious again the next moment.... But, as I say, we must also include in the unconscious the psychoid functions that are not capable of consciousness and of whose existence we have only indirect knowledge.

We now come to the question: in what state do psychic contents find themselves when not related to the conscious ego? (This relation constitutes all that can be called consciousness.) ...But from certain experiences—some of them known already to Freud—it is clear that the state of unconscious contents is not quite the same as the conscious state. For instance, feeling-toned complexes in the unconscious do not change in the same way that they do in consciousness. Although associations may enrich them, they are not corrected, but are conserved in their original form, as can easily be ascertained from the continuous and uniform effect they have upon the conscious mind. Similarly, they take on the uninfluenceable and compulsive character of an automatism, of which they can be divested only if they are made conscious. This latter procedure is rightly regarded as one of the most important therapeutic factors. In the end such complexes—presumably in proportion to their distance from consciousness—assume, by self-amplification, an archaic and mythological character and hence a certain numinosity, as is perfectly clear in schizophrenic dissociations. Numinosity, however, is wholly outside conscious volition, for it transports the subject into a state of rapture, which is a state of will-less surrender.

...Evidently the unconscious state is different after all from the conscious. Although at first sight the process continues in the unconscious as though it were conscious, it seems, with increasing dissociation, to sink back to a more primitive (archaic-mythological) level, to approximate in character to the underlying instinctual pattern, and to assume the qualities which are the hallmarks of instinct: automatism, nonsusceptibility to influence, all-or-none reaction, and so forth.

Insofar as what is conscious was once a content of the unconscious, it remains in essence part of the latter, although in principle distinct from it. Despite the separation, the whole is maintained. This recalls the ancient speculation about the micro- and macrocosmos. In Indian tradition it is Atman-atmân: the world-soul and the soul of the individual. The latter is a part of the former, not in an arithmetical sense, but rather in the form of a faithful image of it in miniature. The collective unconscious is both the expression of human experience generally and, on the level of the individual, the possibilities that exist in all of us personally. The archetype itself cannot be represented as an image, insofar as it is the possibility of all typical representations. The archetypal image or representation in   realized form thus differs essentially from its primal matrix.

This sounds thoroughly abstract and calls for illustration by an example. In Gnosis, there appear archetypal images that are similar to those we encounter in our modern dreams or fantasies. We are separated by roughly two thousand years and great cultural differences from the time of the Gnostics. There would be no hope of understanding their earlier ideas, were we not possessed of an equivalent matrix capable of producing similar ideas and images. The difficulty that impedes understanding of ancient Gnostic texts consists solely in the variation of the temporally determined contents that fill the forms—the cultural language of the times. It is thus necessary to study the intellectual environment in which the Gnostics lived, not because that environment produced the contents of their experience, but because their environment supplied the vocabulary they employed to express experience.

Shared archetypal ideas supply the foundation for understanding human expression across time and cultures. The unconscious is a medium sui generis, independent of time and space; it is perpetually actualized in individual consciousness.

Yet because we are parts of the pleroma, the pleroma is also in us.

Even in the smallest point is the pleroma endless, eternal, and entire, since small and great are qualities which are contained in it. It is that nothingness which is everywhere whole and continuous. Only figuratively, therefore, do I speak of created being as a part of the pleroma. Because, actually, the pleroma is nowhere divided, since it is nothingness. We are also the whole pleroma, because, figuratively, the pleroma is the smallest point (assumed only, not existing) in us and the boundless firmament about us. But wherefore, then, do we speak of the pleroma at all, since it is thus everything and nothing?

We have to go back to Chinese Taoism to understand what our Basilides (or Jung) is teaching here. His pleroma corresponds approximately to the Tao. The latter cannot be defined, but only described in images and in terms of its effects. Chuang Tzu says:[67] "When this (subjective) and that (objective) are both without their correlates, that is the very 'Axis of Tao.'" "Tao is obscured by our inadequate understanding, and words are obscured by flowery expressions." The limitations are not initially based in the Tao of existence.

Among the men of old their knowledge reached the extreme point. What was that extreme point? Some held that at first there was not anything. This is the extreme point, the utmost point to which nothing can be added. A second class held that there was something, but without any responsive recognition of it (on the part of men).

Jung, in a late work, *Synchronicity: An Acausal Connecting Principle,*[68] dealt extensively with this idea and its history in the West, as precursor of the synchronicity idea; the interested reader may wish to consult this work. Marcel Granet[69] provides a detailed description of the complexity of the material to which the Tao refers. He writes, "At the basis of all Taoist ideas is found the concept of order, of the whole, of responsibility, and of efficacy." The concept of the Tao, which to an extent exceeds that of the pleroma, is important in our context, because it likewise stems from experience. It is difficult to illustrate the concept by means of individual quotations. It is necessary to get a feel for the manner of Chinese thinking in order to understand it.[70] Lao-tse says of it in the Tao Te Ching:

> Something mysteriously formed,
> Born before heaven and Earth.
> In the silence and the void,
> Standing alone and unchanging,
> Ever present and in motion.
> Perhaps it is the mother of ten thousand things.
> I do not know its name
> Call it Tao.[71]

And in a later section of the Tao Te Ching:

> All things arise from Tao.
> They are nourished by Virtue.
> They are formed from matter.
> They are shaped by environment.[72]

This all-pervading something that the Chinese call Tao is everywhere and continuous; it is the contingent, that which is sheer presence, which merely is.[73]

The Upanishads[74] have much to say about this issue. It will be recalled that it was from this source that Jung borrowed the concept of the "self," because there was in German no way to express the unfathomable wholeness of the human being and the world. According to the famous fourteenth Khanda of the Chāndogya Upanishad:[75]

> He [the Brahman] is my self within the heart, smaller than a corn of rice, smaller than a corn of barley,[76] smaller than a mustard seed,

smaller than a canary seed or the kernel of a canary seed. He also is my self within the heart, greater than the earth, greater than the sky, greater than heaven, greater than all these worlds.

The idea that the whole is always contained in the smallest part plays a role once again in modern physics. Correspondences of this sort between archetypal ideas and physics warrant the assumption that our psyche is tuned to the environment. Thus, Jung's Basilides continues:

I speak of it to make a beginning somewhere, and also to free you from the delusion that somewhere, either without or within, there standeth something fixed, or in some way established, from the beginning. Every so-called fixed and certain thing is only relative. That alone is fixed and certain which is subject to change.

We speak as if our soul were inside. This is by no means obvious! First of all, the individual originally existed within a participation mystique (Lévy-Brühl),[77] or archaic identity, with his environment, which can once again be observed in every small child. This is an a priori unity between object and subject. Even among cultured peoples this condition persists to an extraordinary degree. Inside and outside seem connected or conjoined. Between any two people there can exist shared unconscious contents, with magical effects. Between a person and an object there can arise in the same way a dependence of the former on the latter, in which case it becomes a fetish. We therefore can feel or say, "I am very attached to so-and-so, or such-and-such. A part of my soul is secretly contained in this person or thing. If I lose it, I lose a part of myself." Furthermore, our God-image is placed into the external. This is a doubtful exteriorization because the God-image represents the supreme intensification of life, the source of an enhanced vitality. Insofar as God is understood dynamically, he corresponds to the soul as the personification of a central unconscious content. If—and to the extent that—he is not experienced as an inner dynamic, he is projected outward, binding the individual magically to his object world. This leaves the individual dependent on whether the object behaves in accord with expectations.

In the process of psychic integration in the individual, Gnosis represents a specific stage. In the religions of antiquity, this libido animated the statues of divinities as the bearers of projections. In Gnosis, libido in this sense was largely internalized—it apparently involved a minimum of cultural objects and external rites, though scholars continue to argue about this issue. Nevertheless, the Gnostics did not develop a psychology, but projected and formed their experiences in terms of mythical and theological statements. The next stage is that of alchemy, in which matter itself takes on a divine, numinous quality, and the God-image is found in the lapis philosophorum. From here on, as Jung pointed out repeatedly, a direct line runs to modern materialism, in which money, technology, and material well-being are "pseudo-deified"—that is, attributed redemptive powers.

Resistance against adopting the perspective of analytical psychology toward Gnosis, or religious dogmas, shows the extent to which people remain dependent on the magical projection of a God-image. The difficulty involved in any attempt to retrieve the projection consists in overcoming the fear that everything might dissolve into nothingness when the projection is withdrawn. And everything does indeed dissolve into nothingness, insofar as it is no longer an external object that orients discussion—strictly speaking, and without regard to the subject. It would be very awkward for our theological faculties at the universities if they were not to be able to summon their God from the outside and put him under the microscope of reason. Unable to summon God from outside, they would need to begin with the self—the internal fact—and that would be embarrassing.

To make this point is not to surrender to subjectivism. Nevertheless, both outer and inner can only be perceived via the psyche.[78] Jung designates this "esse in anima," and ultimately what it means is the primacy of the psyche.

Why is it that Pleroma, an expression for the unconscious (as should now be apparent), and creatura, an expression of the individual consciousness, cannot simply be designated in these more familiar terms? In the first place, we are dealing in these sermons with Jung's spontaneous fantasy, which creates a neutral language and its own expressions. Second, there is the danger of following Freud in understanding the unconscious as the personal unconscious. Jung's fantasies are like primal volcanic eruptions, laying as yet no claim to any scientific status. Achieving that status, then, was Jung's task for the remainder of his life. If today we are in the position to use scientific terms, then this is due to Jung's scientific endeavors—the results of which are there for us in his works.

What is changeable, however, is creatura. Therefore is it the one thing which is fixed and certain; because it hath qualities: it is even quality itself.

Consciousness undergoes transformation not only from antiquity to the modern era, but also during the course of an individual life. To trace the history of religion is also to produce an image of the secular transformations of the collective consciousness. Transformation is the essence of consciousness. Just as life is an energetic process, so, as Jung demonstrated,[79] is the life of the psyche a process of continual change along the gradient of psychic energy. It is therefore not surprising that the idea of sacrifice and transformation plays a central role in Christianity, and is the subject of ritual repetition in the mass.[80] During the mass, the Son of God is ritually sacrificed, as well as being consumed bodily by the believers. In engaging in these acts, they take part in the divine, which is to say in self-becoming. The process of transformation aims naturally at an unfolding of the personality carried by the individual; this is termed by Jung "individuation."[81] On the other hand, as suggested above, the contents of the unconscious that do not come into contact with consciousness change very little. Jung explains:[82]

> Consciousness is something like perception, and like the latter is subject to conditions and limitations. You can, for instance, be conscious at various levels, within a narrower or wider field, more on the surface or deeper down. These differences in degree are often differences in kind as well, since they depend on the development of the personality as a whole; that is to say, on the nature of the perceiving subject.
>
> The intellect has no interest in the nature of the perceiving subject so far as the latter only thinks logically. The intellect is es-

sentially concerned with elaborating the contents of consciousness and with methods of elaboration. A rare philosophic passion is needed to compel the attempt to get beyond intellect and break through to a "knowledge of the knower." Such a passion is practically indistinguishable from the driving force of religion; consequently this whole problem belongs to the religious transformation process, which is incommensurable with intellect. Classical philosophy subserves this process on a wide scale, but this can be said less and less of the newer philosophy. Schopenhauer is still—with qualifications—classical, but Nietzsche's Zarathustra is no longer philosophy at all: it is a dramatic process of transformation that has completely swallowed up the intellect. It is no longer concerned with thought, but, in the highest sense, with the thinker of thought—and this on every page of the book. A new man, a completely transformed man, is to appear on the scene, one who has broken the shell of the old and who not only looks upon a new heaven and a new earth, but has created them.

The question ariseth: How did creatura originate? Created beings came to pass, not creatura; since created being is the very quality of the pleroma, as much as non-creation which is the eternal death. In all times and places is creation, in all times and places is death. The pleroma hath all, distinctiveness and non-distinctiveness.

Distinctiveness is creatura. It is distinct. Distinctiveness is its essence, and therefore it distinguisheth. Therefore man discriminateth because his nature is distinctiveness. Wherefore also he distinguisheth qualities of the pleroma which are not. He distinguisheth them out of his own nature. Therefore must he speak of qualities of the pleroma which are not.

Here Jung (or, the voice speaking the sermons) draws a clear distinction between the created being and created beings. Had we thought it possible to regard creature as equivalent to consciousness, then we would already be confronted with a problem. It would be better to regard the creature as a universal principium individuationis, which emerges from the self and is the cause of individual empirical consciousness. The unconscious as a whole has inherent within it a disposition to create consciousness. The unconscious self, on the other hand, has the inherent capacity to produce a holistic individual. The unconscious consists of luminosities,[83] seeds of consciousness that correspond to the archetypes. They possess not only a certain brightness, but also numinosity. They are the flash points of the psyche, the contents of which make the unconscious tangible. Among these sparks, one is allotted a dominant role, from which emerges the self, the inconceivable wholeness of the individual out of consciousness and the unconscious, which cannot be distinguished from the God-image.

The defining characteristic of consciousness is to distinguish. Something can become conscious only when it is separated out from the overall context (pleroma). The historical Gnostic Basilides says in this connection:

> Jesus, therefore, became the first-fruits of the distinction of the various orders of created objects, and his Passion took place for not any other reason than the distinction which was thereby brought about in the various orders of created objects that had been confounded together. For in this manner (Basilides) says that the entire Sonship, which had been left in Formlessness for the purpose of conferring benefits and receiving them, was divided into its component elements, according to the manner in which also the distinction of natures had taken place in Jesus.[84]

Jung explains in this connection:[85] "Jesus is thus the prototype for the awakening of the third sonship slumbering in the darkness of humanity. He is the 'spiritual inner man.'" The unconscious formlessness, amorphia, in which the third sonship finds itself is practically equivalent to agnosia, unconsciousness. This initial condition of things corresponds to the potential of unconscious contents. Jesus, for the historical Basilides, is the principium individuationis, which awakens these seeds to life. He awakens them to reality through his suffering of oppositions. The deed that he accomplishes is exemplary for unconscious humanity. In this regard, he represents the archetypal image of the self.

Regarding these thorny discussions on the nature of the unconscious and the emergence of consciousness, Jung writes[86] that psychology, in comparison to the other natural sciences, finds itself in an awkward situation,

> because it lacks a base outside its object. It can only translate itself back into its own language, or fashion itself in its own image. The more it extends its field of research and the more complicated its objects become, the more it feels the lack of a point which is distinct from those objects. And once the complexity has reached that of the empirical man, his psychology inevitably merges with the psychic process itself. It can no longer be distinguished from the latter, and so turns into it. But the effect of this is that the process attains to consciousness. In this way, psychology actualizes the unconscious urge to consciousness. It is, in fact, the coming to consciousness of the psychic process, but it is not, in the deeper sense, an explanation of this process, for no explanation of the psychic can be anything other than the living process of the psyche itself. Psychology is doomed to cancel itself out as a science and therein precisely it reaches its scientific goal.

This elaboration by Jung strikes me as extraordinarily important for an understanding of what psychology is, as well as of that which lies beyond its reach. Since all psychology up to the discovery of the unconscious[87] was essentially a psychology of consciousness, based on the assumption that it was possible to disregard the observer, this prejudice continues to the present day. All modern psychologists whose knowledge is confined to consciousness and for whom unconscious psychic material does not exist are "psychologists without soul." If we were to apply here Jung's ideas about theology as science, it would transcend itself, becoming one with the religious process as such. Scholars of Gnosis believe that they can understand the phenomenon of Gnosis entirely in terms of itself. That would only be possible if all such scholars became Gnostics, that is, if they believed in the psyche's power of self-revelation. Their scholarly work would be sublated in the process of their own Gnostic speculation, and feed into the life process of the psyche itself. Students of Gnosis lack sufficient awareness of their own presuppositions, with the result that their findings are often very subjective. Others, trying to avoid that problem, choose only to present the facts, without evaluation and without placing them in context. This approach is without spirit.

Given the premises noted by Jung, it is clear that only in a very limited sense can the psychology of the unconscious search for causes or goals of the psychic process, as opposed to trying to render it accessible to conscious understanding through comparisons with ideas from other times and places. Because this approach is the same as the psychic process itself, so is the pursuit of it the activity of the human spirit itself.

What use, say ye, to speak of it? Saidst thou not thyself, there is no profit in thinking upon the pleroma?

That said I unto you, to free you from the delusion that we are able to think about the pleroma. When we distinguish qualities of the pleroma, we are speaking from the ground of our own distinctiveness and concerning our own distinctiveness. But we have said nothing concerning the pleroma. Concerning our own distinctiveness, however, it is needful to speak, whereby we may distinguish ourselves enough. Our very nature is distinctiveness. If we are not true to this nature we do not distinguish ourselves enough. Therefore must we make distinctions of qualities.

We must accept the circumstance that only by way of consciousness is it possible to say anything about "the unconscious" (pleroma). Even a dream or a Gnostic revelation, which we regard as having originated in the unconscious, is no longer unconscious, but a product of the unconscious as apprehended by consciousness. We mark a fundamental distinction between these products and consciousness because, as they are expressed in symbolic form, they initially appear beyond conscious understanding. The language spoken by consciousness is logical and conceptual, while the expressions of the unconscious are symbolic. To be made comprehensible to consciousness, they must first be supplemented—as it were, translated—by similar images bearing the same meaning. Consciousness clearly attempts to resolve these images in terms of its concepts. If it is honest, it must concede that success in this endeavor is extremely rare because the image is highly intuitive, including somehow within itself the whole, while concepts work by drawing distinctions.

The paradigmatic Gnostic representation of distinction appears in the myth of Sophia. The story of Sophia is told in several similar and subtly different forms within the Gnostic texts. In the *Pistis Sophia*,[88] Sophia, finding herself in the thirteenth aeon, looks up into the heights at the command of the first mysterium and sees the light of the curtain of the treasury of light. Thereupon, she and begins to extol the superior light. For this she is hated by the twelve archons, or cosmic powers, which seek to rob her of the light. She is cast into the material chaos and into darkness. She cries out for the light of the lights that she saw initially and is sent a redeemer, named Jesus.

In the Ptolemaic Gnostic system described by Irenaeus,[89] Sophia is the final and youngest aeon, searching passionately for her Father in order to comprehend his greatness. Because this is an impossible undertaking—given the depth of the profundity and the unfathomability of the Father—she falls into a state of extreme distress. "She was ever stretching herself forward [and] there was danger lest she should at last have been absorbed by his sweetness, and resolved into his absolute essence," had she not encountered the power Horos, who established limits for her.[90]

In the report on the Valentinians by Hippolytus,[91] Sophia is the twelfth and youngest aeon. She wants to emulate the Father by producing an offspring—without a conjugal partner—who would be in no way inferior to his own product. But she is unable to equal the power of the "Unbegotten One," with the result that the offspring she does bring forth is a formless abortion. This causes unrest within the pleroma, which was beset by uncertainty. The Father brings forth Christ and the Holy Spirit to mark a distinction from Sophia's miscarriage.

Gnostic testimony represents the emergence of consciousness as a mistake of creation. This may strike us as surprising, considering that the goal of evolution seemingly centers on the human becoming equipped with consciousness.[92] I have no way of resolving this contradiction, other than to assume that the Gnostics regarded "the great theater of the world" from a different perspective than that of modern mind. They perceived it from the standpoint of the self. The evidence for this comes from the numerous symbols of the self we find in their systems. Becoming conscious, from this point of view, entails the destruction of an original wholeness. This is the source of the Gnostics' negative view of the world. Consciousness is reflected in the incomplete, presumptuous demiurges that create a flawed world. Thus, the Gnostic is to have as little to do with the world as possible, for the sake of saving his original essence and returning it to the pleroma. This is also the reason why the Gnostics created a magnificent doctrine of anthropos,[93] of the "true man," of the God-man.

During this modern age in which the conscious individual self-identifies as the "supreme God", a careful examination of the Gnostic message of the divine man can be of benefit. At a time when people are seeking salvation entirely in worldly materialism, the Gnostic message can sharpen our appreciation of the incompleteness of creation and the transience of the material.

> *What is the harm, ye ask, in not distinguishing oneself? If we do not distinguish, we get beyond our own nature, away from creatura. We fall into indistinctiveness, which is the other quality of the pleroma. We fall into the pleroma itself and cease to be creatures. We are given over to dissolution in the nothingness. This is the death of the creature. Therefore we die in such measure as we do not distinguish. Hence the natural striving of the creature goeth towards distinctiveness, fighteth against primeval, perilous sameness. This is called the PRINCIPIUM INDIVIDUATIONIS. This principle is the essence of the creature. From this you can see why indistinctiveness and nondistinction are a great danger for the creature.*

The reference here is once again to the danger already noted in Jung's text: It is quite fruitless to think about the pleroma, for this would mean self-dissolution. As a psychiatrist, Jung was well positioned to understand the meaning of "self-dissolution in the pleroma," namely, psychosis. That is the great danger faced by all of those who follow their own revelation unreflectedly. The church fathers' fear of leaving believers to their own devices is unmistakable in their representation of the Gnostics. The ship of the church, sailing over the rough seas of this world, is supposed to offer safe passage.[94] It is this same fear, perhaps, that Martin Buber felt in regard to Jungian psychology. To be noted in this connection, however, is that Buber misunderstands analytical psychology, which does not deny support to the individual, but provides it in the form of a connection to the self. What, then, would be the danger of the church also acting to mediate the necessary security? I have no doubt about the sincerity of its message—not to interfere with the "lovers of the soul"—but there are concerns about the mediators. When the mediators themselves are lacking in the appropriate instincts, they lead the flock into the abyss whether or not they bear the right teaching. Ultimately the question is whether anyone is entitled to lead others, or whether it should be the self exclusively that bears this responsibility?

The Gnostics begin by affirming the second alternative, which is why the self takes on such great significance in their systems. No doubt, many individuals are lacking in the ability to follow the self. "Those who do not have to leave father and mother are certainly safest with them."[95] It is not yet appreciated that it is the individual's job to stand on his own two feet, separate from all others. Collective identities remain opposed to the fulfillment of this task, such as membership in organizations, allegiance to "-isms" and the like. Writes Jung:[96]

> Such collective identities are crutches for the lame, shields for the timid, beds for the lazy, nurseries for the irresponsible but they are equally shelters for the poor and weak, a home port for the shipwrecked, the bosom of a family for orphans, a land of promise for disillusioned vagrants and weary pilgrims, a herd and a safe fold for lost sheep, and a mother providing nourishment and growth. It would therefore be wrong to regard this intermediary stage as a trap; on the contrary, for a long time to come it will represent the only possible form of existence for the individual, who nowadays seems more than ever threatened by

anonymity. Collective organization is still so essential today that many consider it, with some justification, to be the final goal; whereas to call for further steps along the road to autonomy appears like arrogance or hubris, fantasticality, or simply folly.

A person's individual aspect dies to the extent that it is not distinguished from the environment and the unconscious. It is lost either to the outer or the inner. The principle of individuation involves the overcoming of identity with the persona[97] and dissociation from the "mother." Although a certain degree of adaptation to society is necessary, too much conformity signifies a loss of self to the collectivity. The battle for deliverance from the mother[98] signifies the overcoming of the original identity with the unconscious. The overcoming of agnosia is the primary concern of Gnosis. At this point analytical psychology and Gnosis meet. The experts are still arguing over whether the Gnostic sects lived together in tight secret societies, and the surviving textual sources allow no resolution of the question. This much is certain: their revelatory texts present the "secret" responsible for holding the community together. In a similar manner to the alchemists, we find here the demand that the secret not be betrayed to anyone who is unworthy of it. This is not a case of secretiveness for its own sake, but a necessary part of maintaining identity. It remains a question how much access the church fathers had to Gnostic texts in their opposition to the Gnostics, and whether they really understood the ideas they attacked, or took note exclusively of their perceivable deviations from orthodoxy. It is indeed remarkable that, among the documents found at Nag Hammadi, only isolated texts can be attributed to particular sects as they were described by ancient critics.

Here, as noted above, the speaker of the sermon elucidates creatura as the principium individuationis. "The man, therefore, who, driven by his daimon, steps beyond the limits of the intermediary stage, truly enters the 'untrodden, untreadable regions,' where there are no charted ways and no shelter spreads a protecting roof over his head. There are no precepts to guide him when he encounters an unforeseen situation—for example, a conflict of duties," writes Jung.[99] The conflict of duties is one in which an opposition cannot be resolved by collective resources, because each of the alternatives has its justification. "[The ego] becomes aware of a polarity superordinate to itself."[100]

We must, therefore, distinguish the qualities of the pleroma. The qualities are PAIRS OF OPPOSITES, such as:

> *The Effective and the Ineffective.*
> *Fullness and Emptiness.*
> *Living and Dead.*
> *Difference and Sameness.*
> *Light and Darkness.*
> *The Hot and the Cold.*
> *Force and Matter. Time and Space.*
> *Good and Evil.*
> *Beauty and Ugliness.*
> *The One and the Many, etc.*

The pairs of opposites are qualities of the pleroma which are not, because each balanceth each.

After Jung affirms that the pleroma has no qualities—because each balances the other—a list of the "balanced" qualities is given. These are pairs of opposites, or Gnostic syzygies, that mutually transcend each other in the pleroma and therefore are not accessible to distinguishing perception. As soon as these pairs of opposite cross the threshold into consciousness, they are activated. Since consciousness draws the distinction, it perceives the contents of the unconscious as paradox. Since consciousness, unlike the unconscious, strives for unambiguousness; the oppositional component of a content that has become conscious—the other pole of the duality—must fall back into the unconscious, whereupon its compensatory function gets underway. The pairs of opposites bring to expression the polar structure of the psyche.[101]

The polarity of the unconscious is thus not only a danger for consciousness (dissolution, conflict of duties), but also protects it from becoming too one-sided. Precisely because of its exclusiveness, consciousness is under constant threat of separating too completely from its foundation in instinct. The products of the unconscious work continually to draw it back to a healthy middle position. The feared "lawlessness" of trusting in the self thus does not end up in anarchy or libertinism, as Martin Buber thinks. The psyche, the totality of conscious and unconscious processes, is a self-regulating, homeostatic system. If that were not the case, humanity would have long since died out, a victim of self-annihilation. Human life vegetated for millions of years in a kind of twilight condition, in which survival was ensured by inborn behaviors and their mental equivalents.

These polarities are not fundamentally characteristics of the unconscious, but are bound to the fact of distinction as such. A content can only be perceived by being distinguished from its surroundings. Many analysands have trouble with way their dreams, instead of being "whole," appear as isolated fragments out of context. If we wanted to draw the "whole" dream into consciousness, it would bring the whole unconscious with it, which is impossible because it would result in the dissolution of consciousness. As soon as a content has a characteristic attributed to it, the opposite must be represented by its surroundings, or else it would not be perceptible. Therefore, Jung says:

As we are the pleroma itself, we also have all these qualities in us. Because the very ground of our nature is distinctiveness, therefore we have these qualities in the name and sign of distinctiveness.

This is probably the deeper sense of Heraclitus's famous words:

War is both king of all and father of all, and it has revealed some as gods, others as men; some it has made slaves, others free.[102]

As soon as an opposition becomes conscious, a conflict is already implied. In most cases it fails to overcome the threshold to consciousness because the unacceptable side is immediately absorbed by the unconscious. If this continues to happen over a long period of time, the unconscious constructs a counter-position: it forms a shadow of consciousness. Both collectively in our civilization and among individuals, this process is quite active, which is why the unconscious is generally subject to a negative judgment and is rejected or negated. People are not aware that the unconscious has become a hostile factor, because it is left out of consideration. The danger of a vicious circle is imminent, leading to a split within the collective as within the individual (neurosis). Consciousness continually judges the content as acceptable or unacceptable. And the result:

> *[This] meaneth:*
>
> *These qualities are distinct and separate in us one from the other; therefore they are not balanced and void, but are effective. Thus are we the victims of the pairs of opposites. The pleroma is rent in us.*
>
> *The qualities belong to the pleroma, and only in the name and sign of distinctiveness can and must we possess or live them. We must distinguish ourselves from qualities. In the pleroma they are balanced and void; in us not. Being distinguished from them delivereth us.*

The first case, "qualities are distinct and separate in us one from the other," results in a civil war in one's own soul, because repressing the conflict is not a solution; it continues to exist in the unconscious. The "civil war" usually takes the form of a neurotic split between a conscious light side and a reactive dark side. In the positive case, as occurs in some neuroses, the inner split leads to the issue becoming conscious, because the repressed conflict makes itself unpleasantly apparent, and thus is taken note of.

"For a naïve consciousness that sees everything in black and white, even the unavoidable dual aspect of 'man and his shadow' can be transcendent in this sense and will consequently evoke paradoxical symbols," writes Jung.[103]

> We shall hardly be wrong, therefore, if we conjecture that the striking contradictions we find in our spirit symbolism are proof that the Holy Ghost is a complexio oppositorum (union of opposites). Consciousness certainly possesses no conceptual category for anything of this kind, for such a union is simply inconceivable ex-

cept as a violent collision in which the two sides cancel each other out. This would mean their mutual annihilation.

But the spontaneous symbolism of the complexio oppositorum points to the exact opposite of annihilation, since it ascribes to the product of their union either everlasting duration, that is to say incorruptibility and adamantine stability, or supreme and inexhaustible efficacy.

Thus the spirit as a complexio oppositorum has the same formula as the "Father," the auctor rerum, who is also, according to Nicholas of Cusa, a union of opposites.

In the first book of his *De docta ignorantia* ("On learned ignorance"), Nicholas of Cusa defines God as the absolute maximum, the actual infinity, to be determined by neither more or less, nor by any sort of opposite, nor by affirmation or denial. All oppositions are contained within him (coincidentia oppositorum). Cusanus was probably not fully aware of the true magnitude of this truth. Jung understood his statement as an expression of the nontransparency of the unconscious.

The second case ("the qualities belong to the Pleroma") is the ideal case: to identify oneself with none of the oppositions, but to remain between them. "Not to allow oneself to be influenced by the pairs of opposites," Jung writes, "but to be nirdvandva (free, untouched by the opposites), to raise oneself above them, is an essentially ethical task, because deliverance from the opposites leads to redemption."[104] This amounts to a crucifixion, with all the attendant torments. The sermon immediately supplies an example:

When we strive after the good or the beautiful, we thereby forget our own nature, which is distinctiveness, and we are delivered over to the qualities of the pleroma, which are pairs of opposites. We labor to attain to the good and the beautiful, yet at the same time we also lay hold of the evil and the ugly, since in the pleroma these are one with the good and the beautiful. When, however, we remain true to our own nature, which is distinctiveness, we distinguish ourselves from the

good and the beautiful, and, therefore, at the same time, from
the evil and the ugly. And thus we fall not into the pleroma,
namely, into nothingness and dissolution.

The dead who went to Jerusalem were good Christians, striving for
the good and the beautiful, as befitted good Christians. Have we not
already noted how many infamies—not only in the Crusades—have
been committed in the name of Christianity? The more we try to
achieve the good and the beautiful, the more we are afflicted by the
evil and the ugly, and we cannot help doing both with the same
fervor.

In his book *Aion*, Jung refers to the synchronicity between the
age of Pisces, expressed in the two fish swimming in opposite directions to each other, and the moral problem of opposites in
contemporary Christianity. The Christian religion is characterized
like no other by the moral problem, so much so that the question
sometimes arises as to whether it is possible to go on describing it as
a monotheism. In Manichaeism the opposition is worked out consistently. No wonder that the Christians condemned as an arch-
heresy the religion of Mani, because they frequently came very close
to it. Dualism is the expression of this psychic structure.

Erich Neumann wrote a pamphlet ("Tiefenpsychologie und
Neue Ethik") that seemed to Jung off the mark, prompting Jung to
respond to it in a letter dated June 3, 1957:[105]

For it is not really a question of a "new" ethic. Evil is and remains what you know you shouldn't do. But unfortunately,
man overestimates himself in this respect: he thinks he is free to
choose evil or good. He may imagine he can, but in reality, considering the magnitude of these opposites, he is too small and
impotent to choose either the one or the other voluntarily and
under all circumstances. It is rather that, for reasons stronger
than himself, he does or does not do the good he would like, in
exactly the same way that evil comes upon him as a misfortune.

An ethic is that which makes it impossible for him deliberately to do evil and urges him—often with scant success—to do
good. That is to say, he can do good but cannot avoid evil even

though his ethic impels him to test the strength of his will in this regard. In reality he is the victim of these powers. He is forced to admit that under no circumstances can he avoid evil absolutely, just as on the other side he may cherish the hope of being able to do good. Since evil is unavoidable, he never quite gets out of sinning and this is the fact that has to be recognized. It gives rise not to a new ethic but to differentiated ethical reflections such as the question: How do I relate to the fact that I cannot escape sin?

The ethical problem is central to individuation, because only against the backdrop *of its opposite* does any virtue attain its value for the individual. Were we to consist exclusively of either virtues or of vices, the distinction itself would be devalued. The wholeness of the personality, which is the goal of individuation, thus consists of a great many opposites. The latter are no longer in a state of latency—as they are in the pleroma—but in conscious awareness, where they appear to be mutually exclusive; this leads to division within the individual. The uniting of the opposites is not possible by intellectual processes, and thus is clouded in mystery.[106] Self-becoming, writes Jung,[107] is a mysterious combined process of consciousness and the unconscious, resulting in a unified, harmonious personality:

> It turns out that all archetypes spontaneously develop favourable and unfavourable, light and dark, good and bad effects. In the end we have to acknowledge that the self is a complexio oppositorum precisely because there can be no reality without polarity. We must not overlook the fact the opposites acquire their moral accentuation only within the sphere of human endeavor and action, and that we are unable to give a definition of good and evil that could be considered universally valid. In other words, we do not know what good and evil are in themselves. It must therefore be supposed that they spring from a need of human consciousness and that for this reason they lose their validity outside the human sphere. That is to say a hypostasis of good and evil as metaphysical entities is inadmissible because it would deprive these terms of meaning. If we call everything that God does or allows "good,"

then evil is good too, and "good" becomes meaningless. But suffering, whether it be Christ's passion or the suffering of the world, remains the same as before. Stupidity, sin, sickness, old age, and death continue to form the dark foil that sets off the joyful splendour of life.

Thou sayest, ye object, that difference and sameness are also qualities of the pleroma. How would it be, then, if we strive after difference? Are we, in so doing, not true to our own nature? And must we nonetheless be given over to sameness when we strive after difference?

Ye must not forget that the pleroma hath no qualities. We create them through thinking. If, therefore, ye strive after difference or sameness, or any qualities whatsoever, ye pursue thoughts which flow to you out of the pleroma; thoughts, namely, concerning nonexisting qualities of the pleroma. Inasmuch as ye run after these thoughts, ye Fall again into the pleroma, and reach difference and sameness at the same time. Not your thinking, but your being, is distinctiveness. Therefore not after difference, as ye think it, must ye strive; but after YOUR OWN BEING. At bottom, therefore, there is only one striving, namely, the striving after your own being. If ye had this striving ye would not need to know anything about the pleroma and its qualities, and yet would ye come to your right goal by virtue of your own being. Since, however, thought estrangeth from being, that knowledge must I teach you wherewith ye may be able to hold your thought in leash.

The speaker delivering the sermons to the dead (be it Jung, Basilides, or some other entity) never said that *difference* was a quality of the Pleroma; in particular he insisted that the pleroma has no characteristics ("the pleroma hath no qualities"), that we just speak of them ("Therefore must he speak of qualities of the pleroma"), that we must speak of them due to our nature ("he distinguisheth them out of his own nature"). Now he says that the qualities of the pleroma come out of thinking.

Here it is necessary to add a historical note. Before Jung had fully clarified his description of types, he had equated introversion with the thinking type: "This concentration on the inner world of thought is nothing else than introversion," he said in an address in 1913.[108] He recognized later that extraversion and introversion are both orientations that are independent of the functions.[109] Thinking can be extraverted in one person, introverted in another. The qualities of the pleroma, according to a yet later understanding, derive from introverted feeling, which judges the value of something. This type of feeling separates out the qualities of the pleroma and strives to follow only those that confirm it. But this leads to one-sidedness, as described, and to the attendant consequences. For this reason one should not choose according to principles of some sort, but according to one's being. This striving for one's own being is the initial formulation of the later concept of "individuation."

Individuation would be the natural development of the individual toward an inner goal, in the absence of any internal or external influences. But such influences do divert the individual from his immanent goal, with the effect that he is estranged from his being. This is why he needs instruction.

Since the dead are Christians, their understanding of Christianity has estranged them from their being. This includes their understanding of sexuality, which even today remains quite unnatural. This includes the way the masculine principle of logos is over-valued. This includes the one-sided striving to be good, along with the baneful consequences described. This includes rationality, which rejects the irrational as unprovable superstition. People's strongest drive is the drive for individuation—even when unrecognized. Every deviation from the immanent goal entails sickness (neurosis) or stunted development—ultimately, in other words, suffering.

Sermo II

> *In the night the dead stood along the wall and cried: We would have knowledge of god. Where is god? Is god dead?*
>
> *God is not dead. Now, as ever, he liveth. God is creatura, for he is something definite, and therefore distinct from the pleroma. God is quality of the pleroma, and everything which I said of creatura also is true concerning him.*
>
> *He is distinguished, however, from created beings through this, that he is more indefinite and indeterminable than they. He is less distinct than created beings, since the ground of his being is effective fullness. Only in so far as he is definite and distinct is he creatura, and in like measure is he the manifestation of the effective fullness of the pleroma.*
>
> *Everything which we do not distinguish falleth into the pleroma and is made void by its opposite. If, therefore, we do not distinguish god, effective fullness is for us extinguished.*
>
> *Moreover god is the pleroma itself, as likewise each smallest point in the created and uncreated is the pleroma itself.*

The dead pose the decisive question of whether God is dead. Let us see what Jung has to say:[110]

Modern iconoclasts are unconscious of the [God] in whose name they are destroying old values. Nietzsche thought himself quite conscious and responsible when he smashed the old tablets, yet he felt a peculiar need to back himself up with a revivified Zarathustra, a sort of alter ego, with whom he often identifies himself in his great tragedy Thus Spake Zarathustra. Nietzsche was no atheist, but his God was dead. The result of this demise was a split in himself, and he felt compelled to call the other self "Zarathustra" or, at times, "Dionysus." In his fatal illness he signed his letters "Zagreus," the dismembered God of the Thracians. The tragedy of Zarathustra is that, because his God died, Nietzsche himself became a god; and this happened because he was no atheist. He was of too positive a nature to tolerate the urban neurosis of atheism. It seems dangerous for such a man to assert that "God is dead": he instantly becomes the victim of inflation. Far from being a negation, God is actually the strongest and most effective "position" the psyche can reach, in exactly the same sense in which Paul speaks of people "whose God is their belly" (Phil. 3:19). The strongest and therefore the decisive factor in any individual psyche compels the same belief or fear, submission or devotion which a God would demand from man. Anything despotic and inescapable is in this sense "God," and it becomes absolute unless, by an ethical decision freely chosen, one succeeds in building up against this natural phenomenon a position that is equally strong and invincible. If this psychic position proves to be absolutely effective, it surely deserves to be named a "God," and what is more, a spiritual God, since it sprang from the freedom of ethical decision and therefore from the mind. Man is free to decide whether "God" shall be a "spirit" or a natural phenomenon like the craving of a morphine addict, and hence whether "God" shall act as a beneficent or a destructive force.

However indubitable and clearly understandable these psychic events or decisions may be, they are very apt to lead people to the false, unpsychological conclusion that it rests with them to decide whether they will create a "God" for themselves or not. There is no question of that, since each of us is equipped with a psychic disposition that limits our freedom in high degree and makes it practically illusory... "Principalities" and "powers" are always with us; we have no need to create them even if we could. It is merely incumbent on us to choose the master we wish to serve, so that his service shall be our safeguard against being mastered by the "other" whom we have not chosen. We do not create "God," we choose him.

Though our choice characterizes and defines "God," it is always man-made, and the definition it gives is therefore finite and imperfect. (Even the idea of perfection does not posit perfection.) The definition is an image, but this image does not raise the unknown fact it demonstrates into the realm of intelligibility, otherwise we would be entitled to say that we had created a God. The "master" we choose is not identical with the image we project of him in time and space. He goes on working as before, like an unknown quantity in the depths of the psyche... But because this inner is intrinsically free and not subject to our will and intentions, it may easily happen that the living thing chosen and defined by us will drop out of its setting, the man-made image, even against our will. Then, perhaps, we could say with Nietzsche, "God is dead." Yet it would be truer to say, "He has put off our image, and where shall we find him again?" The interregnum is full of danger, for the natural facts will raise their claim in the form of various -isms, which are productive of nothing but anarchy and destruction because inflation and man's hybris between them have elected to make the ego, in all its ridiculous paltriness, lord of the universe. That was the case with Nietzsche, the uncomprehended portent of a whole epoch.

The individual ego is much too small, its brain is much too feeble, to incorporate all the projections withdrawn from the world. Ego and brain burst asunder in the effort; the psychiatrist calls it schizophrenia. When Nietzsche said "God is dead," he uttered a truth which is valid for the greater part of Europe. People were influenced by it not because he said so, but because it stated a widespread psychological fact.

This is the real "death of God," for which neither Nietzsche nor Jung can be held responsible. It is the sickness of our time, and the two prophets diagnosed it. Jung experienced it firsthand during his youth in his father, who was a Protestant minister and was destroyed by it.

Jung tells how his confirmation ceremony with his father left him cold:[111]

> But what was the purpose of this wretched memorial service with the flat bread and the sour wine? Slowly I came to understand that this communion had been a fatal experience for me. It had proved hollow; more than that, it had proved to be a total loss. I knew that I would never again be able to participate in this ceremony. "Why, that is not religion at all," I thought. "It is an absence of God; the church is a place I should not go to. It is not life which is there, but death."

I was seized with the most vehement pity for my father. All at once I understood the tragedy of his profession and his life. He was struggling with a death whose existence he could not admit. An abyss had opened between him and me, and I saw no possibility of ever bridging it, for it was infinite in extent. I could not plunge my dear and generous father, who in so many matters left me to myself and had never tyrannized over me, into that despair and sacrilege which were necessary for an experience of divine grace. Only God could do that....

My sense of union with the Church and with the human world, so far as I knew it, was shattered. I had, so it seemed to me, suffered the greatest defeat of my life. The religious outlook which I imagined constituted my sole meaningful relation with the universe had disintegrated; I could no longer participate in the general faith, but found myself involved in something inexpressible, in my secret, which I could share with no one. It was terrible and—this was the worst of it—vulgar and ridiculous also, a diabolical mockery.

Later on, he writes:[112]

Several times my father had a serious talk with me. I was free to study anything I liked, he said, but if I wanted his advice I should keep away from theology. "Be anything you like except a theologian," he said emphatically. By this time there was a tacit agreement between us that certain things could be said or done without comment. He had never taken me to task for cutting church as often as possible and for not going to Communion any more. The farther away I was from church, the better I felt... Looking back, I now see how very much my development as a child anticipated future events and paved the way for modes of adaptation to my father's religious collapse as well as to the shattering revelation of the world as we see it today—a revelation which had not taken shape from one day to the next, but had cast its shadows long in advance.[113] I would remain passive during his [the father's] outbursts of rage, but when he seemed to be in a more accessible mood I sometimes tried to strike up a conversation with him, hoping to learn something about his inner thoughts and his understanding of himself. It was clear to me that something quite specific was tormenting him, and I suspected that it had to do with his faith. From a number of hints he let fall I was convinced that he suffered from religious doubts. This, it seemed to me, was bound to be the case if the necessary experience had not come to him. From my attempts at discussion I learned in fact that something of the sort was amiss, for all my questions were met with the same old lifeless theological answers, or with a resigned shrug which aroused the spirit of contradiction in me. I could not understand why he did not seize on these opportunities pugnaciously and come to terms with his situation. I saw that my critical questions made him sad, but I nevertheless hoped for a constructive talk, since it appeared almost inconceivable to me that he should not have had experience of God, the most evident of all experiences...[114] I tried, no doubt very clumsily, to convey these obvious truths to him, with the hopeful intention of helping him to bear the fate which had inevitably befallen him. He had to quarrel with somebody, so he did it with his family and himself. Why didn't he do it with God, the dark author of all created things, who alone was responsible for the sufferings of the world? God would assuredly have sent him by way of an answer one of those magical, infinitely profound dreams which He had sent to me even without being asked, and which had sealed my fate...[115] These fruitless discussions exasperated my father and me, and in the end we abandoned them, each burdened with his own specific feeling of inferiority. Theology had alienated my father and me from one another. I felt that I had once again suffered a fatal defeat, though I sensed I was not alone. I had a dim premonition that he was inescapably succumbing to his fate. He was lonely...[116] Once I heard him praying. He struggled desperately to keep his faith. I was shaken and outraged at once, because I saw how hopelessly he was entrapped by the Church and its theological thinking. They had blocked all avenues by which he might have reached God directly, and then faithlessly abandoned him...[117] I was...sure that none of the theologians I knew had ever seen "the light that shineth in the darkness" with his own eyes, for if they had they would not have been able to teach a "theological religion," which seemed quite inadequate to me, since there was nothing to do with it but believe it without hope. This was what my father had tried valiantly to do, and had run aground...[118] I recognized that this celebrated faith of his had played this deadly trick on him, and not only on him but on most of the cultivated and serious people I knew. The arch sin of faith, it seemed to me, was that it forestalled experience.[119]

His father's depressive moods became both more frequent and more intense, as did his hypochondria. He complained of feeling that he had "stones in his stomach." He became bed ridden and, at just 53, died a premature death.

I have quoted these passages about the fate of Jung's father and his fatal struggle over his faith in such detail because it is not a single, unique case.

Let us turn back to revelation—or, better, the teachings—of the Sermons. At first glance, the declaration "God is creatura" might be shocking. It likewise explains that he is distinct from the pleroma—which he also is—in that he is something determinate, yet obviously a content of the Pleroma. The speaker of the sermons terms this a quality. But God distinguishes himself from a creature in that he is less clearly defined and less determinate than a creature. The ground of his being is effective fullness. To understand this better, consider what Jung had to say about "The Relativity of the God-Concept in Meister Eckhart":[120]

The "relativity of God," as I understand it, denotes a point of view that does not conceive of God as 'absolute,' i.e., wholly 'cut off' from man and existing outside and beyond all human conditions, but as in a certain sense dependent on him; it also implies a reciprocal and essential relation between man and God, whereby man can be understood as a function of God, and God as a psychological function of man... Hence, for our psychology, which as a science must confine itself to empirical data within the limits set by cognition, God is not even relative, but a function of the unconscious—the manifestation of a dissociated quantum of libido that has activated the God image. From the metaphysical point of view God is, of course, absolute, existing in himself. This implies his complete detachment from the unconscious, which means, psychologically, a complete unawareness of the fact that God's action springs from one's own inner being. The relativity of God, on the other hand, means that a not inconsiderable portion of the unconscious processes is registered, at least indirectly, as a psychological content. Naturally this insight is possible only when more attention than usual is paid to the psyche, with the consequence that the contents of the unconscious are withdrawn from projection into objects and become endowed with a conscious quality that makes them appear as belonging to the subject and as subjectively conditioned.

Effective void is the nature of the devil. God and devil are the first manifestations of nothingness, which we call the pleroma. It is indifferent whether the pleroma is or is not, since in everything it is balanced and void. Not so creatura. In so far as god and devil are creatura they do not extinguish each other, but stand one against the other as effective opposites. We need no proof of their existence. It is enough that we must always be speaking of them. Even if both were not, creatura, of its own essential distinctiveness, would forever distinguish them anew out of the pleroma.

Everything that discrimination taketh out of the pleroma is a pair of opposites. To god, therefore, always belongeth the devil.

This inseparability is as close and, as your own life hath made you see, as indissoluble as the pleroma itself. Thus it is that both stand very close to the pleroma, in which all opposites are extinguished and joined.

Since becoming conscious always takes the form of oppositions becoming distinct from each other, it is revealing on a logical plane that for God as well, in becoming distinct from the pleroma, it is likewise necessary for an opposed figure to arise. If philosophers define God as the summum bonum, then his counterpart is the infimum malum, the devil. Our speaker is a Gnostic who imparts knowledge to the dead, that is, knowledge from the depths. If God, according to this teaching, is effective fullness, so is his counterpart effective void. Since they are not in the pleroma, but are instead creatures, so are they effective opposites.

This doctrine stands in a certain contrast to the orthodox version of "dear God" as the all-powerful. He appears to have a secret counterpart, with the ability to thwart all his good intentions. In Gnostic systems this idea is developed rather consistently—as mentioned previously, the visible world is to some extent a misadventure committed by an overbearing, incompetent demiurge. As a result of this incomplete creation, darkness came into the world—darkness in the form of matter itself, above all—which is beyond redemption. The unrecognizable father, who is there in the background, is designated summum bonum—a designation according to the teaching of the Sermons that is utterly vacuous, because his pleroma has no qualities. Only where something becomes conscious is it possible for qualities to be recognized.

Just as "God" exceeds conscious comprehension, so does the "devil." We know just as little about how and in what form he becomes manifest. As a created being, he is just as much principium individuationis as is God. Dualism appears to be unavoidable, and in the Iranian and Manichean religion, this idea is consistently manifest. Christianity, although it takes itself to be a monotheism, displays dualistic aspects as well—not only in the Old Testament and the Garden of Eden story, but likewise around the coming of the new era and in Gnosticism. In Pseudo-Clementine, we read: "God by His Son created the world as a double house...For the prince of this world and of the present age is like an adulterer, who corrupts and violates the minds of men, and, seducing them from the love of the true bridegroom, allures them to strange lovers."[121]

Epiphanius says of the Ebionites that two were called, side by side: the one Christ, and the other the devil.[122] As the "ruler of this world" (John 14:30), the devil is once again connected to matter and the creation. He is "the son of perdition, who opposes and exalts himself against every so-called god or object of worship, so that he takes his seat in the temple of God, proclaiming himself to be God" (2 Thessalonians 2:4).

In John's revelation he becomes the antichrist, clearly drawing a contrast with the luminous figure of Christ. And when it is said, "And the great dragon was thrown down, that ancient serpent, who is called the Devil and Satan, the deceiver of the whole world—he was thrown down to the earth, and his angels were thrown down with him," it may be that the heavens are being purified of "vermin" (12:12). But this polarity nonetheless remains in the individual. "Who is the liar but he who denies that Jesus is the Christ? This is the antichrist, he who denies the Father and the Son" (1 John 2:22). This concept is represented explicitly in the Valentinian system. We read in Irenaeus' critical recension of Valentinus' words:[123]

> Christ also was not produced from the Aeons within the Pleroma, but was brought forth by the mother who had been excluded from it, in virtue of her remembrance of better things, but not without a kind of shadow. He, indeed, as being masculine, having severed the shadow from himself, returned to the Pleroma; but his mother being left with the shadow, and deprived of her spiritual substance, brought forth another son, namely, the Demiurge, whom he [Valentinus] also styles the supreme ruler of all those things which are subject to him (princeps huius mundi).

Jung further amplifies this subject:[124]

> The devil is the aping shadow of God [simia Dei], the ἀντίμιμον πνεῦμα, in Gnosticism and also in Greek alchemy. He is "Lord of this world" [John 14:30] in whose shadow man was born, fatally tainted with the original sin brought about by the devil. Christ, according to the Gnostic view, cast off the shadow he was born with and remained without sin. His sinlessness proves his essential lack of contamination with the dark world of nature-bound man, who tries in vain to shake off this darkness... Man's connection with physis, with the material world and its demands, is the cause of his anomalous position: on the one hand he has the capacity for enlightenment, on the other he is in thrall to the Lord of this world... Christ on the contrary lives in the Platonic realm of pure ideas whither only man's thought can reach, but not he himself in his to-

tality. Man is, in truth, the bridge spanning the gulf between "this world"—the realm of the dark Tricephalus—and the heavenly Trinity.

And elsewhere, he states:[125]

Antimimos, the imitator and evil principle [in Zosimos], appears as the antagonist of the Son of God: he too considers himself to be God's son. Here the opposites inherent in the deity are clearly divided... He is the spirit of darkness in a man's body, compelling his soul to fulfill all his sinful tendencies.

Jung explains again, in *Aion*:[126]

One must, however, take evil rather more substantially when one meets it on the plane of empirical psychology. There it is simply the opposite of good. In the ancient world the Gnostics, whose arguments were very much influenced by psychic experience, tackled the problem of evil on a broader basis than the Church Fathers. For instance, one of the things they taught was that Christ "cast off his shadow from himself." If we give this view the weight it deserves, we can easily recognize the cut-off counterpart in the figure of Antichrist. The Antichrist develops in legend as a perverse imitator of Christ's life. He is a true antimimon pneuma, and imitating spirit of evil who follows in Christ's footsteps like a shadow following the body...

For anyone who has a positive attitude towards Christianity the problem of the Antichrist is a hard nut to crack. It is nothing less than the counterstroke of the devil, provoked by God's Incarnation; for the devil attains his true stature as the adversary of Christ, and hence of God, only after the rise of Christianity, while as late as the Book of Job he was still one of God's sons and on familiar terms with Yahweh. Psychologically the case is clear, since the dogmatic figure of Christ is so sublime and spotless that everything turns dark beside it. It is, in fact, so one-sidedly perfect that it demands a psychic complement to restore the balance... The coming of the Antichrist is not just a prophetic prediction—it is an inexorable psychological law whose existence, though unknown to the author of the Johannine Epistles, brought him a sure knowledge of the impending enantiodromia. Consequently he wrote as if he were conscious of the inner necessity for this transformation, though we may be sure that the idea seemed to him like a divine revelation. In reality every intensified differentiation of the Christ-image brings about a corresponding accentuation of its unconscious complement, thereby increasing the tension between above and below.

Jung never tired of calling attention to the psychological law in question here, and of combatting the Christian tendency to belittle the devil. It earned him widespread hostility in theological circles. The instruction of the dead is that which, in compensation, he was obliged to convey to our Christian civilization—and it was what no one wanted to hear. In this sense, the dead represent traditional Christianity that had run out of steam and lost its bearings. For Jung, it was a source of genuine distress that he had to make the world aware of this uncomfortable truth. The spirits of the dead themselves, as we have seen, thrust the task upon him. Clearly, I can only begin to suggest in this book what an accomplishment it was for Jung to meet this task.

God and devil are distinguished by the qualities fullness and emptiness, generation and destruction. EFFECTIVENESS is common to both. Effectiveness joineth them. Effectiveness, therefore, standeth above both; is a god above god, since in its effect it uniteth fullness and emptiness.

This is a god whom ye knew not, for mankind forgot it. We name it by its name ABRAXAS. It is more indefinite still than god and devil.

That god may be distinguished from it, we name god HELIOS or Sun. Abraxas is effect. Nothing standeth opposed to it but the ineffective; hence its effective nature freely unfoldeth itself. The ineffective is not, therefore resisteth not. Abraxas standeth above the sun and above the devil. It is improbable probability, unreal reality. Had the pleroma a being, Abraxas would be its manifes-

tation. It is the effective itself, not any particular effect, but effect in general.

It is unreal reality, because it hath no definite effect.

It is also creatura, because it is distinct from the pleroma.

The sun hath a definite effect, and so hath the devil. Wherefore do they appear to us more effective than indefinite Abraxas.

It is force, duration, change.

The dead now raised a great tumult, for they were Christians.

Now I must first say something about Abraxas (or Abrasax) in the history of religion, before we attempt to understand the way Abraxas is used here. Jung probably knew the name from the monograph by Albrecht Dietrich,[127] which was found in his library. It is also possible that he was aware of what Richard Reitzenstein—whom he held in high esteem—had written on the issue in his 1904 book *Poimandres*,[128] of which Jung likewise possessed a copy. This god was never especially prominent. It may be that the name was constructed so that the numerical values assigned to the letters added up to the number of days in a year: alpha = 1; beta = 2; rho = 100; alpha = 1; sigma = 200; alpha = 1; zeta = 60, for a total of 365. This made him a temporal god in terms of magic,[129] similar to the lion-headed Aion. Of greater interest to us here would be his role in the teachings of the Gnostic Basilides. Yet, in this we are disappointed, because he appears there in only a very subordinate status, while for Jung's speaker in the sermons he is a supreme god.

In the report by Irenaeus[130] he is the leader of the 365 heavens, and for Epiphanius,[131] this is the why the human body is composed of 365 parts. According to Hippolytus,[132] the followers of Basilides possess a great book in which Abraxas is a significant ruler over the 365 heavens. In the Nag Hammadi text, Apocalypse of Adam, the name comes up as a savior.[133] From this we may conclude that, at most, this Sermon incorporates distant echoes of Gnosticism, and is in essence an independent autonomous creation.

In our text Abraxas is effectiveness as such, that is, the dynamic. This identity is constantly evoked by a specific content. If he is creative, then we call him God or Helios, the Sun. If he is destructive, we call him the devil. The dynamic as such is not predetermined as to quality. It comes into being by way of the tension between opposites, and leads to transformation.

We are told that a great tumult arises among the dead. What is it that disturbs them in this teaching? All religions have a tendency to act as if they had existed since the beginning of the world and will survive until it comes to an end. This is why archaic language is used in worship services. The idea is that the truths of the religion remain valid from one eternity to another. Yet, as we learn from the history of religion, religions come into existence and flourish, and then decline. The question arises as to how it is possible at all for a religion to maintain that it is eternal, in complete opposition to reality. Religion just is the expression of a universally valid and eternal fundamental truth, yet one subject to transformation over time in how it is formulated. In this sense, Jung did not announce any "new" truths. He had to take the "old" truths and reformulate them in the language of our time, because they were no longer being understood. This is the same thing that happens to religions. Jung writes:[134]

> The Christian nations have come to a sorry pass; their Christianity slumbers and has neglected to develop its myth further in the course of the centuries. Those who gave expression to the dark stirrings of growth in mythic ideas were refused a hearing; Gioacchino da Fiore, Meister Eckhart, Jacob Boehme, and many others have remained obscurantists for the majority. The only ray of light is Pius XII and his dogma [*Assumptio Mariae*, 1950]. But people do not even know what I am referring to when I say this. They do not realize that a myth is dead if it no longer lives and grows.
>
> Our myth has become mute, and gives no answers. The fault lies not in it as it is set down in the Scriptures, but solely in us, who have not developed it further, who, rather, have suppressed any such attempts. The original version of the myth offers ample points of departure and possibilities of development... Today we are compelled to meet that question; but we stand empty-handed, bewildered, and perplexed, and cannot even get it into our heads that no myth will come to our aid alt-

hough we have such urgent need of one. As the result of the political situation and the frightful, not to say diabolic, triumphs of science, we are shaken by secret shudders and dark forebodings; but we know no way out, and very few persons indeed draw the conclusion that this time the issue is the longsinceforgotten soul of man.

As a result of the great emphasis placed on the eternal validity of the Christian truth, the latter became permanent in the form of dogma, even though it is precisely a reformulation and further elaboration that would make it possible for progressive development to occur. There is no genuine duration in the soul, but only a kind of "fleeting equilibrium," representative of balance. Everything has a before and an after, and anything that is not in a process of transformation is dead. Life consists of constant change. This is true both in the large and the small. When Jung referred to ancient Egyptian precursors of the trinity dogma, he found little understanding among the theologians, although he had underlined specifically what was new in Christianity. The dynamic according to which development takes place in the image of God, as he demonstrated in *Answer to Job*,[135] encountered rejection and contradiction among theologians. In this we have the great tumult that had been predicted. Jung has more to say about Abraxas in the third Sermon.

Sermo III

Like mists arising from a marsh, the dead came near and cried: Speak further unto us concerning the supreme god.

Hard to know is the deity of Abraxas. Its power is the greatest, because man perceiveth it not. From the sun he draweth the summum bonum; from the devil the infimum malum; but from Abraxas LIFE, altogether indefinite, the mother of good and evil.

Smaller and weaker life seemeth to be than the summum bonum; wherefore is it also hard to conceive that Abraxas transcendeth even the sun in power, who is himself the radiant source of all the force of life.

Abraxas is the sun, and at the same time the eternally sucking gorge of the void, the belittling and dismembering devil.

The power of Abraxas is twofold; but ye see it not, because for your eyes the warring opposites of this power are extinguished.

What the god-sun speaketh is life. What the devil speaketh is death.

But Abraxas speaketh that hallowed and accursed word which is life and death at the same time.

Abraxas begetteth truth and lying, good and evil, light and darkness, in the same word and in the same act. Wherefore is Abraxas terrible.

As the supreme god, Abraxas represents a projection in theological language of a fundamental phenomenon of life that transcends consciousness. It is only to be expected therefore that it has received a variety of historical characterizations. For Aristotle,[136] it is that "which causes motion but is itself unmovable and exists as actuality." Plato[137] defines the soul as "that which moves itself," in which all movement finds its origin and is therefore immortal. According to Empedocles,[138] love (*philia*) and hate (*neikos*) "For if both once it was, and will be; never, I think, Will be the age eternal void of both of these." In Schopenhauer[139] it is the transcendent will; in Henri Bergson the *élan vitale*.

Jung had already spoken, in his *Psychology of Dementia Praecox* (1907),[140] of the psychic energy of the complex. In *Transformations and Symbols of the Libido* (1912), he defined the latter as the concept of intention as such, cleansing it of the sexual connotation it had been given by Sigmund Freud. This is the approach to psychic phenomena from the point of view of energetics. In a subsequent essay, "The Theory of Psychoanalysis" (1913),[141] he defined libido as passionate desire, corresponding to the classical sense of the term. In the most extensive work on this issue, "On Psychic Energy" (1928),[142] he also refers to the precursors of this concept, in which the beginnings of religious symbol formation are bound up precisely with this idea of energy. Ethnologists have had an extremely difficult time explaining such concepts in a way that is accessible to our way of understanding. The life of primitive peoples revolves to a considerable degree around such a "diffused, all-pervasive, invisible, manipulable and transferable life-energy and universal force,"[143] as, for example, wakanda among the Dakotas. Similar concepts include churinga among Australian aborigines, the Native American wakan, and mana in Melanesia. Mana has been described as,

> a power or influence, not physical, and in a way supernatural; but it shows itself in physical force, or in any kind of power or influence which a man possesses. This mana is not fixed in anything, and can be conveyed in almost anything.[144]

Behind this is the view of,

> a diffused substance or energy upon the possession of which all exceptional power or ability or fecundity depends. The energy is...mysterious and incomprehensible; but it is so because it is vastly powerful, not because the things that manifest in it are unusual and "supernatural" or such as "defeat reasonable expectation."[145]

For primitive peoples what is perceived in connection to the object is a psychological phenomenon, because, not yet making use of abstract concepts, they live in a world of associations. These expressions have much more the status of associations grounded in the perception of phenomenal relationships than concepts in modern sense of the term. In a later cultural stage, symbolic relationships took over.

Psychic phenomena are always perceived as dynamic, and for this, Abraxas is the most personal expression. This dynamic is a characteristic of the unconscious, which has not yet become accessible as an object of consciousness.

It is splendid as the lion in the instant he striketh down his victim.

It is beautiful as a day of spring. It is the great Pan himself and also the small one. It is Priapos.

It is the monster of the under-world, a thousand-armed polyp, coiled knot of winged serpents, frenzy.

It is the hermaphrodite of the earliest beginning.

It is the lord of the toads and frogs, which live in the water and go up on the land, whose chorus ascendeth at noon and at midnight.

It is abundance that seeketh union with emptiness. It is holy begetting.

It is love and love's murder.

It is the saint and his betrayer.

It is the brightest light of day and the darkest night of madness. To look upon it, is blindness.

To know it, is sickness.

To worship it, is death.

To fear it, is wisdom.

To resist it not, is redemption.

God dwelleth behind the sun, the devil behind the night. What god bringeth forth out of the light the devil sucketh into the night. But Abraxas is the world, its becoming and its passing. Upon every gift that cometh from the god-sun the devil layeth his curse.

Everything that ye entreat from the god-sun begetteth a deed of the devil.

Everything that ye create with the god-sun giveth effective power to the devil.

That is terrible Abraxas.

It is the mightiest creature, and in it the creature is afraid of itself. It is the manifest opposition of creatura to the pleroma and its nothingness.

It is the son's horror of the mother. It is the mother's love for the son.

It is the delight of the earth and the cruelty of the heavens. Before its countenance man becometh like stone.

Before it there is no question and no reply.

It is the life of creatura.

It is the operation of distinctiveness. It is the love of man.

It is the speech of man.

It is the appearance and the shadow of man. It is illusory reality.

Now the dead howled and raged, for they were unperfected.

In the moment that it strikes down its prey, the lion is accumulated force. It is the animal of high noon and the heat of the sun. Then follow a series of libido symbols meant to deliver the vaguely perceived Abraxas to clarity. The lion is the "king of beasts," and plays a very prominent role in alchemy (Cantilena Riplaei).[146] The spring day brings the rebirth of all nature. The Aniada of Paracelsus, an aid to longevity in the form of a universal remedy, is meant to be gathered "in the true May."[147] The great Pan is the divine force in nature. Part buck, he is the god of the shepardesses, responsible for fertility. Later on, via popular etymology (pan = all), he became the great Pan, the god of all. Another fertility god is Priapos, designated as *praesentissimum numen* ("most omnipresent power") and extolled in the *Carmina Priapea*.[148] He is portrayed with an erect member, signifying potency, vigor, and vitality. Hermaphroditus, in alchemy, is the numinous product of the unification of opposites. He is also the primal human, before sexual differentiation, the androgynous Anthropos of Gnosis. As the lord of the toads and frogs, he assisted in the evolution from water to land. He is the unification of the opposites full and empty. Thus he is the hieros gamos, the holy wedding as such, inclusive of love and its opposite, the saint and his betrayer. Alcmaeon of Croton (about 460 BCE),[149] reported of the Pythagoreans that there are, pairs of cognate principles, bounded and unbounded, odd and even, one and many, right and left, male and female, resting and moving, straight and curved, light and darkness, good and bad, square and oblong.... For both, however (Alcmaeon as well as the Pythagoreans in general), it is evident that these oppositions supply the primeval basis (the principles) of things.

The sermons have already listed pairs of opposites (the Effective and the Ineffective, Fullness and Emptiness, Living and Dead, etc.) as qualities of the pleroma. If he repeats some of them here, it is now from the perspective of energy. There it was light and dark, here the brightest light (consciousness) and the deepest night of insanity (agnosia); there it is static principles, as those of the Pythagoreans, here the dynamic of the psyche.

Abraxas is such an indeterminate dynamic that it cannot be seen, because we can only see and recognize it in determinate form, as an object or symbol, or as directed desire. Abraxas bears unmistakable similarities to the alchemists' spirit Mercury.[150] This is a Proteus, of whom Jung says in summary:

> (1) Mercurius consists of all conceivable opposites. He is thus quite obviously a duality, but is named a unity in spite of the fact that his innumerable inner contradictions can dramatically fly apart into an equal number of disparate and apparently independent figures.
> (2) He is both material and spiritual.
> (3) He is the process by which the lower and material is transformed into the higher and spiritual, and vice versa.
> (4) He is the devil, a redeeming psychopomp, an evasive trickster, and God's reflection in physical nature.[151]
> (5) He is also the reflection of a mystical experience of the artifex that coincides with the opus alchymicum.
> (6) As such, he represents on the one hand the self and on the other the individuation process and, because of the limitless number of his names, also the collective unconscious.

The alchemists made a tremendous effort to capture this contradictory and elusive spirit in symbols. It is that which is effective as such, which inspires fear in human beings, causing them to need religio—which is to say, to persist in careful and conscientious observation. Rudolf Otto[152] designated it the numinous, a dynamic existence or effect that does not stem from caprice. The effect seizes and rules over the experiencing subject, making the subject more its victim than its creator. It is either the characteristic of a visible object or the influence of an invisible presence that works a change in consciousness. Jung bases his concept of religio on the derivation by Cicero (*De inventione rhetorica* II, p. 147): religion is that which a certain higher nature (termed divine) faces with care and sacred reserve,[153] demonstrating clearly that the concept indicates a universal human disposition and not a profession of faith. Thus is "the fear of the Lord the beginning of knowledge" (Proverbs 1:7).

To cease resisting is to do the will of God, which signifies redemption. The Gnostics did not think of "the redeemer, who bore the sins of the world," saying rather with the Gnostic Markos that, "the knowledge of the unspeakable Greatness is itself perfect redemption."[154] Abraxas is in their system the unspeakable greatness that is to be known in order to follow its will. In the Gospel of Truth[155] the redeemer is both the power of the word, which emerges out of the pleroma toward knowledge of the father of truth, and the process of redemption itself.[156]

The Sun is the benevolent side of God, the devil the sinister side. The becoming and dying away of the world take place within this tension; this is Abraxas, the blind disposition, as it were, of nature. When events turn toward the one pole, an enantiodromia sets in, a reversal toward the other: this is the dread Abraxas. "Every psychological extreme secretly contains its own opposite or stands in some sort of intimate and essential relation to it," writes Jung.[157]

Indeed, it is from this tension that it derives its peculiar dynamism. There is no hallowed custom that cannot on occasion turn into its opposite,[158] and the more extreme a position is, the more easily may we expect an enantiodromia, a conversion of something into its opposite. The best is the most threatened with same devilish perversion just because it has done the most to suppress evil.

Jung borrowed the concept of enantiodromia ("running counter to")[159] from the philosophy of Heraclitus, according to which everything that is goes over into its opposite.

> But perhaps Nature has a liking for opposites and produces concordance out of them and not out of similars, just as for instance she brings male together with female and not each with members of the same sex, and composes the first concord by means of opposites and not similars. Art, too, seems to imitate Nature in doing this... It was this same thing which was said in Heraclitus the Obscure: Things taken together are whole and not whole, something which is being brought together and brought apart, which is in tune and out of tune: out of all things can be made a unity, and out of a unity, all things.[160]

Viewed psychologically, this is the emergence of unconscious oppositions, specifically in temporal succession (Saul-Paul). Jung, with his keen intuition, discovered in this a fundamental psychological truth, which in this form finds no place in Western Christianity: and so, the dead "howled and raged."

The images that follow represent the dynamic of libidinal nature. In part, the dynamic signifies self-sustaining and self-propagating life, and in part the blind disposition of nature, either unconscious or in opposition to consciousness. Yet in the domain of the drives the opposites hold each other in check and compensate each other. No doubt, humanity, given its drives, is rooted in the animal world, and like all natural beings would like to have them fully gratified. On the other side, however, is a cultural drive that seeks to domesticate the animal drives, in order to redirect the freed-up libido to creative endeavors. According to experience, these two basic drives exist in conflict with each other and are the most common cause of neurosis—the civil war in one's own psyche. "Too much of the animal distorts the civilized man," writes Jung,[161] "too much civilization makes sick animals."

Abraxas is a force of nature, with no awareness of what is specifically human, and with no morality. All oppositions are contained in this force in equal measure. This is why it is wonderful and sublime, but also cruel and relentless, like all nature. Thus is the individual petrified in its presence, and unable to solve its riddles. A dream brought this reality home to Jung. He tells that on a trip to Tunisia in 1920,[162]

I dreamt that I was in an Arab city, and as in most such cities there was a citadel, a casbah. The city was situated in a broad plain, and had a wall all around it. The shape of the wall was square, and there were four gates.

The casbah in the interior of the city was surrounded by a wide moat (which is not the way it really is in Arab countries). I stood before a wooden bridge leading over the water to a dark, horseshoe-shaped portal, which was open. Eager to see the citadel from the inside also, I stepped out on the bridge. When I was about halfway across it, a handsome, dark Arab of aristocratic, almost royal bearing came toward me from the gate. I knew that this youth in the white burnoose was the resident prince of the citadel. When he came up to me, he attacked me and tried to knock me down. We wrestled. In the struggle we crashed against the railing; it gave way and both of us fell into the moat, where he tried to push my head under water to drown me. No, I thought, this is going too far. And in my turn I pushed his head under water. I did so although I felt great admiration for him; but I did not want to let myself be killed. I had no intention of killing him; I wanted only to make him unconscious and incapable of fighting.

Then the scene of the dream changed, and he was with me in a large vaulted octagonal room in the center of the citadel. The room was all white, very plain and beautiful. Along the light--colored marble walls stood low divans, and before me on the floor lay an open book with black letters written in magnificent calligraphy on milky-white parchment. It was not Arabic script; rather, it looked to me like the Uigurian script of West Turkestan, which was familiar to me from the Manichaean fragments from Turfan. I did not know the contents, but nevertheless I had the feeling that this was "my book," that I had written it. The young prince with whom I had just been wrestling sat to the right of me on the floor. I explained to him that now that I had overcome him he must read the book. But he resisted. I placed my arm around his shoulders and forced him, with a sort of paternal kindness and patience, to read the book. I knew that this was absolutely essential, and at last he yielded.

In this dream, the Arab youth was the double of the proud Arab who had ridden past us without a greeting. As an inhabitant of the casbah he was a figuration of the self, or rather, a messenger or emissary of the self. For the casbah from which he came was a perfect mandala: a citadel surrounded by a square wall with four gates. His attempt to kill me was an echo of the motif of Jacob's struggle with the angel; he was—to use the language of the Bible—like an angel of the Lord, a messenger of God who wished to kill men because he did not know them.

Actually, the angel ought to have had his dwelling in me. But he knew only angelic truth and understood nothing about man. Therefore he first came forward as my enemy; however, I held my own against him. In the second part of the dream I was the master of the citadel; he sat at my feet and had to learn to understand my thoughts, or rather, learn to know man.

Obviously, my encounter with Arab culture had struck me with overwhelming force. The emotional nature of these unreflective people who are so much closer to life than we are exerts a strong suggestive influence upon those historical layers in ourselves which we have just overcome and left behind, or which we think we have overcome. It is like the paradise of childhood from which we imagine we have emerged, but which at the slightest provocation imposes fresh defeats upon us.

Abraxas, a parallel to the young Arab prince in the dream, is pure, uncivilized nature in us. When Rousseau calls for a "retour à la nature," or when we hear from ethnologists of the "noble savages," these are both signs of a secret desire for the uncorrupted primal man in all of us, just as God made him on the sixth day of creation. This "true man" in us remains buried under the rubble of millennia of culture, calling for redemption. In many of their systems, the Gnostics developed a comprehensive theology of primal man. It is the moment of creation when a subject first encountered the magnificence of the world and, like Adam, gave names to the animals and the birds (Genesis 1:19).

The more we distance ourselves from this natural man via the civilizing process, the more powerfully wells our desire for the paradise of unquestioned being, threatening consciousness with the danger that it will be overwhelmed by the primitive being within us. It was through this dynamic that libertine sects, insofar as they existed among the Gnostics, were undone.

Particularly interesting in this context is a sect mentioned by Epiphanius,[163] which appeals to an unknown text called the book of Noria. We now also find in the Nag Hammadi collection a short document of similar name: "The Thought of Norea."[164] The name of Norea appears elsewhere, as well: she is named as Seth's sister,[165] or elsewhere, as his wife.[166] According to Epiphanius' statement, Noria is Noah's wife.[167] This Noria repeatedly burned Noah's arc because he listened to the Archon,[168] while Noria listened to and revealed the higher powers. In "The Thought of Norea" found in the Nag Hammadi texts, Norea is the soul lost in the world that redeems herself and others through knowledge. What was stolen from the supernal mother by the powers that created the world must be returned to her out of the emanations of the men and women.[169]

We witness through such constructive consideration the spiritual background of the Gnostic systems—systems that appeared outwardly to the church fathers as abominations. There is a much deeper background to the Gnostic "perversions" than the church fathers realized.

Sermo IV

The dead filled the place murmuring and said: Tell us of gods and devils, accursed one!

The god-sun is the highest good; the devil is the opposite. Thus have ye two gods. But there are many high and good things and many great evils. Among these are two god-devils; the one is the BURNING ONE, *the other* THE GROWING ONE.

The burning one is EROS, who hath the form of flame. Flame giveth light because it consumeth.

The growing one is the TREE OF LIFE. It buddeth, as in growing it heapeth up living stuff.

Eros flameth up and dieth. But the tree of life groweth with slow and constant increase through unmeasured time.

Good and evil are united in the flame.

Good and evil are united in the increase of the tree. In their divinity stand life and love opposed.

Why are the dead murmuring and calling the teacher accursed? Obviously, he has touched one of their "sore spots"!
"Through centuries of educational training, Christianity subdued the animal instincts of antiquity and of the ensuing ages of barbarism," writes Jung,[170]

to the point where a large amount of instinctual energy could be set free for the building of civilization. The effect of this training showed itself, to begin with, in a fundamental change of attitude, namely in the alienation from reality, the otherworldliness of the early Christian centuries. It was an age that strove after inwardness and spiritual abstraction. Nature was abhorrent to man. One has only to think of the passage in St. Augustine quoted by Jacob Burckhardt: "And men go forth, and admire lofty mountains and broad seas...and turn away from themselves" [Confessions, 10, c. 8].

But it was not only the aesthetic beauty of the world that distracted their senses and lured them away from concentrating on a spiritual and supramundane goal. There were also daemonic or magical influences emanating from nature herself...

The world and its beauty had to be shunned, not only because of their vanity and transitoriness, but because love of created nature soon made man its slave. As St. Augustine says (X, 6): "...they love these things too much and become subject to them, and subjects cannot judge."[171] One would certainly think it possible to love something, to have a positive attitude towards it, without supinely succumbing to it and losing one's power of rational judgment. But Augustine knew his contemporaries, and knew furthermore how much godliness and godlike power dwelt in the beauty of the world.

> Since you alone govern the universe, and without you nothing rises into the bright realm of light, and nothing joyous or lovely can come to be...

Thus Lucretius extols "alma Venus" as the ruling principle of nature. To such a daimonion man falls an abject victim unless he can categorically reject its seductive influence at the outset. It is not merely a question of sensuality and of aesthetic corruption, but—and this is the point—of paganism and nature-worship. Because gods dwell in created things, man falls to worshipping them, and for that reason he must turn away from them utterly lest he be overwhelmed. In this respect the fate of Alypius is extremely instructive. If the flight from the world is successful, man can then build up an inner, spiritual world which stands firm against the onslaught of sense-impressions. The struggle with the world of the senses brought to birth a type of thinking independent of external factors. Man won for himself that sovereignty of the idea which was able to withstand the aesthetic impact, so that thought was no longer fettered by the emotional effect of sense-impressions, but could assert itself and even rise, later, to reflection and observation. Man was now in a position to enter into a new and independent relationship with nature, to go on building upon the foundation which the classical spirit had laid, and to take up once more the natural link which the Christian retreat from the world had let fall. On this newly-won spiritual level there was forged an alliance with the world and nature which, unlike the old attitude, did not collapse before the magic of external objects, but could regard them with the steady light of reflection. Nevertheless, the attention lavished upon natural objects was infused with something of the old religious piety, and something of the old religious ethic communicated itself to scientific truthfulness and honesty... The newly-won rational and intellectual stability of the human mind nevertheless managed to hold its own and allowed it to penetrate further and further into depths of nature that early ages had hardly suspected. The more successful the penetration and advance of the new scientific spirit proved to be, the more the latter—as is usually the case with the victor—become the prisoner of the world it had conquered... The world had not only been deprived of its gods, but had lost its soul. Through the shifting of interest from the inner to the outer world our knowledge of nature was increased a thousandfold in comparison with earlier ages, but knowledge and experience of the inner world were correspondingly reduced. The religious interest, which ought normally to be the greatest and most decisive factor, turned away from the inner world, and the great figures of dogma dwindled to strange and incomprehensible vestiges, a prey to every sort of criticism. Even modern psychology has the greatest difficulty in vindicating the human soul's right to existence, and in making it credible that the soul is a mode of being with properties that can be investigated, and therefore a suitable object for scientific study; that it is not something attached to an outside, but has an autonomous inside, too, and a life of its own; that it is not just an ego-consciousness, but an existent which in all its essentials can only be inferred indirectly.

I want as much as possible to allow Jung to express himself in his own words, to illustrate for the reader how this teaching from the Sermons came to be elaborated in his life's work as a whole. Thus, I will let Jung continue,[172]

The sun...is the only truly "rational" image of God, whether we adopt the standpoint of the primitive savage or of modern science. In either case the sun is the father-god from whom all living things draw life; he is the fructifier and creator, the source of energy for our world. The discord into which the human soul has fallen can be harmoniously resolved through the sun as a natural object which knows no inner conflict. The sun is not only beneficial, but also destructive; hence the zodiacal sign for August heat is the ravaging lion which Samson slew [Judges 14:6] in order to rid the parched earth of its torment. Yet it is in the nature of the sun to scorch, and its scorching power seems natural to man. It shines equally on the just and the unjust, and allows useful creatures to flourish as well as the harmful. Therefore the sun is perfectly suited to represent the visible God of this world, i.e., the creative power of our own soul, which we call libido, and whose nature it is to bring forth the useful and the harmful, the good and the bad... Our physiological life, regarded as an energy process, is entirely solar.

The speaker of the Sermons calls the harmful effects of the Sun, the devil. In addition, there are two ambivalent gods—or, better, daimons—that he calls god-devils. Eros, as flame, is that which burns. "Earth-bound desire," writes Jung,[173] "sensuality in all its forms, attachment to the lures of this world, and the incessant dissipation of psychic energy in the world's prodigal variety, are the main obstacle to the development of a coherent and purposive attitude." Object relations have always been expressed symbolically in sexuality, which is why certain theories reduce all of the essential sexual functions to sexuality. "'Eros is a mighty daemon,' as the wise Diotima says to Socrates," quotes Jung,[174] "We shall never get the better of him, or only to our own hurt. He is not the whole of our inward nature, though he is at least one of its essential aspects."

If it were merely a physical drive, to be suppressed—that is, repressed—by Christian morality as depicted above, then the problem should have been taken care of given today's more liberal views. But to think this way would be to forget that morality is a function of the human psyche, not something brought down from Mt. Sinai on tablets and imposed on the people—as Jung pointed out to Neumann in the letter quoted above.[175] Morality is an instinctive counterbalance to behavior.

Toward the end of his life, Freud counterposed the pleasure principle to the destructive instinct, or the death drive. This is not a genuine opposition, because every beginning has an end anyway and every process is an energetic phenomenon, which feeds for its energy off the tension. The Sermon opposes eros to that which grows, which is striking insofar as Jung, late in life, opposed eros to logos.[176] The former describes the female consciousness, which is characterized by the binding force of eros, the relationship function. Logos, bearing on matters of discrimination and knowing, characterizes male consciousness. "In women...Eros is an expression of their true nature, while their Logos is often only a regrettable accident," because it is comprised, not of judgments but opinions. The latter are a priori assumptions, laying claim, as it were, to absolute truth. "In men, Eros...is usually less developed than Logos." In this undeveloped state, it clouds a man's judgment through resentment and sentimentality. In developed form, it lends an aspect of relationship and relatedness to male consciousness. Eros and logos represent two poles, like female and male, or yin and yang.

In his Late Thoughts,[177] Jung writes about eros from the distance of age:

In classical times, when such things were properly understood, Eros was considered a god whose divinity transcended our human limits, and who therefore could neither be comprehended nor represented in any way. I might, as many before me have attempted to do, venture an approach to this daimon, whose range of activity extends from the endless spaces of the heavens to the dark abysses of hell; but I falter before the task of finding the language which might adequately express the incalculable paradoxes of love. Eros is a kosmogonos, a creator and father-mother of all higher consciousness. I sometimes feel that Paul's words—"Though I speak with the tongues of men and of angels, and have not love"—might well be the first condition of all cognition and the quintessence of divinity itself. Whatever the learned interpretation may be of the sentence "God is love," the words affirm the complexio oppositorum of the Godhead. In my medical experience as well as in my own life I have again and again been faced with the mystery of love, and have never been able to explain what it is. Like Job, I had to "lay my hand on my mouth. I have spoken once, and I will not answer." (Job 40:4 f.)

Here is the greatest and smallest, the remotest and nearest, the highest and lowest, and we cannot discuss one side of it without also discussing the other. No language is adequate to this paradox. Whatever one can say, no words express the whole. To speak of partial aspects is always too much or too little, for only the whole is meaningful. Love "bears all things" and "endures all things" (1

Cor. 13:7). These words say all there is to be said; nothing can be added to them. For we are in the deepest sense the victims and the instruments of cosmogonic "love." I put the word in quotation marks to indicate that I do not use it in its connotations of desiring, preferring, favoring, wishing, and similar feelings, but as something superior to the individual, a unified and undivided whole. Being a part, man cannot grasp the whole. He is at its mercy. He may assent to it, or rebel against it; but he is always caught up by it and enclosed within it. He is dependent upon it and is sustained by it. Love is his light and his darkness, whose end he cannot see. "Love ceases not"—whether he speaks with the "tongues of angels," or with scientific exactitude traces the life of the cell down to its uttermost source. Man can try to name love, showering upon it all the names at his command, and still he will involve himself in endless self-deceptions. If he possesses a grain of wisdom, he will lay down his arms and name the unknown by the more unknown, ignotum per ignotius—that is, by the name of God. That is a confession of his subjection, his imperfection, and his dependence; but at the same time a testimony to his freedom to choose between truth and error.

Eros played a central role in Jung's life, beginning with a dream he had in childhood of an underground enthroned phallus[178]—Marie-Louise von Franz[179] offered a detailed interpretation of this, pointing to the significance it had in Jung's life. This early dream also contained the kernel of Jung's later break with Freud—it brought home to him that eros (as well as sexuality) represents a deus absconditus, a chthonic counterpart to the Christian God in heaven, manifest both biologically as a drive and intellectually as creativity.

Freud may have raised sexuality to the status of an omnipresent power. But for Freud—in accord with the materialist bias of the nineteenth century—it was an omnipresence understood exclusively in biological terms. "Basically, he wanted to teach," writes Jung,[180]

or so at least it seemed to me—that, regarded from within, sexuality included spirituality and had an intrinsic meaning. But his concretistic terminology was too narrow to express this idea. He gave me the impression that at bottom he was working against his own goal and against himself; and there is, after all, no harsher bitterness than that of a person who is his own worst enemy... Freud never asked himself why he was compelled to talk continually of sex, why this idea had taken such possession of him... He was blind toward the paradox and ambiguity of the contents of the unconscious, and did not know that everything which arises out of the unconscious has a top and a bottom, an inside and an outside.

Only in one sense do growth and eros form an opposition; for the rest they are compensatory. In an extended work, "The Philosophical Tree" (1945),[181] Jung showed how the process of psychological growth could be imagined like a tree or flower. This image is common among Christians in the form of a lighted Christmas tree. The historical parallels are so multifaceted that they represent the entire individuation process. Jung explains:[182]

In so far as the tree symbolizes the opus and the transformation process 'tam ethice quam physice' (both mentally and physically) it also signifies the life process in general. Its identity with Mercurius, the *spiritus vegetativus*, confirms this view. Since the opus is a life, death, and rebirth mystery, the tree as well acquires this significance and in addition the quality of wisdom, as we have seen from the view of the Barbeliots reported in Irenaeus: "From man [= Anthropos] and Gnosis is born the tree, which they also call Gnosis" (Adversus haereses, I, 29, 3) In the Gnosis of Justin, the angel Baruch, named the 'wood of life,' is the angel of revelation, just as the sun-and-moon tree in the Romance of Alexander[183] foretells the future. However, the cosmic associations of the tree as world-tree and world-axis take second place among the alchemists as well as in modern fantasies, because both are more concerned with the individuation process, which is no longer projected into the cosmos.

It may not be altogether apparent to lay persons how eros could be connected to the philosophical tree. It may take us too far afield to repeat what Jung said about it in the chapter, "The Rose-Colored Blood and the Rose,"[184] but I must include a portion of it here. He writes:[185]

It seems as though the rose-coloured blood of the alchemical redeemer was derived from a rose mysticism that penetrated into
alchemy, and that, in the form of the red tincture, it expressed the
healing or whole-making effect of a certain kind of Eros. The
strange concretism of this symbol is explained by the total absence
of psychological concepts... Since the stone represents the homo
totus, it is only logical for Dorn to speak of the "putissimus homo"
when discussing the arcane substance and its bloody sweat, for that
is what it is all about. He is the arcanum, and the stone and its parallel or prefiguration is Christ in the garden of Gethsemane. This
"most pure" or "most true" man must be no other than what he is,
just as the "argentum putum" is unalloyed silver; he must be entirely man, a man who knows and possesses everything human and is
not adulterated by any influence or admixture from without. This
man will appear on earth "only in the last days." He cannot be
Christ, for Christ by his blood has already redeemed the world
from the consequences of the Fall. Christ may be the "purissimus
homo," but he is not "putissimus." Though he is man, he is also
God, not pure silver but gold as well, and therefore not "putus."
On no account is it a question of a future Christ and salvator mi-
crocosmi, but rather of the alchemical servator cosmi (preserver of
the cosmos), representing the still unconscious ideal of the whole
and complete man, who shall bring about what the sacrificial death
of Christ has obviously left unfinished, namely the deliverance of
the world from evil. Like Christ he will sweat a redeeming blood,
but, as a "vegetabile naturae," it is "rose-colored"; not natural or
ordinary blood, but symbolic blood, a psychic substance, the manifestation of certain kind of Eros which unifies the individual as
well as the multitude in the sign of the rose and makes them whole,
and is therefore a panacea and an alexipharmic...

Love alone is useless if it does not also have understanding.
And for the proper use of understanding a wider consciousness is
needed, and a higher standpoint to enlarge one's horizon. That is
why Christianity as a historical force has not rested content with
admonishing man to love his neighbour, but has also performed a
higher cultural task, which is impossible to overestimate. It has educated man to a higher consciousness and responsibility. Certainly

love is needed for that, but a love combined with insight and understanding. Their function is to illuminate regions that are still dark and to add them to consciousness—regions in the outside world as well as those within, in the interior world of the psyche. The blinder love is, the more it is instinctual, and the more it is attended by destructive consequences, for it is a dynamism that needs form and direction. Therefore a compensatory Logos has been joined to it as a light that shines in the darkness. A man who is unconscious of himself acts in a blind, instinctive way and is in addition fooled by all the illusions that arise when he sees everything that he is not conscious of in himself coming to meet him from outside as a projection upon his neighbour.

Innumerable as the host of the stars is the number of gods and devils.

Each star is a god, and each space that a star filleth is a devil. But the empty-fullness of the whole is the pleroma.

The operation of the whole is Abraxas, to whom only the ineffective standeth opposed.

On this theme, Jung later comments:[186]

The hypothesis of multiple luminosities rests partly...on the quasi-conscious state of unconscious contents and partly on the incidence of certain images which must be regarded as symbolical. These are to be found in the dreams and fantasies of modern individuals, and can also be traced in historical records.

Hippolytus states about the Sethian Gnostics: "The Sethians, then, affirm that the theory concerning composition and mixture is constituted according to the following method: The luminous ray from above is intermingled, and the very diminutive spark is delicately blended in the dark waters beneath; and (both of these) become united, and are formed into one compound mass...[187] For a very diminutive spark, a severed splinter from above like the ray of a star, has been mingled in the much compounded waters of many (existences), as...(David) remarks in a psalm (Psalms 29:3)."[188]

The scintillae can be equated with the archetypes, which themselves possess a certain luminosity or similarity to consciousness, whereby the luminositas corresponds to a numinositas. For the alchemists, it is the vision of the glowing spark in the black arcana. "He beholds the darksome psyche as a star-strewn night sky, whose planets and fixed constellations represent the archetypes in all their luminosity and numinosity. The starry vault of heaven is in truth the open book of cosmic projection, in which are reflected the mythologems, i.e., the archetypes."[189]

Four is the number of the principal gods, as four is the number of the world's measurements.

One is the beginning, the god-sun.

Two is Eros; for he bindeth twain together and outspreadeth himself in brightness.

Three is the Tree of Life, for it filleth space with bodily forms. Four is the devil, for he openeth all that is closed. All that is formed of bodily nature doth he dissolve; he is the destroyer in whom everything is brought to nothing.

For me, to whom knowledge hath been given of the multiplicity and diversity of the gods, it is well. But woe unto you, who replace these incompatible many by a single god. For in so doing ye beget the torment which is bred from not understanding, and ye mutilate the creature whose nature and aim is distinctiveness. How can ye be true to your own nature when ye try to change the many into one? What ye do unto the gods is done likewise unto you. Ye all become equal and thus is your nature maimed.

The whole, as Jung stressed in many places in his work, is four: "Four is the number of the principal gods." It is represented spontaneously in the four directions of the compass, four seasons, four gospels or four evangelists, the four classical elements, four temperaments, four psychological types, etc. The number four thus represents a whole. Nor are all wholes of equal value. Four results from the development of a unity into a multiplicity, as Jung presented it in "A Psychological Approach to the Trinity."[190] Plato's Timaeus[191] begins with the words: "One, two, three, but where, my dear Timaeus, is the fourth...?" In Christianity, the godhead unfolds into the trinity. "But where is the fourth?" This is the question.

Evidently, there is a gap between three and four. The missing fourth thing is something more than merely an additional unity. It poses a difficulty: it exists both in opposition to the three, the trinity, and yet is also as the one that encompasses and completes it. An example of this is the Cabiri scene in Goethe's Faust, where it is said of this fourth, "he must stay yonder, since he for all must ponder." As the fourth function of consciousness, this is the one least accommodated or integrated; it is heavily contaminated by the unconscious and thus retains a degree of autonomy from consciousness. It often goes its own way to an astounding degree; because of the attachment to the unconscious, has about it something of the beyond, something ghostly. In the Christian trinity, the fourth is either the devil or the female. Here, too, it is clear that the reality of evil, as well as the female element, is still largely unconscious. This does not mean that they are any less real; on the contrary, they are more autonomous, and thus removed from the influence of the will. The steps from the one to the four correspond to a differentiation in consciousness. The movement has stretched over millennia of human history, and recapitulates itself in the life of the individual. Jung explains the one is the beginning, "the father," here father-son, which corresponds,[192]

> generally speaking, to a earlier state of consciousness when one was still a child, still dependent on a definite, ready-made pattern of existence which is habitual and has the character of law. It is a passive, unreflecting condition, a mere awareness of what is given, without intellectual or moral judgment...
>
> Legitimate detachment [of the son from the father] consists in conscious differentiation from the father and from the habitus represented by him. This requires a certain amount of knowledge of one's own individuality, which cannot be acquired without

moral discrimination and cannot be held on to unless one has understood its meaning. Habit can only be replaced by a mode of life consciously chosen and acquired... The third step, finally, points beyond the "Son" into the future, to a continuing realization of the "spirit," i.e., a living activity proceeding from "Father" and "Son" which raises the subsequent stages of consciousness to the same level of independence as that of "Father" and "Son"... Accordingly, the advance to the third stage means something like a recognition of the unconscious, if not actual subordination to it.

"One, as the first numeral, is unity," Jung states.[193] "But it is also 'the unity,' the One, All-Oneness, individuality and non-duality—not a numeral but a philosophical concept, an archetype and attribute of God, the monad." The Sun, as the beginning, signifies the origin of life; it is a symbol of the libido and of the collective consciousness. Eros is the combining force, which is needed because with the two, the one is divided, that is, becomes the opposition of the one and other and is what causes doubt to arise. The three, as the dynamic of life, leads the way out of the dilemma. Our space has three dimensions, and represents the reality of consciousness. The four closes the circle into a whole by returning to the beginning, for without destruction there would be no creation and no change. This devil is not evil as such, but the necessary counterpart to the creator.

Viewed from the perspective of energy, symbols most often correspond to a charge, which means that they are interchangeable for each other. The endless variety of symbols can actually be reduced to a very simple root, namely, libido and its characteristics. "But symbols are shaped energies, determining ideas whose affective power is just as great as their spiritual value."[194] On a primitive level, God is viewed as having a purely dynamic nature, that is, God is a divine force, one pertaining to physical and psychic health, to medicine, prosperity, and the fortunes of leadership, a pervasive and omnipresent force like Abraxas. On a higher level, the concentration of unconscious libidinal content gives rise, via the psychic powers of imagination, to a symbol, a God-image, an image of the intensity of life. This unconscious content is easily personified, as we see in general psychic tendency demonstrated by dreams, in which the various actors are each partial personalities.[195] As such, they do not yet have any relationship to the ego, representing instead autonomous complexes. Only to a limited extent is the ego able to impose its will on them, resulting in the existence of a differential in energy between the complex or the partial personality and the ego, which is experienced as divine "influence." This feeling of having been blessed has the character of the flow of life, where there is no resistance to the release of what has been stored up, where the famous "Heinzelmännchen" of German folklore—who are busy at night while people sleep—perform chores without any conscious effort on our part, where things happen "automatically," where spontaneous joy and desire take form. According to Jung,[196]

> This psychological simplification is in accord with the historical attempts of civilization to unify and simplify, in a higher synthesis, the infinite number of gods. We come across this attempt even in ancient Egypt, where the boundless polytheism of local-demon worship finally made simplification necessary. The various local gods, such as Amon of Thebes, Horus of the East, Horus of Edfu, Khnum of Elephantine, Atum of Heliopolis, etc., were all identified with the sun-god, Ra....
>
> A similar fate befell Hellenic and Roman polytheism, brought on by the syncretic strivings of the later centuries. Splendid evidence for this is given by the beautiful prayer of Lucius to the Queen of Heaven (the moon):
>
>> Queen of heaven, whether thou be named Ceres, bountiful mother of earthly fruits, or heavenly Venus, or Phoebus' sister, or Prosperina, who strikest terror with midnight ululations..., thou that with soft feminine brightness dost illume the walls of all cities (Apuleius, XI, 2) (cf. 5, 1-3).[197]
>
> These attempts to reunite the basic archetypes after polytheism had multiplied them into countless variants and personified them as separate gods prove that such analogies must forcibly have obtruded themselves at a fairly early date. Herodotus is full of references of this kind, not to mention the various systems known

to the Greco-Roman world. But the striving for unity is opposed by a possibly even stronger tendency to create multiplicity, so that even in strictly monotheistic religions like Christianity the polytheistic tendency cannot be suppressed. The deity is divided into three parts, and on top of that come all the heavenly hierarchies. These two tendencies are in constant warfare: sometimes there is only one God with countless attributes, sometimes there are many gods, who are simply called by different names in different places, and who personify one or the other attribute of their respective archetype.

The multiplicity of gods allows consciousness to keep the many aspects of the psyche in view, paying due tribute to each. This same phenomenon remains evident as the polytheistic religions of antiquity begin to be overlaid by Christian monotheism, and the old gods, no longer the objects of reverence, were demoted to the status of daemons, whose existence is further prolonged in magic.[198] Aspects that were no longer taken into consideration became negative and hostile to life. This is what happened to the Greek Pan who was once in charge of the nature's fruitfulness, but became a devil in the Christian middle ages. In the veneration of saints, Catholicism was able to absorb a remnant of polytheism, fending off the negative consequences of monotheism.

Equality shall prevail not for god, but only for the sake of man.

For the gods are many, whilst men are few. The gods are mighty and can endure their manifoldness. For like the stars they abide in solitude, parted one from the other by immense distances. But men are weak and cannot endure their manifold nature. Therefore they dwell together and need communion, that they may bear their separateness. For redemption's sake I teach you the rejected truth, for the sake of which I was rejected.

The collective unconscious is comprised of a large number of numinosities and luminosities, similar to the constellations filling the night sky; these luminosities corresponding to the archetypes. They are the energy centers of the field of the collective unconscious.[199] Consciousness emerges from them. A child's consciousness consists at first in a number of islands of consciousness, and only over time do these slowly merge together into a continent. The same occurs in daily life in the way that one knows something in one context, but not in another—thus, the right hand doesn't know what the left hand is doing. People take on different personas in different situations (ego-shadow-persona), like Dr. Jekyll and Mr. Hyde. For the archetypes to enter into consciousness, it is necessary that they become differentiated, even though their meanings overlap. In the individual, this creates the danger of dissociation, that is, the danger of disintegrating into various partial personalities. This inner multiplicity corresponds to the microcosmic nature of the individual.

This multiplicity is responsible for variation among individuals, which, if the whole being were not also reinforced, would deteriorate into a Babylonian chaos of languages. Hans Trüb's dream, in which he stands alone at the summit of a mountain, surrounded by other mountains, each with one person standing at the top (recounted above), is a warning against the isolation that can result from separation. The individual, in his absolute egoism, stands alone in the icy heights. The shared foundation—the "human, all-too human"—connects him to his fellows, preventing him from becoming a singular eccentric. This is why the path of individuation descends first into the lowlands of what is universally human. The shadow is just the lump of clay out of which the individual is created (Genesis 2:7). The danger of isolation exists precisely in the shadow, the aspects of personality that do not match up with the image one has of oneself, because one appears to oneself to be the "last" or the "ugliest man" (Nietzsche), until noticing that the others are no better, but are merely able to hide and compensate for their inferiority. But there is a great difference between wallowing around with the other members of the collectivity and becoming aware of the weakness that threatens to defeat the ego, which is what allows us to become companionable. This has a redemptive effect, and protects us from the conditions brought on by mass society.

As I mentioned above, Christ stripped from himself his shadow, and in doing so provided a model for what every Christian should do. In psychological terms, this means to repress the shadow, and—since it is a reality—to thereafter spend one's life struggling vainly against it. The new teaching of Jung's Basilides about confronting the "rejected truth" thus appears objectionable.

The multiplicity of the gods correspondeth to the multiplicity of man.

Numberless gods await the human state. Numberless gods have been men. Man shareth in the nature of the gods. He cometh from the gods and goeth unto god.

Thus, just as it serveth not to reflect upon the pleroma, it availeth not to worship the multiplicity of the gods. Least of all availeth it to worship the first god, the effective abundance and the summum bonum. By our prayer we can add to it nothing, and from it nothing take; because the effective void swalloweth all.

The bright gods form the celestial world. It is manifold and infinitely spreading and increasing. The god-sun is the supreme lord of that world.

The dark gods form the earth-world. They are simple and infinitely diminishing and declining. The devil is the earth-world's lowest lord, the moon-spirit, satellite of the earth, smaller, colder, and more dead than the earth.

There is no difference between the might of the celestial gods and those of the earth. The celestial gods magnify, the earth-gods diminish. Measureless is the movement of both.

The gods want to become human; they want to become conscious through humans and find realization. Since consciousness has emerged, human behavior is no longer being guided by instinct; humans are duty bound to realize all of the talents they have been given, which is to lend the gods expression through their lives. The individuation process is not only a process of becoming conscious, but just as much one of realizing inborn potentials. There is a clear distinction between "I do" and "I know what I am doing," and the realization of a mere potentiality through the deed.

When something is realized, it loses its libidinal investment, its charge. No longer is it a cause of invigoration, but becomes instead habitual and banal. Its potential has been spent. The idea that gods can flourish and die is alien to Christians. To Hindus this idea is quite familiar, in their pantheon and the doctrine of kalpas, or cosmic epochs. It is as if the Hindu could assume a particular standpoint in eternity, from which it was possible to follow the procession of archetypes. They come, determine an epoch, then make way for another. We have a similar idea in the astrological ages, when the equinox shifts from one sign to another in the zodiac. The zodiacal symbol is the archetype in the form of a constellation that determines the character of the age.[200]

Because light and dark are in balance, every action undertaken by an individual is compensated by the reaction of the other side. As noted above, Christianity had made an effort, without success, to venerate the summum bonum. Since the powers involved there are greater than the ego, people are unable to cope with them. This teaching in the Sermons appears to be a very pessimistic doctrine, similar to that of Gnosis.

Sermo V

The dead mocked and cried: Teach us, fool, of the church and holy communion.

The world of the gods is made manifest in spirituality and in sexuality. The celestial ones appear in spirituality, the earthly in sexuality.

Spirituality conceiveth and embraceth. It is womanlike and therefore we call it MATER COELESTIS, the celestial mother. Sexuality engendereth and createth. It is manlike, and therefore we call it PHALLOS, the earthly father.

The sexuality of man is more of the earth, the sexuality of woman is more of the spirit.

The spirituality of man is more of heaven, it goeth to the greater. The spirituality of woman is more of the earth, it goeth to the smaller.

Lying and devilish is the spirituality of the man which goeth to the smaller.

Lying and devilish is the spirituality of the woman which goeth to the greater.

Each must go to its own place.

Man and woman become devils one to the other when they divide not their spiritual ways, for the nature of creatura is distinctiveness.

The sexuality of man hath an earthward course, the sexuality of woman a spiritual. Man and woman become devils one to the other if they distinguish not their sexuality.

Man shall know of the smaller, woman the greater.

"Dogma takes the place of the collective unconscious by formulating its contents on a grand scale," writes Jung.[201] He restates the point further, in rather general theoretical terms:[202]

The Catholic way of life is completely unaware of psychological problems in this sense. Almost the entire life of the collective unconscious has been channeled into the dogmatic archetypal ideas and flows along like a well-controlled stream in the symbolism of creed and ritual. It manifests itself in the inwardness of the Catholic psyche. The collective unconscious, as we understand it today, was never a matter of "psychology," for before the Christian Church existed there were the antique mysteries, and these reach back into the grey mists of neolithic prehistory. Mankind has never lacked powerful images to lend magical aid against all the uncanny things that live in the depths of the psyche. Always the figures of the unconscious were expressed in protecting and healing images and in this way were expelled from the psyche into cosmic space.

It is in my view a great mistake to suppose that the psyche of a new-born child is a tabula rasa in the sense that there is absolutely nothing in it. In so far as the child is born with a differentiated brain that is predetermined by heredity and therefore individualized, it meets sensory stimuli coming from outside not with any aptitudes, but with specific ones, and this necessarily results in a particular, individual choice and pattern of apperception. These aptitudes can be shown to be inherited instincts and preformed patterns, the latter being the a priori and formal conditions of apperception that are based on instinct. Their presence gives the world of the child and the dreamer its anthropomorphic stamp. They are the archetypes, which direct all fantasy activity into its appointed paths and in this way produce, in the fantasy-images of children's dreams as well as in the delusions of schizophrenia, astonishing mythological parallels such as can also be found, though in lesser degree, in the dreams of normal persons and neurotics. It is not, therefore, a question of inherited ideas but of inherited possibilities of ideas. Nor are they individual acquisitions but, in the main, common to all, as can be seen from the universal occurrence of the archetypes.

Every archetype is capable of producing both positive, beneficial and negative, unfair effects. From among them, the speaker in the Sermons selects two, namely, spirituality and sexuality. He immediately renders them in symbolic terms, so that it appears we do not know what is meant by them—because they are transcendent in relation to consciousness. Traditionally, we identify heaven with the spiritual and paternal, and the earth with the material and maternal. Here, however, the intellectual is female in its representation, as a vessel or container, as "conception," and sexuality is male, as earth, as the actualizing force. "Archetypes are typical modes of apprehension," writes Jung,[203]

> and wherever we meet with uniform and regularly recurring modes of apprehension we are dealing with an archetype, no matter whether its mythological character is recognized or not.

Alchemy recognized these two complementary aspects of the process: it consisted of work in the laboratory, with all its contingencies of an emotional and daemonic nature, and in the oratorium, in which, by means of scientia or theoria, the opus was assessed and conducted, on the one hand, and the results were interpreted and integrated, on the other. The theoria of the alchemists does not correspond to what we mean by theory today.

The MATER COELESTIS is the maternal side of the godhead, which is not present in Christianity; it is a syzygy of the latter. Yet, while there is no female element in the trinity, holy scripture nonetheless contains abundant references to it. The female element is Wisdom in Proverbs 8:22-23; 30: "The Lord created me at the beginning of his work, the first of his acts of old. Ages ago I was set up, at the first, before the beginning of the earth...then I was there beside him, like a master workman [sic]." In the "Wisdom of Solomon," it is said that "the beginning of wisdom is the most sincere desire for instruction...is assurance of immortality (6: 17-18).[204]

In Ode 33 of the Odes of Solomon, Wisdom (Sophia) says: "I will enter into you, and will bring you forth from perdition, And make you wise in the ways of truth."[205]

In Gnosis, she plays a prominent role as Sophia, and likewise in alchemy as the world soul (anima mundi) or spirit of truth. It would take us too far afield to offer even a preliminary sketch of this figure here. For that I must refer the reader to the second volume of this work. She is the *inflatio* or *inspiratio* of the holy spirit, a clear opposition to the exclusively masculine holy spirit, because she includes within herself the element of eros. The best representation is found in the *Aurora consurgens* attributed to St. Thomas Aquinas,[206] a paraphrase of the Song of Songs. Jung found a part of the psychological significance of this figure reflected in the dogma of the Assumptio Mariae.

The mater coelestis and the Phallos are daemons—intermediate beings between the gods and humans. It is tempting to attribute their dynamic to humans themselves. "Although the strongest instincts undoubtedly demand concrete realization and generally enforce it," writes Jung,[207]

> they cannot be considered exclusively biological since the course they actually follow is subject to powerful modifications coming from the personality itself. If a man's temperament inclines him to a spiritual attitude, even the concrete activity of the instincts will

take on a certain symbolical character. This activity is no longer the mere satisfaction of the instinctual impulses, for it is now associated with or complicated by "meanings." In the case of purely syndromal instinctual impulses, which do not demand concrete realization to the same extent, the symbolical character of their fulfillment is all the more marked. The most vivid examples of these complications are probably to be found in erotic phenomenology. Four stages of eroticism were known in the late classical period: Hawwah (Eve), Helen (of Troy), the Virgin Mary, and Sophia. The series is repeated in Goethe's Faust: in the figures of Gretchen as the personification of the purely instinctual relationship (Eve), Helen as an anima figure; Mary as the personification of the "heavenly," i.e., Christian or religious, relationship; and the "eternal feminine" as an expression of the alchemical Sapientia. As the nomenclature shows, we are dealing with the heterosexual eros or anima-figure in four stages, and consequently with four stages of the Eros cult. The first stage—Hawwah, Eve, earth—is purely biological; woman is equated with the mother and only represents something to be fertilized. The second stage is still dominated by the sexual Eros, but on an aesthetic and romantic level where woman has already acquired some value as an individual. The third stage raises Eros to the heights of religious devotion and thus spiritualizes him: Hawwah has been replaced by spiritual motherhood. Finally, the fourth stage illustrates something which unexpectedly goes beyond the almost unsurpassable third stage: Sapientia. How can wisdom transcend the most holy and the most pure?—Presumably only by virtue of the truth that the less sometimes means the more. This stage represents a spiritualization of Helen and consequently of Eros as such. That is why Sapientia was regarded as a parallel to the Shulamite in the Song of Songs.

The other figure is the masculine-earthy Phallos. He corresponds roughly to a figure recognized by Hippolytus[208] in his report about the Naassenes. The mystery of Isis, he says, is nothing other than,

the seven-robed nature, encircled and arrayed with seven mantles
of ethereal texture—for so they call the planetary stars, allegorizing
and denominating them ethereal robes—is as it were the changeable generation, and is exhibited as the creature transformed by the
ineffable and unportrayable, and inconceivable and figureless one...
And this is the great and secret and unknown mystery of the universe, concealed and revealed among the Egyptians. For Osiris, (the
Naassene) says, it is in temples in front of Isis; and his pudendum
[phallus] stands exposed, looking downwards, and crowned with
all its own fruits of things that are made...and the Greeks, deriving
this mystical (expression) from the Egyptians, preserve it until this
day. For we behold [the] statues of Mercury, of such a figure honoured among them. Worshipping, however, Cyllenius with
especial distinction, they style him Logos. For Mercury is Logos,
who being interpreter and fabricator of the things that have been
made simultaneously, and that are being produced, and that will
exist, stands honoured among them, fashioned into some such figure as is the pudendum of a man, having an impulsive power from
the parts below towards those above.

We recall in this connection Jung's childhood dream of the enthroned,
underground phallus,[209] which I mentioned above. It is the underground counterpart to the Christian creator, a demiurge from out of
the depths. Male sexuality wants to beget and to actualize, especially in
the second half of life. Female sexuality, in the second half of life, seeks
spiritual creation. Male spirituality seeks to generalize the particular,
and to pose the question of meaning in the larger context. Female
spirituality must move on from the general to the particularities of
reality. If the man is petty, then he will become dishonest and devilish;
if the women generalizes too much, then she will overflow with plati-
tudes and clichés. These tendencies come to especially clear expression
in marital disputes. It is necessary for both partners in the relationship
to become conscious of their peculiarity and contrariness.

Man shall distinguish himself both from spirituality and from sexuality. He shall call spirituality Mother, and set her between heaven and earth. He shall call sexuality Phallos, and set him between himself and earth. For the Mother and the Phallos are superhuman daemons which reveal the world of the gods. They are for us more effective than the gods, because they are closely akin to our own nature. Should ye not distinguish yourselves from sexuality and from spirituality, and not regard them as of a nature both above you and beyond, then are ye delivered over to them as qualities of the pleroma. Spirituality and sexuality are not your qualities, not things which ye possess and contain. But they possess and contain you; for they are powerful daemons, manifestations of the gods, and are, therefore, things which reach beyond you, existing in themselves. No man hath a spirituality unto himself, or a sexuality unto himself. But he standeth under the law of spirituality and of sexuality.

No man, therefore, escapeth these daemons. Ye shall look upon them as daemons, and as a common task and danger, a common burden which life hath laid upon you. Thus is life for you also a common task and danger, as are the gods, and first of all terrible Abraxas.

These two archetypes, spirituality and sexuality, immeasurably exceed human consciousness. Thus they are never simply at the disposal of the individual. Because consciousness is limited, it runs the risk of transgressing its own boundaries by identifying itself with the one or the other. Simultaneous to the discovery of thought in classical philosophy came the idea, through various sophisms, that it was possible to overstep one's own boundaries. The Gnostics, on the other hand, revered Nous as divine spirit, which required them to draw a distinction between it and themselves. They could nevertheless make use of it to learn more about the riddle of the world. Modern philosophy resisted the limits Kant placed on thinking, Jung says, insisting instead that the human mind was,[210] able to pull itself up by its own bootstraps and know things that were right outside the range of human understanding. The victory of Hegel over Kant dealt the gravest blow to reason and the further development of the German and, ultimately, of the European mind, all the more dangerous as Hegel was a psychologist in disguise who projected great truths out of the subjective sphere into a cosmos he himself had created. We know how far Hegel's influence reaches today...

It is obvious that all philosophical statements which transgress the bounds of reason are anthropomorphic and have no validity beyond that which falls to psychically conditioned statements. A philosophy like Hegel's is a self-revelation of the psychic background and, philosophically, a presumption. Psychologically, it amounts to an invasion by the unconscious. The peculiar high-flown language Hegel uses bears out this view: it is reminiscent of the megalomanic language of schizophrenics, who use terrific spellbinding words to reduce the transcendent to subjective form, to give banalities the charm of novelty, or pass off commonplaces as searching wisdom. So bombastic a terminology is a symptom of weakness, ineptitude, and lack of substance. But that does not prevent the latest German philosophy from using the same crackpot power-words and pretending that it is not unintentional psychology.

The autochthonous reappearance of mythologems out of the collective unconscious is something we observe in the following case of a paranoid psychotics:[211] The patient was an elementary schoolteacher. He produced a doctrine about the primal father, possessed of enormous powers of procreation. At first the primal father had five hundred and fifty membra virilia, which were reduced over time to three. He also had three scrota, each with three testicles. He went into gradual decline caused by the massive production of sperm, until he ultimately shrunk to a clump weighing fifty centners, and was found locked in chains in a ravine. This mythologem contains the motifs of aging and the loss of procreative powers. The patient himself is either the rejuvenated primal father or his avatar. The overstepping of human boundaries in this story, while characteristic of mental illness, is by no means unique to it.

Archetypes and drives are powers existing in the psyche, which are responsible for the highest human accomplishments, but can likewise lead to ruin. The Sermons therefore calls them daemons, representing both a burden and a danger. Should the individual fail to maintain the proper boundaries, he can fall victim to them; he loses his sense of reality, becomes inflated in manner and unhuman. Illness is always simply an exaggeration of the normal, and thus exists the possibility of observing this phenomenon in daily life, when a person becomes obsessed by an archetype or a drive. Having lost track of everything but his own sense of worth, and unable to live normally in self-recognition, he instead propitiates himself with the mana of the archetype.

Keeping ourselves distinct from these powers is not as easy as it may appear. We are still primitive enough to think that we are the inventors of our thoughts. The expression that something "came to mind" can teach us that our ideas are just as much things that arrive in our brains from outside. Anytime we think creatively, as opposed to simply going about our daily lives, an unconscious mind is at work. We call this fantasy. The second half of life is by nature given over more to mental functions than to drives: from nature to culture, from drive to spirit. "Fantasy therefore seems to me," writes Jung,[212]

the clearest expression of the specific activity of the psyche. It is, preeminently, the creative activity from which the answers to all answerable questions come; it is the mother of all possibilities, where, like all psychological opposites, the inner and outer worlds are joined together in living union... Fantasy is for the most part a product of the unconscious. Though it undoubtedly includes conscious elements, it is none the less an especial characteristic of fantasy that it is essentially involuntary and, by reason of its strangeness, directly opposed to the conscious contents...

The relation of the individual to his fantasy is very largely conditioned by his relation to the unconscious in general, and this in turn is conditioned in particular by the spirit of the age. According to the degree of rationalism that prevails, the individual will be more disposed or less to have dealings with the unconscious and its products. Christianity, like every closed system of religion, has an undoubted tendency to suppress the unconscious in the individual as much as possible, thus paralyzing his fantasy activity.

Man is weak, therefore is communion indispensable. If your communion be not under the sign of the Mother, then is it under the sign of the Phallos. No communion is suffering and sickness. Communion in everything is dismemberment and dissolution.

Distinctiveness leadeth to singleness. Singleness is opposed to communion. But because of man's weakness over against the gods and daemons and their invincible law is communion needful. Therefore shall there be as much communion as is needful, not for man's sake, but because of the gods. The gods force you to communion. As much as they force you, so much is communion needed, more is evil.

In communion let every man submit to others, that communion be maintained; for ye need it.

In singleness the one man shall be superior to the others, that every man may come to himself and avoid slavery.

In communion there shall be continence. In singleness there shall be prodigality. Communion is depth.

Singleness is height.

Right measure in communion purifieth and preserveth.

Right measure in singleness purifieth and increaseth. Communion giveth us warmth, singleness giveth us light.

Humans are social beings. This may seem a simple statement, yet just as complex is the psychology of the community. "There is no better means of intensifying the treasured feeling of individuality than the possession of a secret which the individual is pledged to guard," Jung writes.[213]

The very beginnings of societal structures reveal the craving for secret organizations. When no valid secrets really exist, mysteries are invented or contrived to which privileged initiates are admitted. Such was the case with the Rosicrucians and many other societies... The need for ostentatious secrecy is of vital importance on the primitive level, for the shared secret serves as a cement binding the tribe together. Secrets on the tribal level constitute a helpful compensation for lack of cohesion in the individual personality, which is constantly relapsing into the original unconscious identity with other members of the group...

The secret society is an intermediary stage on the way to individuation. The individual is still relying on a collective organization to effect his differentiation for him; that is, he has not yet recognized that it is really the individual's task to differentiate himself from all the others and stand on his own feet... Nevertheless it may be that for sufficient reasons a man feels he must set out on his own feet along the road to wider realms. It may be that in all the garbs, shapes, forms, modes, and manners of life offered to him he does not find what is peculiarly necessary for him. He will go alone and be his own company. He will serve as his own group, consisting of a variety of opinions and tendencies—which need not necessarily be marching in the same direction. In fact, he will be at odds with himself, and will find great difficulty in uniting his own multiplicity [gods!] for purposes of common action...

A great many individuals cannot bear this isolation. They are the neurotics, who necessarily play hide-and-seek with others as well as with themselves, without being able to take the game really seriously. As a rule they end by surrendering their individual goal to their craving for collective conformity—a procedure which all the opinions, beliefs, and ideals of their environment encourage. Moreover, no rational arguments prevail against the environment. Only a secret which the individual cannot betray—one which he fears to give away, or which he cannot formulate in words, and which therefore seems to belong to the category of crazy ideas—can prevent the otherwise inevitable retrogression.

"Although the conscious achievement of individuality is consistent with man's natural destiny, it is nevertheless not his whole aim," writes Jung in another place.[214]

> It cannot possibly be the object of human education to create an anarchic conglomeration of individual existences. That would be too much like the unavowed ideal of extreme individualism, which is essentially no more than a morbid reaction against an equally futile collectivism. In contrast to all this, the natural process of individuation brings to birth a consciousness of human community precisely because it makes us aware of the unconscious, which unites and is common to all mankind. Individuation is an at-one-ment with oneself and at the same time with humanity, since oneself is part of humanity.

Isolation in egoism and massing together in the collective are the two opposed dangers threatening the individual. Jung devoted an entire chapter on the threat modern society poses to the individual in his essay "The Undiscovered Self."[215]

> The bigger the crowd the more negligible the individual becomes. But if the individual, overwhelmed by the sense of his own puniness and impotence, should feel that his life has lost its meaning—which, after all, is not identical with public welfare and higher standards of living—then he is already on the road to State slavery and, without knowing it or wanting it, has become its proselyte. The man who looks only outside and quails before the big battalions has nothing with which to combat the evidence of his senses and his reason. But that is just what is happening today: we are all fascinated and overawed by statistical truths and large numbers and are daily apprised of the nullity and futility of the individual personality, since it is not represented and personified by any mass organizations... In this way the individual becomes more and more a function of society, which in its turns usurps the function of the real life carrier, whereas, in actual fact, society is nothing more than an abstract idea like the State. Both are hypostatized, that is, have

become autonomous. The State in particular is turned into a quasi-animate personality from whom everything is expected.

Sermo VI

The daemon of sexuality approacheth our soul as a serpent. It is half human and appeareth as thought-desire.

The daemon of spirituality descendeth into our soul as the white bird. It is half human and appeareth as desire-thought.

The serpent is an earthy soul, half daemonic, a spirit, and akin to the spirits of the dead. Thus too, like these, she swarmeth around in the things of earth, making us either to fear them or pricking us with intemperate desires. The serpent hath a nature like unto woman. She seeketh ever the company of the dead who are held by the spell of the earth, they who found not the way beyond that leadeth to singleness. The serpent is a whore. She wantoneth with the devil and with evil spirits; a mischievous tyrant and tormentor, ever seducing to evilest company. The white bird is a half-celestial soul of man. He bideth with the Mother, from time to time descending. The bird hath a nature like unto man, and is effective thought. He is chaste and solitary, a messenger of the Mother. He flieth high above earth. He commandeth singleness. He bringeth knowledge from the distant ones who went before and are perfected. He beareth our word above to the Mother. She intercedeth, she warneth, but against the gods she hath no power. She is a vessel of the sun. The serpent goeth below and with her cunning she lameth the phallic daemon, or else goadeth him on. She yieldeth up the too crafty thoughts of the earthy one, those thoughts which creep through every hole and cleave to all things with desirousness. The serpent, doubtless, willeth it not, yet she must be of use to us. She fleeth our grasp, thus showing us the way, which with our human wits we could not find.

With disdainful glance the dead spake: Cease this talk of gods and daemons and souls. At bottom this hath long been known to us.

It is generally accepted that the serpent is a symbol of sexuality. But it is also much more than this. It is the image of the spinal cord and the lower nerve centers, and in this corresponds to,

> what is totally unconscious and incapable of becoming conscious, but which, as the collective unconscious and as instinct, seems to possess a peculiar wisdom of its own and a knowledge that is often felt to be supernatural... Its unrelatedness, coldness, and danger-ousness express the instinctuality that with ruthless cruelty rides roughshod over all moral and any other human wishes and consid-erations and is therefore just as terrifying and fascinating in its effects as the sudden glance of a poisonous snake.
>
> In alchemy the snake is a symbol of Mercurius non vulgi, which was bracketed with the god of revelation, Hermes. Both have a pneumatic nature. The serpens Mercurii is a chthonic spirit who dwells in matter, more especially in the bit of original chaos hidden in creation, the massa confusa or globosa.[216]

The snake signifies,

> psychic experiences that suddenly dart out of the unconscious and have a frightening or redeeming effect... The Gnostics favoured it because it was an old-fashioned symbol for the "good" genius loci, the Agathodaimon, and also for their beloved Nous... The snake does in fact symbolize "cold-blooded," inhuman contents and tendencies of an abstractly intellectual as well as a concretely ani-mal nature: in a word, the extra-human quality in man... It expresses his fear of everything inhuman and his awe of the sub-lime, of what is beyond human ken. It is the lowest (devil) and the highest (son of God, Logos, Nous, Agathodaimon).

"The snake symbolizes the numen of the transformative act as well as the transformative substance itself, as it particularly clear in alchemy," Jung writes elsewhere.[217]

> As the chthonic dweller in the cave she lives in the womb of moth-er earth, like the Kundalini serpent who lies coiled in the abdominal cavity... The image of the consuming change that dis-

solves the phenomenal world of individual psychic existence originates in the unconscious and appears before the conscious mind in dreams and shadowy premonitions. And the more unwilling the latter is to heed this intimation, the more frightening become the symbols by which it makes itself known. The snake plays an important role in dreams as a fear-symbol. Because of its poisonousness, its appearance is often an early symptom of physical disease. As a rule, however, it expresses an abnormally active or "constellated" unconscious and the physiological symptoms—mainly abdominal—associated therewith... The unconscious insinuates itself in the form of a snake if the conscious mind is afraid of the compensating tendency of the unconscious, as is generally the case in regression. But if the compensation is accepted in principle, there is no regression, and the unconscious can be met halfway through introversion.

The snake, as the presence of spirit in the material, represents, on the one hand, the same fascination it evinces, occasioning all the complications that come of projection. On the other, it stands for the fear of concrete reality, which would lead to full incarnation. The sermon thus designates it "wishful thinking." If the individual follows it in a careful and deliberate fashion, it becomes the guide to expanded consciousness. As long as we fail to recognize a projection, we are compulsively bound to the objects. Then our psyche and our values remain still in the external world. We have not yet extricated ourselves from the entanglements of our environment. We are plagued by fears and covetousness. Our personality is dissociated among a thousand worldly things. This is the courting of the world as a woman, seductive at first but afterward an empty trough full of worms.

We have already encountered the white bird in the dream Jung had a few years prior to writing the Septem Sermones.[218] I drew on material from Greek mythology to amplify the dream, and thus interpreted it. Now I add to the interpretation material from Jung's lifework. In his essay "The Psychological Aspects of the Kore,"[219] he reveals a whole series of dreams,[220] so that the one about the white bird no longer stands alone. These dreams are concerned with the idea of the anima, the "femme à homme" of male psychology, representing the highest and lowest, the spiritual and material, phantasmal and banal. Her theriomorphic forms refer to the fact that she is only part human. In dream four, she appears as a living Madonna figure: "Instead of a child, she holds in her arms a sort of flame or a snake or a dragon."

This son alludes to mystical and Gnostic speculation about the redemptive serpent and the nature of the redeemer as fire. In dream six, the behavior of a female snake is tender and insinuating, and she speaks in a human voice. Only "accidentally" does she have the form of a snake. In dream seven, it is a bird, speaking in the same voice, that proves helpful in trying to rescue the dreamer from a dangerous situation. As snake, she appears in a negative role, as bird in a positive one, making it clear that the two are related. In dream five, she is a "distinguished" woman clad in black, with red hair, kneeling in a dark chapel, with a fascinating air and surrounded by the spirits of the dead. The earthly serpent-soul in our text is related to the spirits of the dead, with whom it swarms around among earthly things, provoking our desire. As a female serpent, she seeks out the company of the dead who failed to find the way over into individual being. She is a spirit of the collectivity, the spirit of gravity, unable to lift herself above material reality.

She appears as a snake symbolizing mercury for the alchemists, at the start of work with the retort. She represents all the illusions of Maia, to whom we so easily fall victim only to withdraw all the more disappointed. Thus she is a whore, who tempts with empty promises in order, like Circe, to transform her victim into a pig, which explains why she makes her appearance in league with the devil and surrounded by evil spirits. She uses her fascination to seduce the man into the basest community, revealing herself as tyrant and torturer who knows how to entangle him in his own projections, which he is powerless to resist. She is the factor responsible for projections, as so beautifully depicted in Indian philosophy in the figure of Maia. It is she who produces the world of reality, the force manifest in the wonders of the universe. She is neither existent nor nonexistent, for her magical power vanishes the moment the truth breaks forth. By these means she draws the man into life and ensnares him, when because of his tie to the mother, he would prefer remaining in the realm of the possible. She is responsible for the innumerable complications and conflicts he encounters in life, until the insight dawns that his conscious knowledge is illusionary, and he begins to pull off the veils in which she has wrapped him.

In the Book Baruch by the Gnostic Justin,[221] the female power, Eden, is initially a virgin, but underneath a snake. She is the soul and the earth. Above her stands the "father of all becoming," Elohim, the spirit. The two figures ignite in mutual desire, the result of which is Adam, the first human. They each beget twelve angels, also called "trees." The "tree of life" is the third paternal angel, Baruch; the "tree of the knowledge of good and evil" is the third maternal angel, Naas (= snake). Naas gives Eden access to all manner of punishments to punish the spirit of Elohim in humanity. He commits adultery with Eve; he engages in homosexuality with Adam. From this moment on, mankind is dominated by evil and by good. This is why the soul is directed against spirit, and spirit against soul. They diverge from each other in their strivings, just as Elohim, in striving upward toward the "good," wanted to leave Eden behind.

The emphasis in this text is on the opposition between the female Melusine, signifying wishful thinking, and the male angel, who is a messenger from the mater coelestis (21, 10). In contrast to *wishful* thinking, he is *actual* thinking. He is a semi-divine soul of humanity, having temporarily descended to our level. In custom he remains with the mother, is chaste and lonely, and sees life by and large from a bird's-eye view, as Jung,[222] prior to the first dream, saw his own past life in overview. He is a spirit with a long temporal view of things. As an ephemeral spirit, he can fly off to underworld of the unconscious, achieving there a secret revitalization, which is what happened to Jung before the Septem Sermones. As noted above, Philemon played an important role in the fantasies that preceded the instructions, and he also figured in a dream: he appeared against the blue sky as a winged male being with the horns of a bull, holding "a bunch of four keys, one of which he clutched as if he were about to open a lock." Philemon, as Jung called him, was an illuminating and revelatory spirit, who

brought home to me the crucial insight that there are things in the psyche which I do not produce, but which produce themselves and have their own life. Philemon represented a force which was not myself. In my fantasies I held conversations with him, and he said things which I had not consciously thought. For I observed clearly that it was he who spoke, not I. He said I treated thoughts as if I generated them myself, but in his view thoughts were like animals in the forest, or people in a room, or birds in the air, and added, "If you should see people in a room, you would not think that you had made those people, or that you were responsible for them." It was he who taught me psychic objectivity, the reality of the psyche.

Through him the distinction was clarified between myself and the object of my thought. He confronted me in an objective manner, and I understood that there is something in me which can say things that I do not know and do not intend, things which may even be directed against me. Psychologically, Philemon represented superior insight.[223]

Jung's many Gnostic revelations, as well as much more, stemmed from this bird spirit, mediating between the individual and the "eternal heavenly queen" Sophia. As the white bird is in relation to the mater coelestis, so is the snake to the Phallus. It either uses guile to paralyze the individual's creative power, or incites it. These are ideas of unruly desire, which everywhere make their presence felt. They compel us to follow the snake. In Jung's fantasies, a black snake appeared with the male and the female figures of Elijah and Salome. Its presence, he wrote, signifies a heroic myth;[224] mythology teaches that the hero and the snake are related. The meaning here bears on the instinctive knowledge that guides the individual and leads him to his destiny.

Sermo VII

Yet when night was come the dead again approached with lamentable mien and said: There is yet one matter we forgot to mention. Teach us about man.

Man is a gateway, through which from the outer world of gods, daemons, and souls ye pass into the inner world; out of the greater into the smaller world. Small and transitory is man. Already is he behind you, and once again ye find yourselves in endless space, in the smaller or innermost infinity. At immeasurable dis-

tance standeth one single Star in the zenith.

This is the one god of this one man. This is his world, his pleroma, his divinity.

In this world is man Abraxas, the creator and the destroyer of his own world.

This Star is the god and the goal of man.

This is his one guiding god. In him goeth man to his rest. Toward him goeth the long journey of the soul after death. In him shineth forth as light all that man bringeth back from the greater world. To this one god man shall pray.

Prayer increaseth the light of the Star. It casteth a bridge over death. It prepareth life for the smaller world and assuageth the hopeless desires of the greater.

When the greater world waxeth cold, burneth the Star.

Between man and his one god there standeth nothing, so long as man can turn away his eyes from the flaming spectacle of Abraxas.

Man here, god there.

Weakness and nothingness here, there eternally creative power. Here nothing but darkness and chilling moisture.

There wholly sun.

Whereupon the dead were silent and ascended like the smoke above the herdsman's fire, who through the night kept watch over his flock.

At the end of the previous instruction, the dead claimed disdainfully that they had long known about gods, daemons, and souls. But now they lament having forgotten man, the most important part—how typical! This speaks to the attitude of Western Christianity in regard to God and human being. Jung explained:[225]

> The West lays stress on the human incarnation, and even on the personality and historicity of Christ, whereas the East says: "With-

out beginning, without end, without past, without future." The Christian subordinates himself to the superior divine person in expectation of his grace; but the Oriental knows that redemption depends on the work he does himself. The Tao grows out of the individual. The imitatio Christi has this disadvantage: in the long run we worship as a divine example a man who embodied the deepest meaning of life, and then, out of sheer imitation, we forget to make real our own deepest meaning—self-realization... The imitation of Christ might well be understood in a deeper sense. It could be taken as the duty to realize one's deepest conviction with the same courage and the same self-sacrifice shown by Jesus.

In a 1956 letter, Jung wrote: [226]

The significance of man is enhanced by the incarnation. We have become participants of the divine life and we have to assume a new responsibility, viz. the continuation of the divine self-realization which expresses itself in the task of our individuation. Individuation does not only mean that man has become truly human as distinct from animal, but that he is to become partially divine as well. This means practically that he becomes adult, responsible for his existence, knowing that he does not only depend on God but that God also depends on man. Man's relation to God probably has to undergo a certain important change: Instead of the propitiating praise to an unpredictable kind or the child's prayer to a loving father, the responsible living and fulfilling of the divine will in us will be our form of worship of and commerce with God. His goodness means grace and light and His dark side the terrible temptation of power.

   Obviously God does not want us to remain little children, looking to their elders to relieve them of their mission.

And in 1957 Jung wrote to a theologian, explaining:[227]

We are cornered by the supreme power of the incarnating Will. God really wants to become man, even if it rends him asunder. This is so no matter what we say... Christ said to his disciples "Ye are gods." The word becomes painfully true. If God incarnates in the empirical man, man is confronted with the divine problem. Being and remaining man he has to find an answer. It is the question of the opposites, raised at the moment when God was declared to be good only. Where then is his dark side? Christ is the model for the human answers and his symbol is the cross, the union of the opposites. This will be the fate of man, and this he must understand if he is to survive at all. We are threatened with universal genocide if we cannot work out the way of salvation by a symbolic death.

The human individual has always been regarded as the microcosm and image of the macrocosm, the universe. The close relationship that exists between the two is described by the term sympathia or correspondentia, signifying the acausal equivalence of events. Earlier, in the Indian Upanishads, we encountered the idea of Atman (world soul) and atman (individual soul), a derivative of the form that remains a part of it. In Chinese, Tao is an untranslatable term for the wholeness of the micro- and macrocosmos, the contingent.[228] This principle says that the whole is contained in the tiniest part of the human soul. For Pico della Mirandola, the world is one being, the corpus mysticum, as it were, of the visible God, as was the body of Christ for the church. Everything that happens in the world, as in an organism, exists in a reciprocal relationship of correspondences that cannot be derived from immanent causality. Because man is made in the image of God (Genesis 1:26), he is "the little God of the world," or the deus terrenus (earthly god), as it was put by the alchemists. Agrippa von Nettesheim held that "everything is filled with gods" and that these gods were distributed in things as divine forces. He believed that things in the underworld possessed a certain force in virtue of which they largely corresponded to the things of the upper world.

Translated into modern terms, the idea of the microcosm, which contains "the images of all creatures," represents the collective unconscious. According to Agrippa, the world soul is a "certain only thing, filling all things, bestowing all things, binding, and knitting together all things, that it might make one frame of the world."[229]

Following Jung's terminology, this sensible coincidence between inner and outer events has been termed synchronicity. It postulates an a priori sense in reference to human consciousness, which appears to exist outside the individual. A modern image of the world must be quaternary, illustrated roughly as follows:

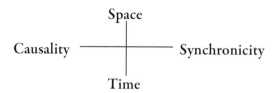

Formulated in this way as the principle of synchronicity, the old idea of micro-macrocosm obtained an empirical foundation. The human individual is in fact the portal between the outer and inner worlds.

The star is, first of all, the star of Bethlehem that showed the way to the wise men from the East to the new king (Matthew 2:2). In a letter to the Ephesians, Ignatius of Antioch writes of the coming of Christ: "How, then, was he manifested to the world? A star shone in heaven beyond the stars, and its light was unspeakable, and its newness caused astonishment, and all the other stars, with the sun and moon, gathered in chorus round this star..."[230] In the so-called Mithras liturgy, one prayer goes: "I am a star, wandering about with you, and shining forth out of the deep"[231] Balaam prophesizes: "I see him, but not now; I behold him, but not near. A star shall come out of Jacob and a scepter will rise out of Israel" (Numbers 24:17). Here the star symbolizes a singular personality.

In ancient Egypt, the stars were the "minions of Osiris," the lord of the underworld. The literature on the dead is replete with sayings about being placed among the stars in the beyond, in the hope of being reborn out of the body of the heavenly goddess.[232] When, during the funeral ceremonies for Julius Caesar, the Romans saw a comet (stella crinita), they took it for a sign that his soul had been taken in among the numina of immortal gods. Augustus himself found it convenient to regard the star's appearance as a favorable omen for himself, and had his helmet adorned with a star. After his death Caesar Augustus's head was lifted into the sky, to dispense favors to the prayerful from a distance.[233] People believed that the soul or the head of the dead emperor had ascended into heaven. It is an article of stoic faith that following death the soul, as fire or flame, rose into the sky.

Horace, taking up the ancient Greek daemon imagery, says in regard to the uniqueness of humans: "Only that spirit can know, who adjusts the affects of our birth-star (qui temperat astrum) / Mortal yet lord over natures of men (naturae deus humanae mortalis) as he walks at our side and / At his caprice makes particular characters cheerful or gloomy (vultu mutabilis, albus et ater)."[234] This recalls the conversation between Wallenstein and his confidant, Field Marshall Illo. Wishing to press the hesitant Wallenstein to action, while the latter awaited a favorable alignment of the stars, Illo declares, "The stars of destiny are in your heart."[235]

Of special interest to us, of course, is what the historical Basilides had to say about this image, as reported by Hippolytus:

> And so there will be the restitution of all things [apokatastasis] which, in conformity with nature, have from the beginning a foundation in the seed of the universe, but will be restored at (their own) proper periods. And that each thing, says (Basilides), has its own particular times, the Saviour is a sufficient (witness) when He observes, "Mine hour is not yet come." And the Magi (afford similar testimony) when they gaze wistfully upon the (Saviour's) star. For (Jesus) Himself was, he says, mentally preconceived at the time of the generation of the stars, and of the complete return to their starting-point of the seasons in the vast conglomeration (of all germs). This is, according to these (Basilidians), he who has been conceived as the inner spiritual man in what is natural (now this is the Sonship which left there the soul, not (that it might be) mortal, but that it might abide here according to nature, just as the first Sonship left above in its proper locality the Holy Spirit, (that is, the spirit) which is conterminous)—(this, I say, is he who has been conceived as the inner spiritual man, and) has then been arrayed in his own peculiar soul.[236]

Basilides' ancient Gnostic doctrine of the three sonships is of particular interest in the present context. According to the text, the third sonship, which remains behind in the formlessness of the world, will be restored "in its time," that is, will be absorbed into the pleroma. There is every reason to suspect the "gravitational body" in this, which is in need of redemption or awakening because it is the light concealed inside material things. This is the "hidden spiritual man," the star, which has taken on a mortal soul.

Among the Nazarene Gnostics, as again reported by Hippolytus,[237] this is called the

> Invisible Point [ameristos stigmé] from which what is least begins to increase gradually. That which is...nothing, and which consists of nothing, inasmuch as it is indivisible...will become through its own reflective power a certain incomprehensible magnitude. This, he says, is the kingdom of heaven, the grain of mustard seed [Matthew 13:31], the point which...no one knows...save the spiritual only.

This point brings together the infinite and the infinitesimal, the macrocosmos and microcosm. Only the spiritual men recognize it, and it is simultaneously that within them which is capable of this knowledge.

Jung taught, "The realization of the self also means a reestablishment of Man as the microcosm, i.e., man's cosmic relatedness. Such realizations are frequently accompanied by synchronistic events."[238] He parenthetically added, "The prophetic experience of vocation belongs to this category." He says elsewhere, in summary: "The star stands for the transcendent totality."[239] As a commentary to one of his own pictures, he writes:[240]

> The sun, too, is a star, a radiant cell in the ocean of the sky. The picture shows the self appearing as a star out of chaos. The four-rayed structure is emphasized by the use of four colours. This picture is significant in that it sets the structure of the self as a principle of order against chaos.

These proverbial locutions are always explained from the perspective of astrology, as if a single star were not sufficient to stand as a person's destiny and inner guide. According to popular belief, for every person there is a star in the heavens that appears with birth and upon death either falls or sets. Thus people say things like "his star is falling" when someone's luck wears out or his fame diminishes. Or, his star "hasn't risen yet" or "is rising," when a person's time has not yet come, or his

success is just beginning to be apparent. A "star" is what we call someone who has become famous for some accomplishment, a successful
artist, for example. We speak of people's "lucky star," which accompa-
nies them through life or through a specific period. The fortunate child
is "born under a lucky star." Being "guided by a lucky star," means to
have achieved some unanticipated success. To be "under a bad star" is to
suffer bad luck or failure. The seafarer is "lit by a star" when he does not
lose his way. "To reach for the stars" is to want something impossible,
to set one's sites too high. At the same time, someone who has fallen in
love "plucks a star from the sky" for the beloved.[241]

The sole and impossibly distant star at its zenith is the transcendental particularity of a person—the expression and symbol of the
eternal in the individual, which stands superior to mortality and provides orientation and hope through the vagaries of life. This is his
God—his individual God, his leader and his goal—that shines for him
beyond death. Prayer enhances the light of the star: it elucidates it by
the concentration of spirit. By withdrawing projections from the great
world, the world becomes unattractive and cold. The individual and his
own one God finally become one, insofar as the drivenness of life
(Abraxas) ceases. Out of the weakness, vanity, darkness, and dank
coldness of the individual, there arises the eternal creativity and light of
his God.

By way of this quite personal God, the unredeemed dead ascend
like smoke, because they have received an answer to their burning
question.

I do not claim to have here offered an exhaustive interpretation of
the *Septem Sermones ad Mortuos*—a complete interpretation can only
be conveyed by the life and work of Jung himself. However, I do hope
that my interpretation has given readers a clearer sense of the development of Jung's psychology. I also hope it has prepared the ground for
the next volume of this work, which is dedicated to Jung's understanding of Gnosis and alchemy.

Notes and Bibliography

Notes

Editorial Note: This English edition is based on a translation of the original work prepared by Don Reveau; it incorporates minor revisions to the German edition. The primary Gnostic texts cited by Dr. Ribi, including the Nag Hammadi Codices, and the writings of Irenaeus and Hippolytus, are all available online at: gnosis.org/library.

Foreword (by Lance S. Owens)

[1] Letter of Nov 13, 1960. Eugene Rolfe, *Encounter with Jung* (Boston: Sigo Press, 1989), 158.

[2] C. G. Jung, *The Red Book: Liber Novus*, ed. Sonu Shamdasani, tr. John Peck, Mark Kyburz, and Sonu Shamdasani (New York: W.W. Norton & Co, 2009). (Hereafter, *Liber Novus.*)

[3] Jung usually employed the German term *die Gnosis* in his references to the historical tradition; the word can be translated in English either as *Gnosis* or *Gnosticism*. However, specialists in Gnostic studies have recently questioned usage of the generic term "Gnosticism," arguing that the word did not exist anciently; it was a polemical term coin in the seventeenth century by Protestant theology. Over subsequent centuries, the term became synonymous with "heresy"—a pervasive bias strongly rejected by most current scholarship. Historians point out that many second-century Gnostics simply considered themselves Christians; others were called (and called themselves) *gnostikoi*, "Gnostics." I will preferential employ the term "Gnosis" in reference to the tradition, following a usage common in European languages, and generally avoid the polemical term Gnosticism. By "classical Gnostic tradition," I refer to manifestations in the first three centuries CE. See, Karen L. King, *What Is Gnosticism?* (Cambridge: Harvard University Press, 2003), 15ff; Michael Williams, *Rethinking Gnosticism* (Princeton: Princeton University Press, 1996), 51ff; and the balanced response to this terminological controversy in, Marvin W. Meyer & Willis Barnstone, eds., *The Gnostic Bible* (Boston: Shambhala, 2003), 8-16.

[4] C. G. Jung, *Memories, Dreams, Reflections*, ed. Aniela Jaffe (Rev. ed., Pantheon, 1993), 201. (Hereafter, MDR.)

[5] Ribi gives the first detailed summary of Jung's alchemical notebooks, 138ff. The bibliography provides a catalog description of the notebooks. Several photographs of the notebooks appear in, Sonu Shamdasani, *C. G. Jung: A Biography in Books* (New York: W.W. Norton, 2012), 172-88. (Hereafter, *Biography in Books.*)

[6] As a result of this study, Dr. Ribi's library contains a comprehensive collection of the manuscript facsimiles and translations of the Nag Hammadi Gnostic texts; it may

comprise one of the most extensive collections of Nag Hammadi related publications in private collection.

[7] Stephan A. Hoeller, *The Gnostic Jung and the Seven Sermons to the Dead* (Wheaton, IL: Quest, 1982); Stephan A. Hoeller, *Jung and the Lost Gospels* (Wheaton, IL: Quest, 1989); Stephan A. Hoeller, *Gnosticism: New Light on the Ancient Tradition of Inner Knowing* (Wheaton, IL: Quest, 2002).

[8] Marvin Meyer, ed., *The Nag Hammadi Scriptures: The International Edition* (HarperSanFrancisco, 2007).

[9] Marvin W. Meyer, *The Gnostic Gospels of Jesus* (San Francisco: HarperSanFrancisco, 2005), xxiv.

[10] I can give here just a few short examples. In his first recorded seminar at Polzeath, Cornwall in 1923 Jung stated: "Since the world war, the collective unconscious has been constellated as it has not been since the beginning of our era when the world was in a similar state of flux. At that time Gnosticism arose. This came directly from the unconscious; and Christianity was one of the products of Gnosticism. The psychological condition of that time shows remarkable parallelism with our own times." Typescript notes by M. Esther Harding, "Cornwall Seminar given by Carl Gustav Jung, July 1923, Polzeath, Cornwall, England." Beinecke Library, Yale University. In the 1928 seminar he comments, "For the time being we are concerned with the understanding of the unconscious, because we cannot decently live any more without consciousness. That understanding is gnosis..." C. G. Jung, William McGuire, ed.; *Dream Analysis: Notes of the Seminar Given in 1928-1930* (Princeton: Princeton University Press, 1984). In 1933 Jung recommends to his seminar group a reading of G. R. S. Mead's classic compilation of Gnostic literature, *Fragments of a Faith Forgotten* – a work Jung had first studied around 1915. C. G. Jung, *Visions: Notes of the Seminars Given in 1930-1934* (Princeton, 1997), 237-8.

[11] Shamdasani, *Biography in Books*, 121.

[12] H. G. "Peter" Baynes knew well about Jung's Gnostic associations. After Baynes prepared the English translation of the *Seven Sermons to the Dead*, Jung gave him a painting done in the artistic style used in his Red Book, titled "Septem Sermones ad Mortuos." Jung also presented Baynes with an ancient Gnostic gem ring similar to Jung's own; Baynes wore it for the rest of his life. Diana Baynes Jansen, *Jung's Apprentice: A Biography of Helton Godwin Baynes* (Einsiedeln: Daimon Verlag, 2003). A 1943 picture of Baynes wearing the ring appears as frontispiece to the book.

[13] The last disciples to work personally with Jung arrived in a period when his lectures and publications centered on alchemy, and this undoubtedly influenced perceptions about the foundation of his work. Perhaps the most important figure among that final generation was Marie-Louise von Franz, Jung's indispensable collaborator throughout his research into alchemical literature from the late-1930s onward. After Jung's death, Dr. von Franz naturally became a formative force in the perpetuation of his work; she

remained a major influence at the C. G. Jung Institute training program in Zurich up until her death in 1998. Her erudition and close association with Jung's alchemical studies also underscored the role of alchemy as an historical focal point for Jungian commentary, at least in its classical formation. Dr. Ribi commented to me that while von Franz "of course knew everything Jung said about Gnosticism," she never independently studied the Gnostic texts. (Private communication.)

[14] "The main interest of my work is not concerned with the treatment of neurosis, but rather with the approach to the numinous. But the fact is that the approach to the numinous is the real therapy, and in as much as you attain to the numinous experience, you are released from the curse of pathology. Even the very disease takes on a numinous character." Aniela Jaffé, *Was C. G. Jung a Mystic? And Other Essays.* (Einsiedeln: Daimon Verlag, 1989), 16.

[15] Ferne Jensen, ed.; *C.G. Jung, Emma Jung Toni Wolff: A Collection of Remembrances* (The Analytical Psychology Club of San Francisco, 1982), 25.

[16] Martin Buber, *Eclipse of God: Studies in the Relation Between Religion and Philosophy* (Atlantic Highlands, NJ: Humanities Press International, reprint 1988).

[17] In his reply to Buber, Jung rejected the epithet of "Gnostic" as a theological categorization, denied any metaphysical or theological presumptions motivating his empirical psychology, and downplayed his private distribution of the *Seven Sermons* as a "sin of my youth." Of course, one notes Jung was forty-one years old in 1916 when he printed the *Septem Sermones ad Mortuos*, and around forty-seven when he allowed H.G. "Peter" Baynes to translate and print the Sermons in English. Jung continued sharing copies with appropriate people into his old age. Though unknown in previous years, the Sermons formed a summary revelation to the mythopoetic experience recorded in *Liber Novus*. C. G. Jung, "Religion and psychology: A reply to Martin Buber" (1952), CW 18, 663-70. [All citations to *The Collected Works of C. G. Jung* (CW) are listed by volume and page number.]

[18] Stephan A. Hoeller, *The Gnostic Jung and the Seven Sermons to the Dead* (Wheaton, IL: Quest, 1982).

[19] "We are at war because that which we consider 'sacred' in our work is under attack *from within*. In this sense it is like a 'Holy War' ... the current third generation battle within the Jungian community is about who gets to tell the 'true' Jungian story and which clan passes on the legitimate Jungian lineage." Barbara D. Stephens, "The Martin Buber-Carl Jung disputations: protecting the sacred in the battle for the boundaries of analytical psychology." *Journal of Analytical Psychology*, 2001, 46, 457.

[20] "Response to Barbara Stephens," *Journal of Analytical Psychology*, 2002, 47:481.

[21] C. G. Jung, *Symbols of Transformation*, CW 5, xxv. The introduction for this revised edition, published in 1956, is signed and dated September 1950.

[22] Ibid.

[23] C. G. Jung, *Psychological Types*, CW 6, 169.

[24] MDR, 189.

[25] MDR, 192.

[26] 30 Jan 1948; Ann Conrad Lammers & Adrian Cunnigham, eds., *The Jung–White Letters* (New York: Routledge, 2007), 117.

[27] C. G. Jung, *Collected Papers on Analytical Psychology* (New York: Moffat Yard and Co., 1917), 443–4.

[28] *Liber Novus*, 222.

[29] *Liber Novus*, 230.

[30] MDR, 4.

[31] *Liber Novus,* 252

[32] *Liber Novus,* 305 n229.

[33] Kurt Plachte was a little-noted theologian and Protestant minister. After surviving four years as a German soldier in World War I, he studied philosophy with Ernst Cassirer in Hamburg; his thesis on Johann Gottlieb Fichte was published in 1922. Plachte's interests seem to have focused on the interplay of symbol and religion; he paraphrased portions of Jung's comment on the "symbol as sensuously perceptible expression" in an essay on Fichte published a few years after this letter. Due to his criticism of National Socialism he was arrested and barred from the ministry in 1936; he died in 1964. Christoph Asmuth, "Wie viele Welten braucht die Welt?: Goodman, Cassirer, Fichte," *Die Philosophie Fichtes im 19. und 20. Jahrhundert.* (Amsterdam: Rodopi, 2010), 63-83.

[34] Gerhard Adler, ed., *C. G. Jung: Letters* (Princeton: Princeton University Press, 1975), vol. 1, 61.

[35] Ibid.

[36] "Psychology and Literature", CW 15, 98.

[37] MDR, 200.

[38] Ibid.

[39] Ibid.

[40] These dates correlate with other evidence presented here. Shamdasani, *Biography in Books*, 122; for dates of military service and Gnostic readings, see also *Liber Novus*, 206; 337 n22.

[41] *Liber Novus,* vii.

[42] These primary records include not only the text of *Liber Novus*, but also the Black Book journals and numerous other archival documents, as referenced and quoted by Sonu Shamdasani in the editorial apparatus to the published edition of *Liber Novus*.

[43] For a summary of the compositional chronology of the sections of *Liber Novus,* see Sonu Shamdasani's "Editorial Note", *Liber Novus,* 225ff.

[44] Barbara Hannah, *Jung: His Life and Work* (New York: G. Putnam's Sons, 1976), 114. Emphasis in the original.

[45] In MDR Jung notes that he first read through the Gnostic texts available in 1911 while working on *Wandlungen und Symbole der Libido*, but was then not able to make much sense of it all. MDR, 163; see also, CW 5, xiii-xxiv.

[46] *Liber Novus*, 232. In his journal, he wrote: "Meine Seele, meine Seele, wo bist du?" A photograph of this journal page appears in Shamdasani, *Biography in Books*, 65.

[47] *Liber Novus*, 207.

[48] A Latin edition appeared in 1859 and this was the edition commonly cited for the next fifty years: L. Duncker & F. G. Schneidewin, ed., *Refutatio Omnium Hæresium* (Göttingen, 1859). The first critical edition in German is: P. Wendland, *Hippolytus Werke III. Refutatio omnium haeresium* (Leipzig, 1916); Jung acquired this edition after 1916 and cited it in his later works. An early English edition appeared in: Macmahon, J. H., Salmond, S. D. F. Transl. *The Refutation of all Heresies by Hippolytus with Fragments from his Commentaries on Various Books of Scripture.* (Edinburgh: T. & T. Clark, 1868); Jung read a 1911 printing of this work around 1939, as indicated by notes made in his alchemical notebook (see Ribi's discussion, 138ff). The first critical English edition is: F. Legge, ed.; *Philosophumena or the Refutation of all Heresies* (London: Soc. for Promoting Christian Knowledge, 1921), and this volume is generally quoted in the English edition of Jung's Collected Works.

[49] Gérard Vallée; *A study in anti-Gnostic polemics: Irenaeus, Hippolytus, and Epiphanius* (Wilfrid Laurier Univ. Press, 1981), 41-2.

[50] Jung eventually read Hippolytus in primary editions; however it is likely his first encounter with Hippolytus came from excerpts in the secondary literature here cited. See supra, note 48.

[51] Wolfgang Schultz, *Dokumente der Gnosis* (Jena: E. Diederichs, 1910).

[52] G. R. S. Mead, *Fragments of a Faith Forgotten* (London: Theosophical Publishing Society, 1900, reprint 1906). Jung had the 1906 edition.

[53] G. R. S. Mead, *Simon Magus: An Essay on the Founder of Simonianism Based on the Ancient Sources With a Re-Evaluation of His Philosophy and Teachings* (London: The Theosophical Society, 1892). The copy in Jung's library contains the library stamp of the H.P.B. (Helena Petrovna Blavatsky) Theosophical Lodge in London, to which Mead belonged. It is unknown how Jung acquired a book from this elite English Theosophical lodge's library, nor what sum of overdue lending fees might now have accumulated.

[54] I offer my thanks to Andreas Jung for his hospitality and assistance – and for our hours of conversation – during my research in Jung's library collection.

[55] Several examples of Jung's marginalia are photographically illustrated in Shamdasani, *Biography in Books*.

[56] This comment is based entirely on anecdotal reports from individuals who are familiar with Jung's library and who have examined large numbers of the books in it. None of them had, however, noted the marginalia in this specific book. Private communications.

[57] Schultz quotes the 1859 edition of Hippolytus, *Refutatio Omnium Haeresium*, ed. Duncker & Schneidewin (Göttingen 1859); this is the same edition used by G.R.S. Mead. Nine of the nineteen chapters in *Dokumente der Gnosis* are based principally on texts preserved by Hippolytus (chapters on Justinus, the Naasenes, the Perates, the Sethians, the Docetists, Simon Magus, Basilides, the School of Basilides, and Marcus). Three are based principally on material found in Irenaeus (on the Ophites, Carpocrates and the Valentinians), two on the *Acts of Thomas*, and one on the *Acts of John*. Chapters on Abraxas and Mithras are based on the work of A. Dieterich (Jung had already studied Dieterich prior to 1911, as cited in *Wandlungen*), and the chapter on Poimandres is based on R. Reitzenstein's work. One chapter is dedicated to Jewish Midrash, citing Jellinek. See, "Nachweis der Quellen", *Dokumente der Gnosis*, 231-41.

[58] Chapter 1 of *Psychological Types* (CW 6) is particularly indebted to material found in Schultz. *Psychological Types* was published in 1921; on the date of its composition, Shamdasani notes, "There is a gap between July 1919 and February 1920 in *Black Book 7*, during which time Jung was presumably writing *Psychological Types*." *Liber Novus*, 305 n230.

[59] The frontispiece art in Schultz's book is based on an engraved Gnostic gem reproduced in Charles King, *The Gnostics and Their Remains* (2nd edition, 1887), 41. Jung had this book in his library. Jung's "Gnostic ring" shows a similar motif, a serpent coiled in a "figure of 8," with a raised head that is surrounded by a crown of eight rays. This specific figure, known as the *Agathodaimon* was associated with Alexandria; a similar figure to the one on Jung's ring is found on examples of Roman imperial coinage minted at Alexandria in the mid-second century.

[60] The dated image of Izdubar appears on folio 36 in the Red Book.

[61] Jung's first citations of Mead are in *Wandlungen und Symbole der Libido* (1912), where he quotes Mead's *A Mithraic Ritual* (London: Theosophical Publishing Society, 1907), and his translation of the Upanishads, G.R.S. Mead and J. C. Chattopadhyaya, *The Upanishads* (London: Theosophical Publishing Society, 1896).

[62] Jung's debt to G.R.S. Mead deserves, and still awaits, a proper evaluation. Mead's writings on Gnosis, which often reflected an astute psychological understanding of the tradition, were uniquely valuable to Jung. Jung had some of Mead's book by 1911, and eventual his library contained a nearly complete collection of Mead's publications, including the several short books published under the series title *Echoes from the Gnosis* (1906-8), and Mead's journal *Quest,* published from 1909 until 1930. Jung quoted most of these works at one time or another in his publications and/or seminars; in addition, at several places in his writings he reflects insightful comments found in Mead's work without giving Mead a citation. An unpublished correspond-

ence between Mead and Jung is preserved in the Jung Archive, ETH. Perhaps indicative of his repect for Mead, around 1930 Jung made a special effort to visit him in London and personally thank him for his work; at the time Mead was both infirm and impoverished. Mead died in 1933. (An account of this visit was conveyed by Jung to Gilles Quispel, who related it to Stephan Hoeller in 1977. Personal communication, Stephan Hoeller.)

[63] C. G. Jung, *Visions: Notes of the Seminars Given in 1930-1934* (Princeton: Princeton Univ. Press, 1997), 237-8.

[64] MDR, 184.

[65] Irenaeus, *Contra Haereses*, I. xxiii. 1-4.

[66] In Greek the word ἐπίνοια (epinoia) has feminine gender and implies both "what is on the mind" and "were it leads;" thus, the fact of thought and the result of conceiving thought.

[67] Irenaeus, *Contra Haereses*, I. xxiii. 2: "He took round with him a certain Helen, a hired prostitute from the Phoenician city Tyre, after he had purchased her freedom, saying that she was the first conception (or Thought) of his Mind, the Mother of All, by whom in the beginning he conceived in his Mind the making of the Angels and Archangels. That this Thought, leaping forth from him, and knowing what was the will of her Father, descended to the lower regions and generated the Angels and Powers, by whom also he said this world was made. And after she had generated them, she was detained by them through envy, for they did not wish to be thought to be the progeny of any other. As for himself, he was entirely unknown by them; and it was his Thought that was made prisoner by the Powers and Angels that has been emanated by her. And she suffered every kind of indignity at their hands, to prevent her reascending to her Father, even to being imprisoned in the human body and transmigrating into other female bodies, as from one vessel into another."

[68] Mead, *Fragments of a Faith Forgotten*, 168. Jung essentially quotes Mead on this point (without citation) in *Mysterium Coniunctionis*, where Jung states the text, "describes a *coniunctio Solis et Lunae*." CW 14, 136.

[69] *Liber Novus*, 236.

[70] *Liber Novus*, 248.

[71] *Liber Novus*, 248, 251 n201, 254 n238. Much later he explaining that, "by Eros I meant the placing into relation." *Mysterium Coniunctionis*, CW 14, 179.

[72] *Liber Novus*, 368.

[73] *Liber Novus*, 233 n49.

[74] *Aion*, CW 9ii, 22. In 1930, Jung related how great poetic creations such as *Shepherd of Hermas*, *The Divine Comedy* and *Faust* all relate, "a preliminary love-episode which culminates in a visionary experience. ...We find the undisguised personal love-episode not only connected with the weightier visionary experience but actually subordinated

to it." ("Psychology and Literature," CW 15, 94.) In 1927 he stated, "Christian and Buddhist monastic ideals grappled with the same problem, but always the flesh was sacrificed. Goddesses and demigoddesses took the place of the personal, human woman who should carry the projection of the anima." ("Mind and Earth," CW 10, 40.) Such remarks may be a reference to Jung's empirical observations about his own experience.

[75] He continues, "In the legend of Simon...anima symbols of complete maturity are found." "Mind and Earth," CW 10, 40. In *Mysterium Coniunctionis* Jung speaks of the alchemical workers, "who in the symbolical realm are Sol and Luna, in the human the adept and his soror mystica, and in the psychological realm the masculine consciousness and feminine unconscious (anima)." He notes first among the classic examples of this, "Simon Magus and Helen." CW 14, 153 and n317.

[76] Jung's commentary on this "remarkable" passage extends over the next pages. In commentary, Jung repeats without citation Mead's 1900 interpretation of Simon as "Sun" and Helena as "Moon;" Jung claims that this text, "describes a *coniunctio Solis et Lunae.*" *Mysterium Coniunctionis*, CW 14, 136 (Greek terms have been transliterated.) For Mead's translation and commentary, probably read by Jung in 1915, see *Fragments of a Faith Forgotten,* 123.

[77] Hippolytus, *Elenchos,* VI.12. Translation by Mead, *Simon Magus.*

[78] "But if it remain in potentiality only, and its imaging is not perfected, then it disappears and perishes, he says... For potentiality when it has obtained art becomes the light of generated things, but if it does not do so an absence of art and darkness ensues, exactly as if it had not existed at all; and on the death of the man it perishes with him." Hippolytus, *Elenchos,* VI. 9. Translation by Mead, *Simon Magus.*

[79] See also the extended quotation of Simon's writings in "Transformation Symbolism in the Mass", CW 11, 236f.

[80] *Liber Novus,* 264.

[81] *Liber Novus,* 359. On first meeting, Jung had titled Philemon as "the Magician." *Liber Novus,* 312.

[82] In the version of the Sermons printed in 1916, Jung attributed the work to Basilides, a second century Alexandrian Gnostic teacher.

[83] *Liber Novus,* 346ff.

[84] *Liber Novus,* 317 n282.

[85] Images of Philemon and Sapientia (*Sophia*) appear on folio 154 on 155 of the Red Book. Painted in 1924, they are a thematic conclusion in the Red Book's transcription; only approximately fifteen more pages would be transcribed into the folio volume over the next six years. At the top of Jung's image of Sophia, Jung scribed a quotation from Paul's first letter to the Corinthians: "The Wisdom of God in a mystery, even the hidden wisdom, which God ordained before the world unto our glory: ...the Spirit

searcheth all things, yea, the deep things of God." On either side of the arch is an inscription from the Revelation of John, 22:17: "The Spirit and the Bride say, Come. And let him that heareth say, Come. And let him that is a-thirst, come. And whosoever will, let him take the water of life freely." Above the arch is the inscription, *"Ave Virgo Virginum"*—"Praise, Virgin of Virgins." *Liber Novus* 317 n283.

[86] Jung began construction of the Tower in 1923. It is unknown when he painted the mural of Philemon, but it was probably before 1930. The Greek inscription on the Tower mural reads: "ΦΙΛΗΜΩΝ ΤΩΝ ΠΡΟΦΗΤΩΝ ΠΡΟΠΑΤΩΡ." (Private communication.) The final word, *Propator*, implies both "forefather" and "the very first" or primal father.

[87] See the "Gnostic aeonology" of Simon Magus, as sketched by G. R. S. Mead, *Simon Magus*, 63.

[88] The Sermons were apparently recorded in the Black Book journals 5 and 6 between about 30 January and 8 February 1916. *Liber Novus* 346 n77; 354 n121.

[89] On the centrality of the myth of the demiurge, see, Karen L. King *What Is Gnosticism?* (Cambridge: Harvard University Press, 2003); and, Michael Williams, *Rethinking Gnosticism* (Princeton: Princeton University Press, 1996).

[90] These arguments are summarized in: Barry Jeromson, "Systema Munditotius and Seven Sermons"; *Jung History* 1:2 (Philemon Foundation, 2005/6), 6-10; and "The sources of Systems Munditotius: mandalas, myths and a misinterpretation"; *Jung History* 2:2 (Philemon Foundation, 2007), 20 - 22. (Online edition available.)

[91] *Liber Novus*, 370.

[92] These entries in Black Book 5 come on 18 January, two days after the 16 January 1916 commentary on Abraxas. Without an explanation about Abraxas, the name would have been meaningless to readers, thus Jung substituted the descriptive term "ruler of this world." *Liber Novus*, 245 n75.

[93] "The spirit of this time would want to make you believe that the depths are no world and no reality." *Liber Novus*, 242 n119.

[94] Shamdasani, *Biography in Books*, 207.

[95] MDR, 201.

[96] "Psychology and Religion," CW 11, 98.

[97] He did occasionally mention it in passing, notably in his first recorded seminar at Polzeath, Cornwall in 1923. See note 10, supra.

[98] MDR, 295ff. Also see Barbara Hannah's account, Barbara Hannah, *Jung: His Life and Work* (New York: G. Putnam's Sons, 1976), 277ff.

[99] MDR, 295–6.

[100] The "Last Quartet" is composed of: *Psychology of the Transference; Aion; Answer to Job; and Mysterium Coniunctionis. Aion* (CW 9ii) was begun in the fall of 1947 and is

the first book entirely written after Jung's illness; it was published in 1951. "The Psychology of the Transference," published in 1946 (CW 16, 163–323) was largely completed prior to the visions, but published in their reflection. Early sections of *Mysterium Coniunctionis* were written before 1945, the final sections and conclusion came after; speaking of this earliest work on the book, Jung said after the visions, "All I have written is correct.... I only realize its full reality now" (Hannah, 279). *Answer to Job* was first published in 1952 (CW 11, 355–470).

[101] Margaret Ostrowski-Sachs, *From Conversations with C. G. Jung* (Zurich: Juris Druck & Verlag, 1971), 68.

[102] For a detailed discussion of this material, see: Lance S. Owens, "Jung and *Aion*: Time, Vision and a Wayfaring Man"; *Psychological Perspectives* (Journal of the C. G. Jung Institute of Los Angeles, 2011) 54:253-89.

[103] Sonu Shamdasani, "Foreword to the 2010 Edition," *Answer to Job* (Princeton: Princeton University Press; Reprint edition, 2010), ix.

[104] William McGuire & R.F.C. Hull, eds., *C. G. Jung Speaking: Interviews and Encounters* (Princeton, NJ: Princeton University Press, 1977), 225.

[105] "All the Christian virtues are needed and something else besides, for the problem is not only moral: we also need the Sophia that Job was seeking. ... [The] higher and 'complete' man is begotten by the 'unknown' father and born from Sophia, and it is he who ... represents our totality, which transcends consciousness." C. G. Jung, *Answer to Job* (Princeton: Princeton University Press, 2nd Edition 1969), 95. (Also, CW 11, 357-470.)

[106] Jung noted that in this proclamation, "Mary as the bride is united with the son in the heavenly bridal-chamber, and as Sophia, with the Godhead. ...It repeats the Old Testament anamnesis of Sophia." *Answer to Job*, 96-7.

[107] "It is psychologically significant for our day that in the year 1950 the heavenly bride was united with the bride-groom. In order to interpret this event, one has to consider ... the prefigurations in the apocalyptic marriage of the Lamb and in the Old Testament anamnesis of Sophia. The nuptial union in the *thalamus* (bridal-chamber) signifies the hieros gamos, and this in turn is the first step towards incarnation, towards the birth of the saviour who, since antiquity, was thought of as the *filius solis et lunae* [the son of the sun and moon], the *filius sapientiae*, [the son of Wisdom] and the equivalent of Christ. Although he is already born in the pleroma, his birth in time can only be accomplished when it is perceived, recognized, and declared by man." *Answer to Job*, 100.

[108] *Aion*, CW 9ii, 174.

[109] *Liber Novus*, 338.

[110] Ibid.

[111] *Liber Novus*, 311.

Chapter 1 – Introduction

[1] G. Quispel, De Hermetische Gnosis in de loop der eeuwen; Tirion,1992.

[2] Alfred Ribi, Zeitenwende: Die geistigen Wurzeln unserer Zeit in Hellenismus, Hermetik, Gnosis und Alchemie; P. Lang, Bern and New York, 2001.

[3] Original German edition: Alfred Ribi, Die Suche nach den eigenen Wurzeln: Die Bedeutung von Gnosis, Hermetik und Alchemie für C. G. Jung und Marie-Louise von Franz und deren Einfluss auf das moderne Verständnis dieser Disziplin. (Bern, Berlin, Frankfurt/M., New York, Paris, Wien: Peter Lang Publishing, Inc., 1999)

[4] In Gnosis und Gnostizismus, ed. by K. Rudolph.

[5] Ibid., pp. 426ff; quoted from Evangelische Theologie 13 (1954), pp. 354-361.

[6] Ibid., p. 428.

[7] Ibid., p. 799.

[8] Studies in Gnosticism and Hellenistic Religions Presented to Gilles Quispel on the Occasion of his 65th Birthday, ed. R. van den Brock and M. J. Vermasern.

[9] Ibid., pp. 1-12.

[10] C. G. Jung, "The Archetypes and the Collective Unconscious," Collected Works (CW), 9/I, pp. 3ff.

[11] "The position of the archetype would be located beyond the psychic sphere, analogous to the position of physiological instinct, which is immediately rooted in the stuff of the organism and, with its psychoid nature, forms the bridge to matter in general." CW 8, § 420.

[12] Maurice Friedman, The Healing Dialogue in Psychotherapy (Lanham, MD: Jason Aronson, 1985), p. 213.

[13] H. F. Ellenberger, The Discovery of the Unconscious (New York: Basic Books, 1970), passim.

[14] A. Ribi, "Die Auffassung C. G. Jungs von der Schizophrenie," passim.

Chapter 2 - Martin Buber versus Carl Gustav Jung

[1] E. L. Fackenheim, "Martin Buber's Concept of Revelation," in Paul Arthur Schilpp and Maurice Friedman, eds., The Philosophy of Martin Buber (London: Cambridge University Press, 1967), p. 281.

[2] Martin Buber, Autobiographical Fragments, in Schilpp and Friedman, p. 4.

[3] Maurice Friedman, Martin Buber's Life and Work. The Early Years 1878-1923 (New York: E. P. Dutton, 1981), pp. 46f.

[4] Martin Buber, "Ein autobiographischer Abriss," in Briefwechsel aus sieben Jahrzehnten, vol. 1 (Gütersloh: Gütersloher Verlagshaus, 1972), pp. 34-37.

[5] Buber, Autobiographical Fragments, p. 5.

[6] Friedman, Buber's Life and Work. The Early Years, p. 330.

[7] CW 5.

[8] Anthropos: Der ewige Mensch. Der ewige, göttliche und kosmische Mensch in Geschichte, Politik und Tiefenpsychologie (Bern and New York: P. Lang, 2002).

[9] Martin Buber, Between Man and Man, chapter one.

[10] Here I am adopting Jung's terminology for the dramatic structure of the dream; in GW 8, §§ 561f. (For readers who are not familiar with Jungian psychology, in the footnotes I indicate the places in the Collected Works where they can find a brief treatment of basic concepts.)

[11] Jung, Symbols of Transformation, CW 5, § 420.

[12] Cf. the significance of the call in Manichaeism and among the Mandaeans.

[13] Schilpp and Friedman, The Philosophy of Martin Buber, p. 637.

[14] Jung, "Psychology and Religion," CW 11, § 6.

[15] Buber, "Replies to My Critics," in Schilpp and Friedman, The Philosophy of Martin Buber, pp. 589ff.

[16] Ibid.

[17] CW 6, § 763.

[18] CW 6, § 812,

[19] CW 6, § 779.

[20] Friedman, The Healing Dialogue, p. 3.

[21] Ibid., p. 179.

[22] Ibid., p. 198.

[23] Ibid., p. 4.

[24] Bergman, "Martin Buber and Mysticism," in Schilpp and Friedman, p. 297. Original: Leipzig, Insel, 1917, pp. 30-32.

[25] Buber, I and Thou, quoted from Friedman, Healing Dialogue, p. 3.

[26] Jung, Mysterium Coniunctionis, CW 14, § 184.

[27] Maurice Friedman's personal notes on the seminar, in Friedman, The Healing Dialogue, p. 147.

[28] Ibid., p. 145.

[29] Martin Buber, "Zu Bergsons Begriff der Intuition," in Werke I; quoted from Friedman, The Healing Dialogue, p. 202.

[30] Ibid., p. 203.

[31] Ibid..

[32] Alfred Ribi, Zeitenwende: Die geistigen Wurzeln unserer Zeit in Hellenismus, Hermetik, Gnosis und Alchemie; P. Lang, Bern and New York, 2001.

[33] The Tavistock Lectures, Lecture III, "On the Theory and Practice of Analytic Psychology," CW 18, § 173.

[34] CW 6, § 814.

[35] M. Friedman, Contemporary Psychology: Revealing and Obscuring the Human (Pittsburgh: Duquesne University Press, 1987), p. 39.

[36] Ibid.

Chapter 3 - Devotio versus Gnosis

[1] Martin Buber, Eclipse of God. Studies in the Relation between Religion and Philosophy (New York: Harper & Brothers, 1952).

[2] K. Kerényi, The Religion of the Greeks and the Romans, trans. By Christopher Holme (New York: Dutton, 1962).

[3] Jung, "Religion and Psychology: A Reply to Martin Buber," CW 18, §§ 1499-1513.

[4] "Jung and Religious Belief," CW 18, §§ 1584-1690.

[5] C. G. Jung, Memories, Dreams, Reflections (abbrev. MDR), recorded and edited by Aniela Jaffé, trans. by Richard and Clara Winston (New York: Vintage Books, 1989), p. 300.

[6] One need not in every case, as one Antimimos analyst thinks.

[7] Marie Louise von Franz, C. G. Jung. His Myth in Our Time, trans. William H. Kennedy (New York: CG Jung Foundation, 1975).

[8] "Face-to-Face" interview, with J. Freeman, in C. G. Jung Speaking: Interviews and Encounters (Princeton: Princeton University Press, 1977), p. 428.

[9] CW 18, § 1589.

[10] Ibid., § 1615.

[11] Jung, Mysterium Coniunctionis, CW 14, p. 336, note 297.

[12] CW 18, § 1637.

[13] Ibid., § 1643.

[14] Ibid., § 1635.

[15] Ibid., § 1595.

[16] Ibid., § 1616.

[17] Ibid., §§ 1637-1638.

[18] Buber, "Supplement: Reply to C. G. Jung," Eclipse of God, p. 176.

[19] Friedman, Martin Buber's Life and Work, p. 169.

[20] Buber, "Replies to My Critics," in Schilpp and Friedman, pp. 715-16.

[21] He is undoubtedly referring to Jung as such a characteristic expression

[22] Bergman, "Martin Buber and Mysticism," in Schilpp and Friedman, The Philosophy of Martin Buber, pp. 297ff.

[23] Buber, "Replies to My Critics," in Schilpp and Friedman, The Philosophy of Martin Buber, pp. 715ff.

[24] Buber, Eclipse of God, pp. 166-167.

[25] E. L. Fackenheim, "Martin Buber's Concept of Revelation," in Schilpp and Friedman, p. 289.

[26] Ibid.

[27] Buber, "Replies to My Critics," in Schilpp and Friedman, pp. 698-99.

[28] Fackenheim, "Martin Buber's Concept of Revelation," in Schilpp and Friedman, p. 277.

[29] Buber, Eclipse of God, pp. 68-69.

[30] Fackenheim, "Buber's Concept of Revelation," in Schilpp and Friedman, p. 296.

[31] Bergman, "Martin Buber and Mysticism," in Schilpp and Friedman, p. 304.

[32] "Individuation, Schuld und Entscheidung. Über die Grenzen der Psychologie," in Die Kulturelle Bedeutung der Komplexen Psychologie. Festschrift zum 60. Gerburtstag von C. G. Jung, pp. 529-555. See also footnote 11, p. 54, in von Franz, Jung, for the claim that Trüb was a feeling type.

[33] Ibid., p. 543.

[34] Ibid., p. 534.

[35] Ibid.

[36] Ibid., p. 532.

[37] Ibid., p. 544.

[38] Ibid., p. 548.

[39] Ibid., p. 538.

[40] Ibid., p. 530.

[41] Martin Buber, Nachlese (Heidelberg: 1966), pp. 146-157.

[42] Trüb, "Individuation, Schuld und Entscheidung," p. 539.

[43] Ibid., p. 540.

[44] Friedman, Contemporary Psychology, p. 44.

[45] Ribi, Die feindlichen Brüder: Extraversion-Intraversion. Zwei komplemetäre Seiten eines einseitigen Weltbildes (Wettingen: Kundschafter, 1993).

[46] Irenaeus, Against Heresies, I 23, 1.

[47] On this issue, see R. Bergmeier, "'Königslosigkeit als nachvalentinisches Heilsprädikat,'" in Novum Testamentum 24 (1982), pp. 316-339.

[48] Bergman, "Martin Buber and Mysticism," in Schilpp and Friedman, p. 306.

[49] "The Relations Between the Ego and the Unconscious," CW 7, §§ 398-400.

[50] Eclipse of God, p. 87.

[51] Friedman, Contemporary Psychology, p. 44.

[52] MDR, p. 256.

[53] "Face-to-Face" interview, in Jung Speaking, p. 431.

[54] CW §§ 8ff.

[55] CW 6, § 60.

[56] On this issue in general, see Ribi, Feindliche Brüder, pp. 63f.

[57] "General Aspects of Dream Psychology," CW 8, § 510.

[58] Bergman, "Martin Buber and Mysticism," in Schilpp and Friedman, p. 300.

[59] CW 6, § 67.

[60] See "On Psychic Energy," CW 8, §§ 1ff, and specially §§ 88.

[61] CW 6, §§ 77-78.

[62] MDR, p. 255; cf. CW 9/I, § 177.

[63] Ribi, Feindliche Brüder, p. 201.

[64] CW 6, § 78. Emphasis added.

[65] CW 6, § 80.

[66] Carl Andresen, Die Kirchen der alten Christenheit. (Stuttgard: W. Kohlhammer, 1971).

[67] Ibid. Carl Andersen (1909-1985) was a noted historian of Christianity, and a professor at Philipps-Universitat Marburg (1956-1961) and Georg-August-Universitat Gottingen (1961-1977)

[68] "Principles of Practical Psychotherapy," CW 16, § 20.

[69] "Psychotherapists or the Clergy," CW 11, §§ 531-532.

[70] As an epigraph to his The Interpretation of Dreams (1903), Freud quoted from Vergil's Aeneid (7, 312):

Flectere si nequeo superos

acheronta movebo.

(If I cannot bend the gods on high, I will at least set Acheron in uproar.)

[71] Jung, "A Psychological Approach to the Trinity," CW 11, § 293.

[72] CW 6, § 417.

[73] Ribi, Feindliche Brüder, p. 84.

[74] H. Bergmann, "Martin Buber and Mysticism," in Friedman and Schilpp, p. 298.

[75] CW 6, §§ 423-427.

[76] Fackenheim, "Buber's Concept of Revelation," in Schilpp and Friedman, pp. 283-284.

[77] To the Rev. Morton T. Kelsey, 3 May 1958, in Letters, p. 435. English original.

[78] "Introduction to the Religious and Psychological Problems of Alchemy," CW 12, §§ 10-11.

[79] Ibid., §§ 14 and 12.

Chapter 4 - On the Nature of Gnosis

[1] Maurice Friedman, Contemporary Psychology, p. 210.

[2] CW 10, §§ 825ff.

[3] CW 10, § 858ff and CW 11, p. 572.

[4] The Eclipse of God, pp. 116f.

[5] "Commentary on 'The Secret of the Golden Flower,'" CW 13, § 69.

[6] CW 11, § 133.

[7] Martin Buber, Eclipse of God, 176.

[8] Friedman, Contemporary Psychology, p. 212.

[9] Buber, "Autobiographical Fragments," in Schilpp and Friedman, p. 10.

[10] Symbols of Transformation, CW 5, § 421.

[11] MDR, p. 67.

[12] Ibid., p. 215.

[13] Buber, Eclipse of God, 104.

[14] MDR, pp. 301-302.

[15] MDR, p. 304.

[16] MDR, p. 311.

[17] CW 6, § 409.

[18] CW 6, §§ 14-15.

[19] "Jung and Religious Belief," CW 18, § 1647.

[20] O. Bardenhewer, Geschichte der altkirchlichen Literatur, vol. 1, pp. 206-262.

[21] Prophets was taken at the time to refer to all the authors of Biblical reports.

[22] "Jung and Religious Belief," CW 18, § 1665.

[23] "Address at the Presentation of the Jung Codex," CW 18, § 1827.

[24] MDR, pp. 332-333.

[25] CW 11, § 168.

[26] Jung, "A Psychological Approach to the Dogma of the Trinity," CW 11, § 203.

[27] Ibid., § 201.

[28] Stromateis I, 9

[29] Stromateis II, 4

[30] Stromateis VII, 10

[31] Quoted in Jung, "A Psychological Approach to the Trinity," CW 11, § 271, note 3.

[32] "Transformation Symbolism in the Mass," CW 11, §§ 441-442.

[33] Ibid., § 438.

[34] Ibid., § 444.

[35] Ibid., § 445.

[36] Ibid., § 446.

[37] Jung, Aion. CW 9/II, § 347.

[38] Ibid., § 428.

[39] J.-M. Sevrin, Le dossier baptismal séthien, p. 211, note 22.

[40] Jung, "Instinct and the Unconscious," CW 8, § 273.

[41] In Archetypal Dimensions of the Psyche (Boston, 1997), p. 373-375. Appeared originally in C. G. Jung und die Theologie, ed. W. Böhme (Stuttgart, 1971).

[1] F. Wisse, "Stalking Those Elusive Sethians," in Rediscovery II, pp. 563-576; quoted in J.-M. Sevrin, Le dossier baptismal Séthien, pp. 5-6.

Chapter 5 - Law versus Personal Responsibility

[2] L'élitisme gnostique et la souillure de la grande église d'après de Nag Hammadi.

[3] Koschorke, Nag Hammadi Studies 12 (Leiden, 1978), 91-174.

[4] Koschorke, p. 178.

[5] Irenaeus, Adversus Haereses III 4, 1.

[6] NHC I 5.

[7] Cf. Hermetica Oxoniensia (HO) III 1: "Les hommes ont établi la loi par opinion.... délaissant la justice véritable et l'âme... 3. C'est pourquoi le ciel est pur de telles lois." J. Paramelle and J. Mahé, Extraits Hermétiques, p. 129.

[8] Jung posed this question to four professors, none of whom were able to give him a satisfying answer. CW 18/II, § 1645.

[9] Quoted from the Revised Standard Version, 1971.

[10] Gospel of the Nazarenes, 41:7.

[11] CH VI 3-6; SH II A 6-10. Cf. G. Fowden, The Egyptian Hermes, p. 102.

[12] E. Benz, Ecclesia spiritualis, p. 9.

[13] Codex XI 1.

[14] NH XI 9, 28; "The Interpretation of Knowledge," in The Nag Hammadi Library in English (Leiden: E. J. Brill, 1977), p. 430.

[15] NH II 58, 22; "The Gospel of Philip," in ibid., p. 135.

[16] NH II 58, 18-22; Ibid.

[17] Sevrin, pp. 209 and 207, A 12.

[18] Just how strict the Gnostics were with themselves is obvious from the few citations that appear in the Bible.

[19] NH VII 61, 29-32 ; "The Second Treatise of the Great Seth," in Nag Hammadi Library, p. 334.

[20] Cf. M. A. Williams, "The Immovable Race. A Gnostic Designation and the Theme of Stability in Late Antiquity," NHS 29 (1985).

[21] Psychology and Religion; CW 11, § 133.

[22] Ibid., § 131.

[23] Jung writes: "The Church knows all about the assimilation of the shadow, i.e., how it is to be repressed and what is evil." CW 18/II, § 1594.

[24] NH XI 22, 18-21; "A Valentinian Exposition," in Nag Hammadi Library, p. 436.

[25] On the "Eglise supérieure" see Tractatus Tripartitus I, ed. R. Kasser, M. Milinine, H.-Ch. Puech, G. Quispel, and J. Zandee, p. 321.

[26] NH VII 60, 25.

[27] Mahé, p. 84.

[28] Against Heresies, I, 5, 1.

[29] Stromateis 3, 4, 2-10, 2.

[30] Against Heresies, I 25, 5.

[31] Against Heresies, I 25, 4.

[32] Against Heresies I, 5, 1.

[33] Ibid., I 5, 5-6.

[34] Ibid., I 6, 1.

[35] Cf. the alchemical in stercore invenitur.

[36] Against Heresies, I 6, 2.

[37] NH IX 29, 22-30, 17; "The Testimony of Truth," in Nag Hammadi Library, p. 407.

[38] Refutatio omnium haeresium, ed. by L. Duncker and F. G. Scheidewin (Göttingen, 1859).

[39] Against Heresies, I 6, 4.

[40] Ibid., ed. by N. Brox (Herder, 1993).

[41] MDR, p. 158.

[42] Origo (Zürich, 1951).

[43] Ibid., p. 45.

[44] Ibid., p. 47.

[45] Ibid., p. 48. This point was also made by G. Quispel in his lecture "Gnosis als Weltreligion": "Gnosis [had] a compensatory function in relation to Christianity."

[46] F. Wisse, Die Sextus-Sprache und das Problem der gnostischen Ethik, quoted in Mahé, L'élitisme gnostique, p. 77.

[47] On the question of baptism and the Gnostics, see J.-M. Sevrin, "Le Dossier Baptismal Séthien," Etudes sur la Sacramentaire Gnostique.

[48] NH IX 69, 7-28; "The Testimony of Truth," in Nag Hammadi Library, p. 414; Birger A. Pearson, in The Coptic Gnostic Library, vol. 5, pp. 189-191.

[49] NH IX 30, 30-31, 5; "The Testimony of Truth," in Nag Hammadi Library, p. 407; Pearson, pp. 125-127.

[50] Cf. the myth of Sophia.

[51] Sevrin, Le dossier baptismal Séthien.

[52] Against Heresies, I 6,4.

[53] TemVer, NH IX, 31,5.

[54] Against Heresies, I, 6,4. On this complex of questions, see J.-M. Sevrin, "Les Noces Spirituelles dans L'Evangile selon Philippe," Le Muséon 87 (1976), pp. 143-193, esp. pp. 148f.

[55] "Femme et Société dans les Notices de Pères contres les Gnostiques," Madeline Scopello, Etudes Coptes III, p. 115.

[56] This is lent especially beautiful expression in the Philipians gospel § 122, 81,34: "Si le mariage de la souillure [= du monde] est caché, combien plus le mariage sans souillure [= céleste] est-il un mystère véritable. Il n'est pas charnel, mais il est pur. Il ne relève pas de la ténèbre ou de la nuit, mais il relève du jour et de la lumière," ibid., p. 165.

[57] Cf. G. Quispel's definition of gnosis as the "mystical projection of the experience of self," in Gnosis als Weltreligion, p. 17.

[58] P. Sloterdijk and H. T. Macho, Weltrevolution der Seele, p. 18: "the reemergence in 1946 of texts that had been lost for ages bore a special significance, as if it were a sign from the depths of time to the survivors of the colossal catastrophe of the "Christian West."

Chapter 6 - Jung and Gnosis

[1] The Facsimile Edition of the Nag Hammadi Codices. Preface by James M. Robinson, p. 3.

[2] "The Jung Codex: The Rise and Fall of a Monopoly," Religious Studies Review 3, (1977), pp. 17-30.

[3] CW, 18, §§1514ff.

[4] 1969 and 1971.

[5] Dall' Asclepius al Crater Hemetis, p. 10.

[6] Gnosis as Weltreligion, p. 29.

[7] De Hermetische Gnosis in de loop der eeuwen.

[8] For the most important dates in Jung's life, see pp. 235f.

[9] The Freud/Jung Letters: The Correspondence between Sigmund Freud and C. G. Jung, ed. William McGuire (Princeton: Princeton University Press, 1974).

[10] MDR, p. 170.

[11] MDR, p. 378; and R. A. Segal, The Gnostic Jung, p. 181. See also the illuminating commentary on the meaning of the Seven Sermons for the life and work of Jung himself by Christine Maillard, Les Sept Sermons aux Morts de Carl Gustav Jung.

[12] An interpretation of the sermons is reserved to a chapter of its own.

[13] MDR, p. 378.

[14] Ibid., p. 188.

[15] "Archetypes of the Collective Unconscious," CW 9/I, §§ 1ff.

[16] MDR, p. 201.

[17] Ibid., p. 202.

[18] Ibid., p. 204.

[19] Ibid.

[20] Ibid., p. 32.

[21] Ibid., pp. 80f.

[22] Alchemical Active Imagination, p. 18.

[23] See Quispel, ed., Hermetische Gnosis in de loop der eeuwen.

[24] Illustrated in "Concerning Mandala Symbolism," CW 9/I, Fig. 36.

[25] Published together with Richard Wilhelm in 1929. Jung's commentary is in CW 13, §§ 1ff.

[26] MDR, p. 205.

[27] Excerpta (Exc.) I, 69.

[28] Exc. V 50.

[29] R. Halleux (Paris 1981) and M. Mertens (Paris 1995).

[30] Exc. V 50. The latest English translation is B. P. Copenhaver, Hermetica, 1994. German: J. Holzhausen, Das Corpus Hermeticum Deutsch, 1997.

[31] Exc. V 198f.

[32] MDR, p. 275.

[33] A. Ribi, "Zum schöpferische Prozess bei C. G. Jung. Aus den Excerptbänden zur Alchemie," Analyt. Psychol., vol. 13 (1982), pp. 201-221.

[34] Exc. VI 93.

[35] CW 11, § 296.

[36] Ibid., §§ 344f.

[37] Katalog 1967, p. 34.

[38] Exc. VII, 110-125.

[39] Exc. VII 134-147.

[40] Exc. VIII, 10-27.

[41] (Exc. VIII 80-82).

[42] Cf. Notes on Lectures given at the ETH Zürich 1933-1940.

[43] Auriferae Artis 1572, p. 199. Typographus Lectori.

[44] Von Franz, Mysterium coniunctionis 14/III, p. 25.

[45] Exc. V 123-131, 162-174.

[46] CW 12, § 464.

[47] CW 14/III, §§ 613-616.

[48] W. Ganzenmuller, "Alchemie und Religion im Mittelalter," Deutsches Archiv für Geschichte des Mittelalters 5, pp. 329-346 (1942).

[49] GW 12, § 1 H.

[50] GW 13, § 299.

[51] CW 12, § 44 H.

[52] "The Visions of Zosimos," CW 13, §§ 85f.

[53] CW 18, §§ 1692-1699.

[54] Typed manuscript in the C. G. Jung Archive of ETH. MDR, p. 65.

[55] CW 11, §§ 169f.

[56] CW 11, §§ 296 f.

[57] CW 9/II.

[58] CW 14.

[59] MDR, 221.

[60] MDR, 297.

[61] CW 9/II, § 267.

[62] Cf. Ps-Demokritos: Physika kai Mystika. M. Berthelot, Coll. Alch. Grecs II 41; Cf. Gnōsis and epistēmē, in G. Fowden The Egyptian Hermes, pp. 100-101.

[63] CW 9/II, § 268.

[64] Ibid., § 269.

[65] Ibid., § 270.

[66] Ibid., § 273.

[67] Ibid., § 274.

[68] Ibid., § 278.

[69] Ibid., § 281.

[70] Ibid., § 283.

[71] CW 9/II.

[72] CW 18, § 1479.

[73] Ibid., § 1480.

[74] Letter to Gilles Quispel of April 21, 1950; Letters, vol. I, p. 553.

[75] CW 18, § 1642.

[76] Ibid., § 1643.

[77] Ibid., § 1647.

[78] Panarion 31, 5, 3; The Panarion of Epiphanius of Salamis, trans. by F. Williams (New York: E. J. Brill), p. 156.

[79] Cf. Gnosis I, S. 303, and F. Williams, ed. I, 156.

[80] Refutatio VII 22.16, Gnosis I 91; Dunker et Schneidewin, Refutatio, p. 364.

[81] CW 9/II, § 119.

[82] CW 9/II, § 299.

[83] Josef Quint, pp. 305, 23-25; 306, 8-12; 308, 7-13.

[84] CW 9/II, § 302-3.

[85] Ibid., § 304.

[86] MDR, p. 331.

[87] CW 7, § 151.

[88] MDR, p. 333.

Chapter 7 - The Septem Sermones ad Mortuos

[1] MDR, pp. 378ff.

[2] C. G. Jung, Analytical Psychology, Notes of the seminar given in 1925, ed. W. McGuire, Bollingen Series XCIX (Princeton: Princeton University Press, 1989), pp. 40f.

[3] MDR, p. 175.

[4] Published in a fourth, revised edition of 1952 as Symbole der Wandlung (Symbols of Transformation), CW 5.

[5] MDR, p. 171.

[6] Marie-Louise von Franz, C. G. Jung. His Myth in Our Time.

[7] MDR, p. 172.

[8] E. Hornung, Das Amduat. Die Schrift des Verborgenen Raumes; 2 vols.

[9] CW 5, § 308; 8, § 68.

[10] J. Ruska, Tabula Smaragdina. Ein Beitrag zur Geschichte der Hermetischen Literatur.

[11] Marie-Louise von Franz, "Projection and Re-Collection in Jungian Psychology," Reflections of the Soul, trans. by W. H. Kennedy (Chicago: Open Court, 1980), p. 150.

[12] K. Kerényi, Religion of the Greeks and Romans, pp. 68-69, 159, 197.

[13] MDR, pp. 172-173.

[14] MDR, pp. 158-159.

[15] MDR, pp. 164-165.

[16] Emma Jung and Marie-Louise von Franz, The Grail Legend (Princeton: Princeton University Press, 1998).

[17] The Coptic Gnostic Library, A Complete Edition of the Nag Hammadi Codices, vol. 2, (Leiden, Boston, Cologne: Brill, 2000), p. 243.

[18] MDR, pp. 190-192.

[19] MDR, p. 162.

[20] MDR, pp. 200-201.

[21] Citations from MDR, pp. 378-390.

[22] Ref. VII, 20.

[23] Adversus haereses I 24, 3-7.

[24] Panarion XXIV 5, 2.4; 7,6.

[25] Ref. VII, 20, 1-27,14.

[26] Clemens of Alexandria, Stromateis. Clément d'Alexandrie, Les Stromates, Stromate V, Introduction, texte critique et index, ed. by A. Le Boulluec, trans. by P. Voulet. Sources Chrétiennes, No. 278, pp. 28-29.

[27] Fragment II, Strom. V1:3, 2-3; Ibid., p. 108.

[28] To Mr. Leonhard, December 5, 1959; C. G. Jung, Letters, volume 2, p. 525. See also the letter to Valentine Brooke, pp. 520ff.

[29] Marie-Louise von Franz, C. G. Jung. His Myth in Our Time, pp. 232ff.

[30] Irenaeus, Adv. Haer. I, 30, 6.

[31] BG 44, 15.

[32] Irenaeus, Adv. Haer. I, 5,4.

[33] Ref. VI, 33.

[34] Pan XXV 2,3.

[35] NHC V 5; 66,29.

[36] NHC II 4; 86,30; 94,22.

[37] A. Ribi, "Morgenerkenntnis und Abenderkenntnis bei Aurelius Augustinus—Wo stehen wir heute?" Address to the Psychological Club of Zurich, 27 June, 1992. In A. Ribi, Ein Leben im Dienst der Seele. Teil II, Gesammelte Aufsätze und Vorträge (Bern, Berlin, Bruxelles, Frankfurt am Main, New York, Oxford, Vienna: P. Lang, 2007), p. 555.

[38] G. Quispel, "Hesse, Jung und die Gnosis. Die 'Septem Sermones ad Mortuos' und Basilides," Eranos, vol. 37, pp. 277-298 (1968).

[39] Fragment 7; Foerster, Gnosis I, p. 105.

[40] Fragment 2: Clemens Alexandrinus Strom. II 114,4, in Ch. Markschies, Valentinus Gnosticus?, pp. 54f.

[41] Aion, CW 9/II, § 370.

[42] W. Schubart, Reallexikon für Antike und Christentum, vol. 1, pp. 271-283.

[43] All the following quotations from the Septem Sermones ad Mortuos are from the English translation prepared by H. C. Baynes, MDR, pp. 378-90.

[44] Stephan A. Hoeller, The Gnostic Jung and the Seven Sermons to the Dead (Wheaton, IL: Quest, 1982).

[45] C. G. Jung, The Red Book: Liber Novus, ed. Sonu Shamdasani, tr. John Peck, Mark Kyburz, and Sonu Shamdasani (New York: W.W. Norton & Co, 2009), 346-354.

[46] Die Kreuzzüge in Augenzeugenberichten, ed. by R. Pernoud; Die Kreuzzüge aus arabischer Sicht, ed. by F. Gabrieli.

[47] Emma Jung and Marie-Louise von Franz, The Grail Legend, p. 95.

[48] Ibid., pp. 131-132.

[49] MDR, p. 333.

[50] "On Psychic Energy," CW 8, § 103.

[51] CW 6, § 741, Definitions.

[52] Selections from The Cherubinic Wanderer, trans. J. E. Crawford Flitch (London, 1032), number 25, 4.

[53] "On the Nature of the Psyche," CW 8, §§ 369-370.

[54] Mysterium coniunctionis. CW 14/II, §§413ff.

[55] Cf. Marie-Louise Franz, Number and Time. Reflections Leading towards a Unification of Psychology and Physics, trans. by Andrea Dykes (London: Rider and Co., 1974).

[56] "On the Nature of the Psyche," CW 8, § 418.

[57] A. Ribi, Anthropos.

[58] W. Y. Evans-Wentz, trans. and ed., The Tibetan Book of the Dead (Oxford, 1957), pp. 11f.

[59] Letters, vol. I, p. 433.

[60] "On the Nature of the Psyche," CW 8, § 430.

[61] Refutation of all Heresies, VII 9,1-4; W. Foerster, vol. I, pp. 87-89.

[62] BG 22, 16-25,10; The Apocryphon of John, The Coptic Gnostic Library, vol. 2, p. 20-26.

[63] NHC XI 3.

[64] J. M. Robinson, The Coptic Gnostic Library, vol. V, p. 225-229; 61, 32-63, 32.

[65] CW 6, §§ 741-742.

[66] "On the Nature of the Psyche," CW 8, §§ 381-384.

[67] Chuang Tzu (The True Classic of Southern (Cultural) Florescence), trans. Lin Yutang.

[68] CW 8, §§ 907ff.

[69] Das chinesische Denken, pp. 227ff, especially p. 228.

[70] J. Needham, Science and Civilization in China, vol. 2, History of Scientific Thought, pp. 36-74.

[71] Lao-tse, Tao te king, translated by Gia Fu Feng, XXV.

[72] Ibid, LI.

[73] Synchronicity: An Acausal Connecting Principle, CW 8, § 955

[74] P. Deussen, Sechzig Upanishads des Veda.

[75] Ibid., p. 110.

[76] Cf. Matthew 13: 31: "The kingdom of heaven is like a grain of mustard seed." Basilides: "the seed of the world [...] as a mustard seed" (Hippolytus, Ref. VII 21,3).

[77] CW 6, § 781.

[78] A. Ribi, Die feindlichen Brüder. Extraversion—Introversion.

[79] Symbols of Transformation, CW 5.

[80] Transformation Symbolism in the Mass, CW 11, §§ 96ff.

[81] CW 6, §§ 757-758.

[82] Foreword to "Introduction to Zen Buddhism, CW 11, §§ 891-892.

[83] "On the Nature of the Psyche," CW 8, § 387.

[84] Hippolytus, Ref. VII, 27, 12. W. Foerster, Gnosis I, p. 99.

[85] Aion, CW 9/II, § 118.

[86] "On the Nature of the Psyche," CW 8, § 429.

[87] H. F. Ellenberger, The Discovery of the Unconscious (New York: Basic Books, 1970).

[88] C. Schmidt and W. Till, Die Pistis Sophia, pp. 26-27.

[89] Irenaeus, Adversus haereses, I 1-9.

[90] Irenaeus, Adversus haereses, I 2, 2.

[91] Ref. VI 30, 6.

[92] MDR, p. 338.

[93] H.-M. Schenke, Der Gott "Mensch" in der Gnosis.

[94] H. Rahner, "Antenna crucis," in Symbole der Kirche, pp. 239ff.

[95] MDR, p. 346.

[96] Ibid., 342-343.

[97] "Definitions," CW 6, §§ 799-800.

[98] Symbols of Transformation, CW 5, §§ 419ff.

[99] MDR, pp. 344-345.

[100] MDR, p. 345.

[101] C. G. Jung, Seminare: Analytische Psychologie, pp. 102ff.

[102] Ancilla to the Pre-Socratic Philosophers. A Complete Translation of the Fragments in Diels, Fragmente der Vorsokratiker, trans. by Kathleen Freeman (Cambridge: Harvard University Press), p. 28.

[103] A Psychological Approach to the Trinity, CW 11, §§ 277-279.

[104] CW 6, § 327.

[105] Letters, volume 2, p. 364.

[106] Mysterium coniunctionis, CW 14.

[107] Aion, CW 9, § 423.

[108] CW 6, § 866.

[109] Ribi, Die feindliche Brüder. Extraversion—Introversion. Zwei komplementäre Seiten eines einseitigen Weltbildes.

[110] "Psychology and Religion," CW 11, §§ 142-145

[111] MDR, pp. 55-56.

[112] MDR, p. 75.

[113] Ibid., p. 91.

[114] Ibid., p. 93.

[115] Ibid.

[116] Ibid.

[117] Ibid.

[118] Ibid., pp. 93-94.

[119] Ibid., p. 94.

[120] CW 6, §§ 412ff.

[121] Recognitions IX 3, 1; 3, 3.

[122] Pan 30: 16, 2.

[123] Irenaeus, Adv. haer. I, 11,1.

[124] A Psychological Approach to the Trinity, CW 11, § 263.

[125] Alchemical Studies, CW 12, § 460.

[126] Aion, CW 9/II, §§ 75 and 77.

[127] Albrecht Dietrich, Abraxas. Studien zur Religionsgeschichte des späten Altertums (Leipzig, 1891).

[128] Reizenstein, pp. 272ff.

[129] H. D. Betz, The Greek Magical Papyri in Translation, p. 331.

[130] Adversus haereses, I 24,7.

[131] Pan. XXIV 7, 6.

[132] Ref. VII 26, 6.

[133] NHC 5, Apocalypse of Adam, 75, 23

[134] MDR, pp. 331-333.

[135] CW 11, p. 385ff.

[136] Metaphysics, 1072b.

[137] Phaedrus, 246a.

[138] Hippolytus, Ref. VII 29, 10.

[139] The World as Will and Representation I, §25.

[140] "The Psychology of Dementia Praecox," CW 3, pp. 3ff.

[141] CW 4, pp. 83ff, esp. 111f.

[142] "On Psychic Energy," CW 8, pp. 3ff.

[143] Arthur Lovejoy, "The Fundamental Concept of the Primitive Philosophy," The Monist, XVI (1906), p. 363; quoted by Jung CW 8, § 116.

[144] Robert Henry Codrington, The Melanesians (Oxford: Oxford University Press, 1891), p. 118; quoted by Jung CW 8, § 123.

[145] Lovejoy, "Fundamental Concept," pp. 380f; quoted by Jung CW 8, § 126.

[146] CW 14/II, §§ 66-70, 77-84, 1757.

[147] Paracelsus as a Spiritual Phenomenon, "The Coniunctio in the Spring," CW 13, § 190.

[148] Poems to the garden god.

[149] F. Howald and M Grünwald, Die Anfänge der Abendlandischen Philosophie, Fragmente und Lehrberichte der Vorsokratiker, p. 31.

[150] CW, 13, esp. § 284.

[151] Cf. Pomaindres c.14 (Nock-Festugière I 11).

[152] The Idea of the Holy: An Inquiry into the Non-Rational Factor in the Idea of the Divine and Its Relation to the Rational, trans. by John W. Harvey (London: Oxford University Press, 1952).

[153] CW 11, § 9.

[154] Irenaeus, Adv. haer. I 21, 4.

[155] Evangelium Veritatis, NHC I 3.

[156] Ibid., 16, 31-171.

[157] CW 5, § 381.

[158] Cf. the black mass.

[159] CW 6, § 708.

[160] 22 Heraclitus B 10, I, from Heraclitus: The Cosmic Fragments, ed. by G. S. Kirk (Cambridge: Cambridge University Press, 1954), pp. 167-168.

[161] CW 7, § 132.

[162] MDR, pp. 242-244.

[163] Pann. XXVI 1, 3f.

[164] NH IX 2.

[165] Hyp. Arch. II 4; 91, 34.

[166] Irenaeus, Against Heresies, I 30, 9.

[167] Epiphanius, 1, 4

[168] Epiphanius, 1, 9

[169] Cf. the sexual fantasies reported by Jan Nelken, in which patients have their semen extracted by an invisible spirit. "Analytischen Beobachtungen über Phantasien eines Schizophrenen," Jahrbuch für psychoanalytische und psychopathologische Forschung, IV (1912), p. 510.

[170] Symbols of Transformation, CW 5, § 107f.

[171] Latin in the original.

[172] Symbols of Transformation, CW 5, § 176.

[173] CW 6, § 391.

[174] On the Psychology of the Unconscious, CW 7, § 33.

[175] Letters, volume 2, p. 364.

[176] Aion, CW 9/II, § 29.

[177] MDR, pp. 353-354.

[178] MDR, p. 12.

[179] C. G. Jung. His Myth in Our Time, pp. 25ff.

[180] MDR, pp. 152-153.

[181] CW 13, pp. 253ff.

[182] CW 13, § 459.

[183] 3, 17, 3. Leben und Taten Alexanders von Makedonien, ed. H. v an Thiel, p. 135.

[184] The Philosophical Tree, CW 13, § 383f.

[185] CW 13, §§ 390-391.

[186] "On the Nature of the Psyche," CW 8, § 388.

[187] Hippolytus, Ref. V 21, 2.

[188] Ibid., 19, 16.

[189] CW 8, § 392.

[190] CW 11, §§ 234f.

[191] In The Collected Dialogues of Plato, ed. by Edith Hamilton and Huntington Cairns (Princeton: Princeton University Press, 1961), p. 1151.

[192] CW 13, §§270f.

[193] MDR, p. 310. See the detailed treatment in von Franz, Number and Time. Reflections Leading towards a Unification of Depth Psychology and Physics, trans. by Andrea Dykes (London: Rider and Co., 1974).

[194] CW 6, § 466.

[195] Ribi, Was Tun mit unseren Komplexen?

[196] CW 5, §§ 147-149

[197] From Lucius Apuleius, The Golden Ass (Metamorphoses).

[198] Betz, The Greek Magical Papyri in Translation.

[199] von Franz, Number and Time, pp. 132f.

[200] Aion, CW 9/II.

[201] The Archetypes and the Collective Unconscious, CW 9/I, § 21.

[202] The Archetypes and the Collective Unconscious, CW 9/I, § 136.

[203] Instinct and the Unconscious, CW 8, § 280.

[204] Quote from the Revised Standard Version of the Bible.

[205] From The Lost Books of the Bible and the Forgotten Books of Eden (New York: Collins-World Publisher, 1974).

[206] Marie-Luise von Franz. CW 14/III.

[207] CW 16, § 361.

[208] Ref. V 7, 23-29; W. Foerster, Gnosis I, pp. 344-345.

[209] MDR, p. 18.

[210] "On the Nature of the Psyche," CW 8, §§ 358 and 360.

[211] Jan Nelken, "Analytischen Beobachtungen," pp. 504-562.

[212] CW 6, §§ 78-80.

[213] MDR, 342-343.

[214] "Psychotherapy Today," CW 16, § 227.

[215] CW 10, § 503.

[216] Aion, CW 9/II, §§ 370-371 and §§ 291 and 293.

[217] Symbols of Transformation, CW 5, §§676, 681, and 587.

[218] MDR, p. 171,

[219] "The Psychological Aspects of the Kore," CW 9/I, §§ 358-381.

[220] With the publication Jung's The Red Book: Liber Novus in 2009, we now discover that the following images were drawn directly from Jung's visions recorded in his Red Book, and not from a series of dreams!

[221] Hippolytus, Ref.V, 26, 1-28.

[222] MDR, pp. 171, 192.

[223] MDR, p. 183.

[224] Ibid., p. 182.

[225] Commentary on "The Secret of the Golden Flower," CW 13, §§80-81.

[226] To Elined Kotsching, June 30, 1956. Letters, vol. 2, p. 316.

[227] CW 18/II, § 1661.

[228] CW 8, §§ 916ff.

[229] Cornelius Agrippa, Of Occult Philosophy, Book II, chapter LVII.

[230] Quoted in Jung, On the Nature of the Psyche, CW 8, § 388.

[231] "A Mithras Liturgy," from the Paris Codex, ed. and trans. by Marvin W. Meyer, line 575.

[232] H. Bonnet, Reallexikon der aegyptischen Religionsgeschichte, p. 749.

[233] Ovid, Metamorphoses, XV 868.

[234] Epistulae II 2, lines 187-189. The Complete Works of Horace, trans. by Charles E. Passage (New York: Frederick Ungar Publishing Co., 1983), p. 355.

[235] Friedrich Schiller, The Robbers and Wallenstein (London: Penguin Books, 1979), p. 254.

[236] Hippolytus, Ref. VII, 24, 4-6.

[237] Hippolytus, Ref. V, 9, 5f.

[238] CW 18, § 1573.

[239] "Concerning Mandala Symbolism," CW 9/I, § 706.

[240] Ibid., § 683.

[241] L. Rohrich, Lexikon der sprichwörtlichen Redensarten, vol. 4, pp. 1016-1017.

Bibliography

1. Texts

Nag Hammadi

Jung Codex (NHC I 1-5):

- Evangelium Veritatis (13) Malinine, M., Puech, H.-Ch., Quispel, G. (editio princeps). Studies from the C. G. Jung Institute VI; Rascher, Zurich, 1956.

- Supplementum Evangelium Veritatis, Codex Jung F. XVII-XVIII (pp. 33-36). Malinine, M., Puech, H.-Ch., Quispel, G., Till, W; Rascher, Zurich and Stuttgart, 1961.

- Nag Hammadi Codex I (The Jung Codex) 2 vols.

- Attridge, H. W., ed. The Gospel of Truth: Attridge, H. W., and MacRae, G. W, pp. 55-122; Brill, Leiden, 1985.

- L'Evangile de Vérité. Menard, J.-E. Nag Hammadi Studies II; Brill, Leiden, 1972.

- Epistula Iacobi Apocrypha, (NHC I 4) Codex Jung F. I-VIII (p. 116). Malinine, M., Puech H.-Ch., Quispel, G., Till, W, Kasser, R., Wilson R. McL.; Rascher, Zurich and Stuttgart, 1968.

- Tractatus Tripartitus, (NHC I 5) Pars I de Supernis. Codex Jung F. XXVI-LII (pp. 51-104). Kasser, P., Malinine, M., Puech, H.-Ch., Quispel, G., Zandee, J., Vycichl, W, Wilson, R. McL.; Francke, Bern, 1973.
  Part II: De Creatione Hominis. Codex Jung F. LII-LXX, pp. 104-140.
  Part III: De Generibus Tribus; Bern, 1975.

Nag Hammadi Codex II 2-7 together with XIII, 2, Brit. Lib. Or. 4926, and Oxy; P. 1, 654, 655. Layton, B., ed. 2 vols.
  Vol. 1:   The Gospel according to Thomas, pp. 38-130
       The Gospel according to Philip, pp. 131-219
       The Hypostasis of the Archons, pp. 220-261.
  Nag Hammadi Studies XX; Brill, Leiden, New York, Copenhagen, Cologne, 1989.
  Barc, B., Hypostase des Archontes (NH II 4).
  Bibliotheque Copte de Nag Hammadi. (BCNH) Section: "Textes" 5 Les Presses de l'Universite Laval, 1980.

Nag Hammadi Codices V, 2-5 and VI with Papyrus
  Berolinensis 8502,1 and 4. Parrot, D. M.; Brill, Leiden, 1979.

Nag Hammadi Codices XI and X.
> Pearson, B. A., ed., Giversen, S., contributor. IX 2: The Thought of Norea,
> pp. 87f. Nag Hammadi Studies XV; Brill, Leiden, 1981.

Nag Hammadi Codices XI, XII, XIII.
> Hedrick, Ch. W, ed. Nag Hammadi Studies XXVIII; Brill, Leiden, New
> York, Copenhagen, Cologne, 1990.
> Codex de Berlin
> Tardieu, M., Sources Gnostiques et Manicheennes 1; Les Editions du Cerf,
> Paris, 1984.

Coptic sources from Nag Hammadi.
> Krause, M., ed., in: Die Gnosis, Vol. II, Part 1; Artemis, Zurich and
> Stuttgart, 1971.

The Nag Hammadi Library.
> Robinson, J. M., ed.; Brill, Leiden, New York, Copenhagen, Cologne, 1977,
> 1988.

Hermetic Texts

Hermetica. The Greek Corpus Hermeticum and the Latin Asclepius in a
New English translation, with notes and introduction; Copenhaver, B. P.,
Cambridge University Press, 1994, [1]1992.

Hermetica. The Ancient Greek and Latin Writings which Contain Religious or Philosophic Teachings Ascribed to Hermes Trismegistus. Scott, W.,
ed., Ferguson, A. S., Addenda, 4 vols. Reprint: Shambala, Boston,1985.

Corpus Hermeticum. Hermes Trismegiste. Nock, A. D., and Festugiere, A.-
J., 4 vols; Les Belles Lettres, Paris, 1945-54.

Das Corpus Hermeticum Deutsch.
> Part 1: Die griechischen Traktate und der lateinische "Asclepius."
> Part 2: Exzerpte, Nag Hammadi-Texte, Testimonien.

Holzhausen, J., trans.. Clavis Pansophiae 7. 1-2; Frommann-Holzboog,
Stuttgart-Bad Cannstatt, 1997.

Asclepius in: Apulei Platonici Madaurensis Opera Quae Supersunt, Vol. III.:
De Philosophia Libri. Moreschini, C., ed.; Bibliotheca Teubneriana,
Stuttgart and Leipzig, 1991.

Asclepius in: Dall' Asclepius al Crater Hermetis. Studi sull' Ermetismo Lati-
no Tardo-Antico e Rinaschimentale (with Italian translation). Moreschini,
C. Bibliotheca di Studi Antichi, vol. 47, pp. 122f.; Giardini, Pisa, 1985.

Mahé, J.-P.: Hermes en Haute-Egypte, Part I.
- L'Ogdoade et L'Enneade, NH VI, 6, pp. 29f.
- La priere d'action de graces, NH VI, 7, pp. 135f.
- Idem, Part II.
- Le fragment grec du discours parfait et l'Asclepius Latin; ed. synoptique de
  NH VI, 8, pp. 45f.; Les Presses de l'Universite Laval, Quebec, Canada,
  1978 and 1982.

Patristic Sources

Die Gnosis, Vol. I: Zeugnisse der Kirchenvater. Foerster, W. ed. and trans.; Artemis,
  Zurich and Stuttgart, 1969.

Irenaeus: Adversus Haereses (Abk. Iren., adv. haer.)
         - Irenaus von Lyon: Adversus haereses, griechisch, lateinisch, deutsch. Brox,
           N., trans. Fontes Christiani, vol. 8/1-4; Herder, Freiburg, 1993-1995.
         - Irenee de Lyon: Contre les Heresies.
           Rousseau, A., trans.; Les Editions du Cerf, Paris, ³1991.
         - Sancti Irenaei: Libros quinque adversus haereses; Harvey; W. W. Typis
           Academicis, Cantabrigiae, 1857.

Clemens von Alexandria. Teppiche (Stromateis). BKV, Vols. 17, 19. Stahlin, 0., ed.
  and trans.; Munich, 1936-1937.

Hippolytos: Refutatio omnium haeresium. Duncker, L., and Schneidewin, F. G.;
  Sumptibus Dieterichianis, Göttingen, 1859.

Hippolytos von Rom: Refutatio omnium Haeresium. Marcovich, M., ed.; Berlin, New
  York, 1986.

Epiphanius of Salamis: The Panarion.
  Book I (Sections 1-46) Williams, F, trans. Nag Hammadi Studies XXXV;
  Leiden, New York, Copenhagen, Cologne, 1987.

Idem: Books II and III (Sections 47-80, De Fide) Williams, E., trans. Nag Hammadi
  and Manichaean Studies XXXVI; Brill, Leiden, New York, Cologne,1994.

Justinus: Saint Justin. Apologies. Wartelle, A., trans., Etudes Augustiniennes; Paris,
  1987.

Coptic-Gnostic Texts

Die Pistis Sophia. Die beiden Bucher des Jeu. Unbekanntes altgnostisches Werk. Till,
  W. and Schmidt, C., ed.; Berlin, ³1962.

Alchemical Texts

Collection des Anciens Alchimistes Grecs. 3 vols. Berthelot, M., and Ruelle, Ch.-Em.,
  ed. Reimpression de l'edition 1888; Zeller, Osnabrock 1967.

Les Alchimistes Grecs. Papyrus de Leyde, Papyrus de Stockholm, Recettes. Vol. 1 R. Halleux, trans. Collection des Universites de France, Bude, G.; Les Belles Lettres, Paris, 1981.

Les Alchimistes Grecs. Zosimos de Panopolis, Mémoires authentiques, Vol. IV, Part 1. Mertens, M., Les Belles Lettres, Paris, 1995.

Artis Auriferae quam Chemiam vocant,
First ed.: Basileae apud Petrum Pernam, 1572.
Second ed.: Basileae, C. Waldkirch, 1593 (2 vols.)
Third ed.: Basileae, C. Waldkirch, 1610 (3 vols.)

Dee, John: Die Monas-Hieroglyphe. Bibliotheca Hermetica; Ansata, Interlaken, 1982.

Musaeum Hermeticum Reformatum et Amplificatum; Francofurti, 1677. Akad. Druck- und Verlagsanstalt, Reprint, Graz, 1970.

Rhenanus Johannes: Harmoniae imperscrutabilis Chymico-Philosophicae sive Philosophorum Antiquorum Consentientium Decades duae apud Com. Eifridum; Francofurti, 1625.

Ruska, J.: Tabula Smaragdina. Ein Beitrag zur Geschich te der Hermetischen Literatur; Winter, Heidelberg, 1926.

Ruska, J.: Turba Philosophorum; Springer, Berlin, 1931.

Theatrum Chemicum, praecipuos selectorum auctorum tractatus de chemiae et lapidis philosophici. Argentorati, E.; Zetzner, 1659-1661. Reprint, Bottega d'Erasmo, Torino, 1981.

2. Unpublished personal excerpts on alchemy by C. G. Jung

These personal notebooks are in the Jung Archive of the Eigenossischen Technischen Hochschule. Use of these materials is made with the permission of the Association of Heirs of C. G. Jung.

Volume I	1935 Treasure hunting
Volume V	1936/37 Extracta
Volume VI	1937/38 Excerpta
Volume VII	1939/40 Extracta philosophica
Volume VIII	1940-52 Extracta philosophica

Excerpts on alchemy by Marie-Louise de Franz

Volume II	
Volume III	Quae ad modum dicendi spectant

Volume IV   Quae ad mercurium spectant
Index Omnium Rerum Alchymicarum. Alchemical glossary.
Faust und die Alchemie. Address to the Psychological Club on October 8,
1949. Typescript. Summary in Collected Works, 18, 1692-1699.

3. List of Sources

Cornelius Agrippa, Of Occult Philosophy, Book II, chapter LVII.

Heinrich Cornelius Agrippa von Nettesheim: De occult a philosophia, libri tres. V.
Perrone Compagni, ed. Studies in the History of Christian Thought, vol.
XLVIII; Brill, Leiden, New York, Cologne, 1992.

Ancilla to the Pre-Socratic Philosophers. A Complete Translation of the Fragments in
Diels, Fragmente der Vorsokratiker, trans. by Kathleen Freeman (Cambridge: Harvard University Press), p. 28.

Andreae, Joh. Val.: Fama Fraternitatis (1614), Confessio Fraternitatis (1615), Chymische Hochzeit: Christiani Rosencreutz. Anno 1459 (1616). R. Van
Dulmen, ed. Calwer, Stuttgart, ³1981.

Andresen, C.: Die Kirchen der alten Christenheit. Die Religionen der Menschheit,
vol. 29, 1/2. Schroder, Ch. M., ed.; Kohlhammer, Stuttgart, Berlin, Cologne,
Mainz, 1971.

Angelus Silesius: Cherubinischer Wandersmann. Rhody, T., ed.; Pattloch, Aschaffen-
burg, 1947.

Die Apokryphen und Pseudepigraphen des Alten Testaments. 2 vols.

Kautzsch, E., ed.; Tubingen, 1900. Reprint, Olms, Hildesheim, 1962.

New Testament Apocrypha in German translation. 2 vols. Hennecke, E., and
Schneemelcher, W., eds.; Mohr, Tubingen, ³1959 and 1964. Schneemelcher,
W., ed.; Mohr, Tübingen, ⁵1987 and 1989.

Augustinus, A.: Bekenntnisse (Confessiones), Thimme, W., trans.; dtv 6120, Munich,
1982.

Bardenhewer, 0.: Geschichte der Altkirchlichen Literatur. 5 vols. Facsimile reprint of
the second edition, 1913; Wissenschaftl. Buchgesell., Freiburg i. Br. and
Darmstadt, 1962.

Benz, E.: Ecclesia spiritualis. Kirchenidee und Geschichtstheologie der Fran-
ziskanischen Reformation; Wissenschaftl. Buchgesell., Darmstadt, 1969.

Bergmann, H.: Martin Buber and Mysticism, in The Philosophy of Martin Buber, Library of Living Philosophers, vol. 12, Schillp, P. A., and Friedman, M., eds. Cambridge Univ. Press, London.

Bergmeier, R.: "Konigslosigkeit" als nachvalentinisches Heilspradikat; Novum Testamentum 24, Leiden, 1982, pp. 316-339.

Betz, H. D.: The Greek Magical Papyri in Translation, Including the Demotic Spells, Vol. 1, The Texts; Chicago, University of Chicago Press, ²1985.

Zürcher Bibel: Die Heilige Schrift des Alten und des Neuen Testaments; Zurich, 1982.

Bonnet, H.: Reallexikon der Aegyptischen Religionsgeschichte; Gruyter, Berlin, New York, ²1971.

Bousset, W.: Hauptprobleme der Gnosis (Forschungen zur Religion und Literatur des Alten und Neuen Testaments 10); Vandenhoek und Ruprecht, Gottingen, 1907.

Broek, R. van den, and Vermaseren, M. J.: Studies in Gnosticism and Hellenistic Religions, prestented to Gilles Quispel on the Occasion of his 65th Birthday. Etudes Preliminaires aux Religions Orientales dans l'Empire Romain, Vol. 91; Brill, Leiden, 1981.

Buber, M.: Autobiographic Fragments, in: The Philosophy of Martin Buber, Library of Living Philosophers, vol. 12, Schillp, P. A., and Friedman, M., eds. Cambridge Univ. Press, London.

Buber, M. Between Man and Man, R. S. Smith, trans. Kegan Paul, London, 1947.

Buber, M. Briefwechsel aus sieben Jahrzehnten, Vol. 1l Gütersloher Verlagshaus, Gütersloh, 1972.

Buber, M.: Eclipse of God. Studies in the Relation between Religion and Philosophy, Harper & Brothers, New York, 1952.

Buber, M.: Nachlese, Heidelberg, 1966.

Buber, M.: Replies to My Critics, in: The Philosophy of Martin Buber, Library of Living Philosophers, vol. 12, Schillp, P. A., and Friedman, M., eds. Cambridge Univ. Press, London.

Chuang Tzu (The True Classic of Southern (Cultural) Florescence), trans. Lin Yutang.

The Cherubinic Wanderer, J. E. Crawford Flitch, trans; London, 1932, number 25, 4.

Clement of Alexandria: The Excerpta ex Theodoto of C. A. Casey, R. P., ed.; Studies and Documents. London, 1934.

Clément d'Alexandrie: Extraits de Théodote. Sagnard, E., trans. Sources Chretiennes 23; Les Edition du Cerf, Paris, 1970.

Clemens of Alexandria, Stromateis. Clément d'Alexandrie, Les Stromates, Stromate V, Introduction, texte critique et index, Le Boulluec, A., ed., Voulet, P., trans.; Sources Chrétiennes.

Codrington, The Melanesians (Oxford: Oxford University Press, 1891), p. 118; quoted by Jung CW 8, § 123.

Copenhaver, B. P.: Hermetica, 1994. German: J. Holzhausen, Das Corpus Hermeticum Deutsch, 1997.

Deussen, P.: Sechzig Upanishads des Veda; Wisschenschaftl. Buchges., Darmstadt, 1963.

Diels, H. and Kranz, W.: Die Fragmente der Vorsokratiker. Griechisch und Deutsch. 3 vols.; Weidmann, Berlin, [10]1961.

Dieterich, A.: Abraxas. Studien zur Religionsgeschichte des spateren Alterturns. Festschrift fur Hermann Usener; Leipzig, 1891.

Dieterich, A.: Eine Mithrasliturgie; Wissenschaftliche Buchges., Darmstadt, 1966. Reprint: Weinreich, Leipzig and Berlin, [3]1923.

Dschuang Dsi: Das wahre Buch vom südlichen Blütenland (Nan Hua Dschen Ging). Wilhelm, R., trans.; Diederichs, Düsseldorf and Cologne, 1951.

Meister Eckehart: The Essential Sermons, Commentaries, Treaties, and Defense; Colledge, E., and McGinn, B., trans.; Paulist Press, New York, 1981.

Ellenberger, H. E. The Discovery of the Unconscious (New York: Basic Books, 1970).

Evans-Wentz, W. Y. trans. and ed., The Tibetan Book of the Dead (Oxford, 1957), pp. 11f.

Fackenheim, E. L. Martin Buber's Concept of Revelation, in Paul Arthur Schilpp and Maurice Friedman, eds., The Philosophy of Martin Buber (London: Cambridge University Press, 1967).

Fowden, G.: The Egyptian Hermes. A Historical Approach to the Late Pagan Mind; Princeton University Press, Princeton, 1993; [1]1986.

Franz, Marie-Louise von: Alchemical Active Imagination; Spring Publications Inc., University of Dallas, Texas; 1979.

Franz, Marie-Louise yon: Archetypische Dimensionen der Seele; Daimon, Einsiedeln, 1994.

Franz, Marie-Louise von: Aurora Consurgens: A Document Attributed to Thomas Aquinas on the Problem of Opposites in Alchemy: A Companion Work to C. G. Jung's Mysterium Conjunctionis (Studies in Jungian Psychology); Inner City Books, Toronto, 2000.

Franz, Marie-Louise von: C. G. Jung. His Myth in Our Time, trans. William H. Kennedy; C. G. Jung Foundation, New York, 1975.

Franz, Marie-Louise von: Number and Time. Reflections Leading towards a Unification of Psychology and Physics, Andrea Dykes, trans.; Rider and Co., London, 1974.

Franz, Marie-Louise von: Projection and Re-Collection in Jungian Psychology, Reflections of the Soul, W. H. Kennedy, trans.; Open Court, Chicago, 1980.

Franz, Marie-Louise von: Spiegelungen der Seele, Projektion und innere Sammlung in der Psychologie C. G. Jungs; Kösel Verlag, Munich, 21988.

Franz, Marie-Louise von: Traum und Tod; Kösel Verlag, Munich, 1984.

Friedman, M.: Contemporary Psychology Revealing and Obscuring the Human; Duquesne University Press, Pittsburg, 1984.

Friedman, M.: The Healing Dialogue in Psychotherapy; Jason Aronson, Lanham, MD, 1985.

Friedman, M.: Martin Buber's Life and Work. 3 vols. (1878-1965); Dutton, New York, 1981 und 1983.

The Freud/Jung Letters: The Correspondence between Sigmund Freud and C. G. Jung, William McGuire, ed.; Princeton University Press, Princeton, 1974.

Ganzenmuller, W: Alchemie und Religion im Mittelalter; Deutsches Archiv für Geschichte des MA 5; 1942, pp. 329-346.

Granet, Marcel: Das chinesische Denken. Porkert, M., ed.; Piper, Munich, 1963.

Heraclitus: The Cosmic Fragments, G. S. Kirk, ed.; Cambridge University Press, Cambridge, 1954.

Hermetica Oxoniensia (HO) III 1: Les hommes ont établi la loi par opinion.... délaissant la justice véritable et l'âme... 3. C'est pourquoi le ciel est pur de telles lois. J. Paramelle and J. Mahé, Extraits Hermétiques.

Histoire des Religions. 3 vols. Encyclopedie de la Pleiade. Puech, H.-Ch., ed. vol. 2: La Gnose, pp. 364f. Doresse, J.: L'Hermetisme Egyptianisant; Paris, 1972, pp. 430f.

Hoeller, S.: The Gnostic Jung and the Seven Sermons to the Dead; Theosophical Publishing House, Wheaton, IL 1982.

Horace, The Complete Works of Horace, Charles E. Passage, trans., Frederick Ungar Publishing Co., New York, 1983.

Hornung, E.: Das Amduat. Die Schrift des Verborgenen Raumes. 2 vols.; O. Harrassowitz, Wiesbaden, 1963.

Howald, E., and Grunwald, M.: Die Anfange der Abendlandischen Philosophie. Fragmente und Lehrberichte der Vorsokratiker; Artemis, Zurich, 1949.

Jung, C. G.: Analytical Psychology, Notes of the Seminar Given in 1925, ed. W. McGuire, Bollingen Series XCIX; Princeton University Press, Princeton; 1989, pp. 40f.

Jung, C. G.: Bibliothek. Katalog; Kusnacht-Zurich, 1967.

Jung, C. G.: Collected Works, 2nd edition, 20 vols., Herbert Reed and others, ed.; Princeton University Press, Princeton, 1966-1992.

Jung, C. G.: Dream Analysis, ed. W. McGuire, Bollingen Series XCIX, Princeton University Press, Princeton, 1984.

Jung, C. G., and Marie-Louise von Franz, The Grail Legend; Princeton University Press, Princeton, 1998.

Jung, C. G.: Jung Speaking. McGuire, W. ed.; New Jersey, 1977.

Jung, C. G.: Letters, 2 volumes, G. Adler, ed.; Princeton University Press, Princeton; 1975-1977.

Jung, C. G.: Memories, Dreams, Reflections, recorded and edited by Aniela Jaffé, trans. by Richard and Clara Winston, Vintage, New York, 1989.

Jung, C. G.: Seminar: Modern Psychology. Notes on Lectures given at the Eidgenossische Technische Hochschule, Zurich. October 1933-July 1935; October 1938-March 1940. 2nd edition 1959; for private use only.

Jung, C. G., The Seven Sermons to the Dead written by Basilides in Alexandria, the City where the East toucheth the West, in Dreams, Memories, Reflections, recorded and edited by Aniela Jaffé, trans. by Richard and Clara Winston; Vintage, New York, 1989.

Kerényi, K., The Religion of the Greeks and the Romans, trans. By Christopher Holme (New York: Dutton, 1962).

Koschorke, K., Nag Hammadi Studies 12 (Leiden, 1978), pp. 91-174.

Die Kreuzzuge in Augenzeugenberichten. Pernoud, R., ed., Thurnau, H., trans.; dtv 763, Munich, 1961.

Die Kreuzzuge aus arabischer Sicht. F. Gabrieli, trans. Bibliothek des Morgenlandes des Artemis Verlag. dtv 4172, Munich, 1976.

Die Kulturelle Bedeutung der Komplexen Psychologie, in honor of the 60th birthday of C. G. Jung; Springer, Berlin, 1935.

Lao-tse, Tao te ching: The Classic Book of Integrity and the Way; Victor H. Mair, trans. Bantam, New York, 1990.

Lattke, M.: Die Oden Salomos in ihrer Bedeutung fur Neues Testament und Gnosis. vol. 1; Editions Universitaires Fribourg Suisse, 1979.

Lovejoy, A. The Fundamental Concept of the Primitive Philosophy, in The Monist, XVI (1906).

Lucius Apuleius, The Golden Ass (Metamorphoses).

Mahé, H.-P.: L'elitisme gnostique et la souillure de la grande eglise d'apres les ecrits de Nag Hammadi. Cahiers de la Revue de Théologie et de Philosophie 17, pp. 65-99, 1993.

Mansfeld, J.: Die Vorsokratiker. Griechisch/Deutsch; Reclam, Stuttgart, 1987.

Markschies, Ch.: Valentinus Gnosticus? Untersuchungen zur valentinianischen Gnosis mit einem Kommentar zu den Fragmenten Valentins. Wissenschaftliche Untersuchungen zum Neuen Testament 65; Mohr, Tubingen, 1992.

Needham, J.: Science and Civilisation in China; Cambridge University Press, Cambridge, 1962.

Nelken, J.: Analytische Beobachtungen uber Phantasien eines Schizophrenen, in: Jb. für psychoanalyt. und psychopathol. Forschung IV (1912), pp. 504-562.

Neumann, E.: Tiefenpsychologie und neue Ethik. Geist und Psyche; Fischer Tb, Frankfurt a.M., 1984.

Origenes: Contra Celsum. Origene: Contre Celse. 5 vols. Borret, M., ed. Sources Chretiennes No. 132, 136, 147, 150, 227; Les Editions du Cerf, Paris 1967-1976.

Otto, R. The Idea of the Holy: An Inquiry into the Non-Rational Factor in the Idea of the Divine and Its Relation to the Rational, trans. by John W. Harvey (London: Oxford University Press, 1952).

Ovid, Metamorphoses, Charles Martin, trans. W. W. Norton, New York, 2004.

Rosch, E., ed.; Wissenschaftl. Buchgesellschah, Darmstadt, 1983. Sammlung Tuscu-
lum. Authorized edition; Artemis Verlags, Munich.

Paramelle, J., and Mahé, J.-P.: Extraits Hermetiques inédits dans un Manuscrit
d'Oxford. Revue des Etudes Grecques. Vol. 104, pp. 109-139; Paris, 1991.

Pearson, B. A., ed., Nag Hammadi Codices IX and X, in The Coptic Gnostic Library,
J. M. Robinson, ed. Brill, Leiden, 1981.

The Collected Dialogues of Plato, Hamilton, E., and Cairns, H, eds. Princeton
University Press, Princeton, 1961.

Plutarch: Über Isis und Osiris. Hopfner, Th., trans.; Prague, 1940. Reprint: Wis-
sensch. Buchges., Darmstadt, 1967.

Quispel, G.: Gnosis als Weltreligion; Origo, Zurich, 1951.

Quispel, G.: Jewish Gnosis and Mandaean Gnosticism. Some Reflections on the
writing Brontè. Les Textes de Nag Hammadi. Colloque du Centre
d'Histoire des Religions. Strasbourg 23-25 October 1974. Menard, J. E., ed.
Nag Hammadi Studies VII, pp. 82-122; Brill, Leiden, 1975.

Quispel, G.: Hermes Trismegistus and the Origins of Gnosticism. Vigiliae Christianae
46, pp. 1-19 (1992).

Quispel, G.: De Hermetische Gnosis in de loop der eeuwen; Tirion, Baarn, 1992.

Quispel, G.: Hesse, Jung und die Gnosis. Die "Septem Sermones ad Mortuos" und
Basilides, Gnostic Studies II, Nederlands Historisch-Archaeologisch Insti-
tut te Istanbul, 1975, pp. 241-258.

Rahner, H.: Symbole der Kirche. Die Ekklesiologie der Vater; Otto Muller, Salzburg,
1964.

Rehm, B., and Strecker, G.: Die Pseudoklementinen. I Homilien; II Rekognitionen in
Rufins Übersetzung. Die Griechischen Christlichen Schriftsteller der ersten
Jahrhunderte; Akademie, Berlin, ²1994.

Reitzenstein, R.: Poimandres. Studien zur griechisch-agyptischen und früh-
christlichen Literatur; Leipzig, 1904. Reprint: Darmstadt, 1966.

Ribi, A.: Anthropos. Der ewige Mensch. Das uralte und das neue Bild vom Menschen;
P. Lang, Bern and New York, 2002.

Ribi, A.: Was tun mit unseren Komplexen; Kösel-Verlag, Munich, 1989.

Ribi, A.: Morgen- und Abenderkenntnis bei Augustinus. Address at the Psycho-
logischen Club Zürich, 1992.

Ribi, A.: Die Auffassung C. G. Jungs von der Schizophrenie. Schweizer Archiv für Neurologie und Psychiatrie; 144, 1993, Number 6, pp. 487-500.

Ribi, A.: Die feindlichen Brüder. Extraversion-Introversion, zwei komplementäre Seiten eines einseitigen Weltbildes; Kundschafter, Wettingen, 1993.

Ribi, A.: Ein Leben im Dienst der Seele. Part II, Gesammelte Aufsätze und Vorträge; P. Lang, Bern, Berlin, Bruxelles, Frankfurt am Main, New York, Oxford, Vienna, 2007.

Ribi, A.: Zeitenwende: Die geistigen Wurzeln unserer Zeit in Hellenismus, Hermetik, Gnosis und Alchemie; P. Lang, Bern and New York, 2001.

Ribi, A.: Zum schöpferische Prozess bei C. G. Jung. Aus den Excerptbänden zur Alchemie, Analyt. Psychol., vol. 13; 1982, pp. 201-221.

Robinson, J. M.: The Jung Codex. The Rise and Fall of a Monopoly. Religious Studies Review 3, 1977, p. 17.30.

Robinson, J. M.: Preface. The Facsimile Edition of the Nag Hammadi Codices. Introduction; Brill, Leiden, 1984.

Robinson, J. M. ed.: The Nag Hammadi Library; Brill, Leiden, New York, Copenhagen, Cologne, 31988.

Rohrich, L.: Lexikon der sprichwörtlichen Redensarten, 4 vols.; Herder, Freiburg, Basel, Wien, 1973.

Rudolph, K., ed.: Gnosis und Gnostizismus. Wege der Forschung, Vol. 257; Wissenschaftliche Buchgesellschaft, Darmstadt, 1975.

Ruska, J.: Tabula Smaragdina. Ein Beitrag zur Geschichte der Hermetischen Literatur, Heidelberg, 1926.

Schiller, F.: The Robbers and Wallenstein; Penguin Books, London, 1979.

Schenke, Hans-Martin: Der Gott "Mensch" in der Gnosis. Ein religionsgeschichtlicher Beitrag zur Diskussion über die paulinische Anschauung von der Kirche als Leib Christi; Vandenhoeck und Ruprecht, Gottingen, 1962.

Schopenhauer, A. The World as Will and Representation, E. F. J. Payne, trans.; Dover Publication, New York, 1958-1959.

Segal, R. A.: The Gnostic Jung. Including "Seven Sermons of the Dead"; Routledge, London, 1992. Therein: Quispel, G.: Jung and Gnosis.

Sevrin, J.-M.: Le dossier baptismal Séthien. Etudes sur la sacramentaire gnostique. BCNH 2; Universite Laval, Quebec, 1986.

Sevrin, J.-M.: Les noces spirituelles dans l'Évangile selon Philippe. Le Museon. Revue d'Études Orientales 87, Louvain, 1974. pp. 143-193.

Sloterdijk, E., and Macho, T. H., eds.: Welt revolution der Seele; Artemis, Zurich, 1993.

Studies in Gnosticism and Hellenistic Religions Presented to Gilles Quispel on the Occasion of his 65 Birthday, ed. R. van den Brock and M. J. Vermasern; Brill, Leiden, 1981.

Suzuki, D. T.: Die Grosse Befreiung. Einführung in den Zen-Buddhismus, with a foreword by C. G. Jung; Rascher, Zurich and Stuttgart, 1958.

Thiel, von, ed.: Leben und Taten Alexanders von Makedonien. Der griechische Alexanderroman nach der Handschrift L. Texte zur Forschung 13; Wissenschaftl. Buchges., Darmstadt, 1983.

Trüb, H.: Individuation, Schuld und Entscheidung. Ober die Grenzen der Psychologie, in: Die Kulturelle Bedeutung der Komplexen Psychologie, Festschrift zum 60. Geburtstag von C. G. Jung, pp. 529-555.

Welling, Georg von: Opus mago-cabbalisticum et theosophicum; Frankfurt u. Leipzig, 1784. Facsimile edition: Stockholm, 1971.

Wickes, F. G.: The Inner World of Man; Henry Holt, New York, 1948.

Williams, M. A.: The Immovable Race. A Gnostic Designation and the Theme of Stability in Late Antiquity. Nag Hammadi Studies XXIX; Brill, Leiden, 1985.

Made in the USA
Charleston, SC
28 July 2013